To Kat,

The one of those sleepless days. You were the one who brought smiles and coffee into the room — and kept my head on straight?

The Other Side

In reading, surely you'll gain a glimpse of the small town boy and his dream to be a surgeon — long before Ean Clarice.

Ralph F. Hudson

Ralph F. Hudson, M.D.

First Printing   November, 2002
Second Printing   December, 2002

ISBN 0-9671762-8-X

Published by:
HEINS PUBLICATIONS
Rev. William A. Heins
2016 Leonard Ct.
Eau Claire WI 54703-9000
Tel. #'s: 715.874.6677; 800.55HEINS (800.554.3467)

TABLE OF CONTENTS

The Beginning of a Journey-Mt. Morris, Illinois
   Birth 1
   The First Letting of Blood 1
   Stop! Go No Further! Beware of Contagion! 2
   Circumcision 3
   First Hospitalization 4
   Dog Days 7
   Down in the Mouth---The Dental Dilemma 7
   A Vision, A Dream 8
The Continuation of a Journey
   U.S. Navy V-12 10
   Medical School---U. of Illinois at Chicago 11
Internship: Milwaukee County General Hospital 14
U.S. Navy---Newport, Rhode Island 20
Henrotin Hospital---Chicago, Illinois 24
Hines Veterans Administration Hospital, Maywood IL . 30
Another New Beginning---Eau Claire, Wisconsin 34
The Colfax Tornado 39
Can the Surgeon be Everything to Everybody? 41
The Annual Deer Hunt 44
Is Football That Important? 46
Go to Jail, Do Not Pass Go 47
Tri-County Memorial Hospital---Whitehall, WI 49
Osseo Area Hospital---Osseo, WI 54
And Back Again to Eau Claire 58
Happy Faces 61
Girl Friends 64
A Digression on Gas 83
The Annual National Guessing Game:
   Influenza Vaccination 85
Some Rambling Thoughts About the O.R. 88
A Softer Side of the O.R.---Daughter Status 94
An Evolution---Changes in Surgical Philosophy 96
Another Digression---Professional Disagreement 102
Great Changes in Surgical Management of
   Breast Problems 104

Bad Communication Can Wreak Havoc 115
The Impact of Age on Breast Malignancy Outcome 117
The Influence of Family History On
   Incidence of Breast Malignancy 120
A Personalization of Family History 121
A Place for Prophylactic Mastectomy 124
The Art of Communication, the Cornerstone of
   the Physician/Patient Relationship 126
Am I Pretty? Am I Handsome? 136
Amputation 139
Quirks of Birth 145
The Darker Days 152
Hernia Concepts 161
Being in the Right Place at the Right Time 164
Unfair! A Family Broken! A Community Awakened .. 170
Would You Operate On the Pope? 176
Yes, Virginia, There Are Bums in this World 179
Loosen Up A Little 182
Vasectomy Can Make a Vas Deferens 186
A Day of Caring 189
Fantasy and the Bear---A Delving Into
   Scientific Research 192
To Be Involved In Your Own Family's Treatment? 195
Support Groups 198
Transportation---Is a Car Just a Car? 201
A Grateful Patient---What Is Acceptable? 203
A Mother Gives Birth. The Role of the Father? 204
We Are Born and We Die---But When?---and How? .. 206
And Then There's Darrel 217
When and Where Is A Physician A Physician? 220
Nepotism---Natural and Neat 226
Potpourri 228
Those Canker Sore Blues 232
A Letter from the Other Side 234
Do I Really Want to Get to that Other Side? 236
The Loneliness of Being a Family Member 240
The Male Curse 243
How Blessed to Have Quality Consultants 246

On the Joys of Visiting the Sick 248
Learning---A Yearning Not Confined
   to the Classroom 252
The Cost! The Cost! 253
The Nature of Healing --- ??? 262
A Time for Reflection 264
A Thought I Leave With You 267

INTRODUCTION/DEDICATION

It is by no means trite to repeat the well-known metaphor that none of us is an island. Sooner or later, it comes to us that we don't live in a vacuum, impervious to others, oblivious to the influence of others. IF, in some way, the thoughts and reflections written herein should have meaning or cause a few heads to turn, it is only fitting that much credit should go to those who have helped me along the way, whether or not they even are aware. In dedication to and with gratitude for, I have the following folks in mind. This treatise is dedicated to:

PEGGY: She, through the years, has tried to understand my varying moods---with occasional success. Somehow, she has had the patience to cope with the demands imposed by my long hours of caring for patients. Amazingly, she has been able to maintain a home more as a castle to retreat to than an impregnable fortress. Without her, the rewards of a medical/surgical practice would have been far less meaningful and perhaps well-nigh impossible. Fortunate I have been that she has helped me, allowed me, or caused me to be the person I always wanted to be.

RICK, JANET, CARYL, LAURA, DEBBIE, DIANE, AND JEFF: Lo, they were all born into a different family, appreciating in varying degrees a father often in absentia. Hopefully, small or large measures of pride might either be created or intensified by reading these thoughts---glimpses into a world in which I may have had a part in helping and influencing the lives of others.

COLLEAGUES, NURSES---YEA, ALL HEALTH CARE WORKERS: All those who have shared in trying to improve the comfort and mobility of patients are remembered with thanks. Again, no person is ever sufficient unto himself/herself. How grateful I am for those who have helped in many ways, who have made my life easier in times of stress.

HENRY J. STENGEL, M.D.: I would honor the memory of the one who treated the 12 year old boy with the fearsome pneumonia, the one who introduced the 18 year old young man to the reality and excitement of the operating room, the one who spoke with vicarious pride of the accomplishments of the young surgeon. In his memory, I would hope that Henry, the astute diagnostician and the purveyor of pearls of wisdom, might read these words in the comfort of his home on the other side.

Front row, L-R: Diane, Laura, Debbie
Back row: Caryl, Janet, Peggy, Ralph, Jeff, Rick

ABOUT THE AUTHOR

Ralph F. Hudson, M.D., was born and raised in Mt. Morris, Illinois, attending elementary school and high school in that community. Pre-medical study was at Duke University, Durham, North Carolina---in the U.S. Navy V-12 program. Medical school education followed at the U. of Illinois College of Medicine, Chicago, Illinois.

Milwaukee County General Hospital was the site of Dr. Hudson's internship. He then served in the U.S. Navy Medical Corps at the Portsmouth, Virginia, naval hospital and the Newport, Rhode Island, naval hospital.

Surgical residency training was combined--- Henrotin Hospital in Chicago, Illinois and Hines V.A. Hospital in Maywood, Illinois. He is a diplomate of the American Board of Surgery.

Ralph Hudson and Peggy Jo Chapman were married in Chicago, Illinois in 1947. They have seven children and ten grandchildren. In 1958, they moved to Eau Claire, Wisconsin---where he engaged in a general surgical practice in partnership with Drs. J. Birney Dibble and William H. Walter. Much of "The Other Side" details medical adventures and changes in health care during three decades until he retired from active practice in 1990.

In addition to an active surgical practice, Dr. Hudson worked with the Wisconsin Medical Society Commission on Safe Transportation to reduce alcohol-related death and injury on the highway. He worked tirelessly, through legislative activism and Letters to the Editor, to keep the specter of alcohol-impaired driving before the public. This activity resulted in a National Citizen Advocate of the Year award in 1990---presented by the National Commission against Drunk Driving. In 1992, he was recognized as a Physician Citizen of the Year by the Wisconsin Medical Society. In retirement, he has been speaking out about the dangers of alcohol poisoning---the all-too-frequent sudden death occurring in young people after consuming beverage alcohol too much, too fast.

Community involvement has been evidenced by membership in many boards and committees. Both Ralph and Peggy have enjoyed their volunteer role as they deliver Meals on Wheels. Together, they have actively participated in community choral groups---and now, in retirement, they are assuming a strong supportive role in encouraging choral music at the University of Wisconsin, Eau Claire.

They both now are learning more about the frailties of the flesh and "The Other Side." When asked about their plans for now and the future, they sum it all up by saying, "Life still is a series of new beginnings---and we're still involved in building tomorrow's memories."

What others have said about Ralph Hudson, M.D.

Whether you are a health care worker or patient, "The Other Side" will give you an appreciation of one person's view of a changing health care system in the last half century. Ralph Hudson presents a picture of change, while pleading that we retain those timeless concerns for the well-being of others. In "The Other Side," idealism is never lost, but is combined nicely with pragmatism.

As a member of the Board of Directors of the Visiting Nurses Association (VNA) from 1990-1996, and as president from 1994-1995, Dr. Hudson had an insightful understanding of changing home health care dynamics in Eau Claire at that time. In all that he did, he had a fascinating way of bringing out the best in people.

Jim Ryder, Director
Eau Claire City-County Health Department

Dr. Hudson had a very positive working relationship with nurses---whom he approached as respected colleagues. He understood nursing's contributions to the healing process and thus valued the importance of good nursing care in striving for positive patient outcomes. There was true collaboration in working together---and this was based on mutual respect, trust, teamwork, and consideration for each other's roles.

Mary Ann Murphy, R.N., M.P.H.
Former Director of Nursing
Eau Claire City-County Health Department

FOREWORD:

Most of us have an insatiable, albeit unspoken desire to be understood---really understood. This thirst to be understood is usually pictured as an accompaniment of emerging adolescence. At age 76, sitting in the forgiving chair of retirement, I have come to believe that the "if only somebody, somewhere would understand me" stretches interminably through the decades, even crescendoing in our last days. Strangely, the stubborn persistence of the yearning to be understood is paralleled by our fear---our disbelief that anybody ever could or would understand. The truth? Before we can even begin to be comforted by another's "I understand you," we must first achieve a reasonable sense of our own self worth.

Clearly, the "foreword" to a book is a thinly-veiled attempt on the part of authors to be understood. Some writers, playing with words and with sufficient ego, may have the vision that they are illuminating the masses with their wisdom. However, most introspective writers, writing out of personal experience, will acknowledge that they're really trying to sort out their own thoughts---and, in the process, gain a sense of calm and reason, a feeling of being on the right page.

After my retirement in 1990, there were those who suggested, even encouraged me to record my medical/ surgical adventures through anecdotes and word pictures. The suggestion was complimentary, but it just didn't ring a bell. Why?

1. I had the feeling that many others had already written such treatises, sometimes tainted by a self-congratulatory theme.

2. I didn't yet have the realization that my practice, my mannerisms had been somewhat unique.

3. There was the fear of breaking patient confidentiality.

4. I wanted to play golf and didn't realize that I might be able to do both.

A cause for reconsideration: From 1995-2002, I found myself trapped on the battlefield with the Philistines, enduring six hip surgeries and, most recently, decompression lumbar laminectomy. A determined and resolute, but stupid stoic, a person rarely acknowledging pain or illness---I suddenly was a bloody casualty, experiencing septic shock, I.C.U., blood loss, the probing of orifices, cardiac arrhythmia, renal shutdown, and the realization of my own mortality. How clearly do I recall my pleas of protest, trying to minimize the importance of the battle. "Hey, no big deal!" How clearly do I also recall the question inevitably to come, "So, how does it feel to be on the other side?" Other side? Other side? I fought back with, "Friends, I always thought we were on the same side." That evasion of the obvious quickly surrendered to a truth known to all patients---that empathetic appreciation of a patient's hurting and bewilderment comes only by walking in his/her moccasins.

As you read the following health-related anecdotes, surrounded by personal philosophical reflections, carry with you:

1. My assurance that EACH person, EACH patient, has been important. The Oklahoma City bombing and the terrorism of Sept. 11,2001, have forced us to appreciate the uniqueness of each life. There is a common denominator that has emerged from the rubble---that, whether banker or janitor, rich or poor, black or white, there is a common sense of being and the inescapable realization that a bit of the eternal rests in all of us, forging a bond which links us together.

2. My assertion that the commonplace, the mundane, the routine---though to some not as important---are often more rewarding than the flashy, the scary, the spectacular. Many people are fascinated by T.V. images of

E.R. and surgical procedures. To be sure, these images are exciting, even titillating, though sadly distorted at times. To be sure, there are procedures which are more complicated and serious than others---but any procedure, exam, or testing carries with it an inherent level of trepidation. Therefore, the terms "minor" and "major" never should have been applied to surgical procedures.

3. An appreciation of generational differences. There always will be evolution and improvements in health care with greater technology and knowledge. I submit to you that dedicated health care workers down through the ages have done the best they could with the imaging and treatment procedures at their disposal. Change isn't always progress, but change is laudable when pain is alleviated and mobility is improved.

Now, walk with me. Explore with me. There is much to be learned from those on the other side---much to be learned from the most unexpected persons and events. Be not afraid to move from side to side---for such movement may result in wisdom and understanding. Many of us have grown up with firm, precise lines determining what is good/evil, right/wrong, moral/immoral, making it easy to determine on which side you might find yourself. These dividing lines may be seen by some as arbitrary, capricious. Has it ever occurred to you that there may also be dividing lines in health care, creating a gulf between the learned and the lowly at times? At age 76, the dividing lines in life are still there, but are less distinct---even a little blurred. Perhaps my writing and your reading also will allow us to appreciate a little more those on the other side in health care.

It is my wish that these memories will let you travel from side to side with ease and will enhance your appreciation of those people who help us and/or need us, whatever the side. Mature, indeed, is the person who can cope with the blurring of dividing lines and yet retain personal principles. Blessed is the person who can empathize with those on the other side. Remember---empathy is just the embodiment of compassionate feelings, augmented by personal experience. As we pursue the odyssey together, perhaps we shall inch a little closer to understanding the person who is on the other side.

A Warning: In reading, you may encounter duplication---either of events or of repetitive phraseology. IF you are alert enough to ascertain such repetition, please---just shrug it off, realizing that all of us, at times, speak with words and phrases which have become comfortable to our own ears.

Further to Clarify: In pursuing any odyssey, it could be terribly confusing if there should be myriad paths. Therefore, I have avoided exploring the other side related to family events, vacations, choral encounters, school and church activities, etc., events which, though meaningful to family, would be inconsequential to those on the other side. That which follows will be confined to one path---related only to health care and the wonderful human body. It isn't that there never will be divergence from this straight and narrow path. Should, however, there be occasional philosophical digressions, even that philosophy shall be related to medical musings. Accounts of family activities, those journeys down other paths, will be found in works long since stored in the Claymore College archives.

Although you will be exposed to anatomy and disease processes, you aren't reading a medical textbook. This isn't any kind of textbook. You will be reading a loosely-woven and sometimes rambling collection of thoughts. Thoughts, by and large, are spontaneous, fragmentary, evanescent---and rarely are complete or all-encompassing. Be aware, therefore, that, for everything said herein, there probably is much more to be said---if only we could have a back porch conversation.

THE BEGINNING OF A JOURNEY---
MT. MORRIS, ILLINOIS.

Birth

In a nutshell, life really is just a series of new beginnings. Sharing a sense of the inevitable with everybody before me and everybody who has come after me, I didn't ask to be born. Regardless, a new promise emerged in the front bedroom at 310 W. Lincoln St., Mt. Morris, Illinois---on October 7, 1925. Why Mt. Morris? In the words of the deadpan, stand-up comedian, "because my mother lived there and I wanted to be close to her."

Yes, I was "born at home." This, of course, was the norm in 1925 but, in later years, I found that this simple fact helped me immeasurably in the taking of medical histories. Somehow, a sort of kinship developed, erasing age differences. To wit, I recall a lady, about age 85, who was reluctant to communicate, perhaps not completely trusting a boyish-looking young M.D. Getting absolutely nowhere in relaxing this dour old lady, I suddenly opened a door with, "Tell me, were you by any chance born at home?" (knowing all along that the answer had to be affirmative). The answer, at first hesitantly, "Why, yes---of course!" "Amazing," I chimed in, "I was, too." What a transformation in communication. With this revelation, I now was seen as not from another planet. We had something in common, but more important---I actually had a mother. It worked every time---and the technique isn't described in books.

The First Letting of Blood

Down through the ages, the letting of blood has

been fearsome, appalling to the uninitiated. After all, whether red blood or blue blood, society would rather have it confined to the cardio-vascular system---not spilled onto the street. Blood letting can be accidental or intentional. Sometimes, blood letting has been weirdly ritualistic. Blood letting even has had a healing intent as practiced by barbers and by the use of leeches.

  To my knowledge, there never has been any organized introduction for surgeons in bloodletting and the development of resiliency to such gore. For me, such introduction occurred in the 1st grade. Even in those years, it was becoming obvious that I had no hope of becoming an orthopedic surgeon. To be one of those guys, you have to be a carpenter of bones and joints---and a carpenter I wasn't. Saws and hammers brought out the klutzy in me. Our 1st grade teacher laid upon us a strange and imaginative curriculum, which included the making of chairs from orange crates. Alas! While trying hard to be a carpenter, I fell against the sharp edge of an orange crate, gashing my scalp and covering the floor with 0 Neg. blood. Carefully stitched and with a turban like bandage, I returned to the classroom---quite pleased and proud that my mishap had made me a celebrity in the eyes of my classmates. Even 3rd graders and teachers passing by took notice. Is there a lesson there somewhere? Even in injury, there are some compensations---in my case, a sense of importance far beyond what was justified. Oh, that we could only see ourselves as others see us!

Stop! Go No Further! Beware of Contagion!

  While incipient dementia is choking out the green grass of present memory, seemingly insignificant events of the past crop up as surely as dandelions in the Spring. Emerging clearly are small town memories. Where else but in small towns? Join me and my friends as we follow the ice truck, retrieving ice chips as the ice delivery man uses the ice pick on huge blocks of ice. It was the day of the delivery man. Look --- on the front porch --- the milk delivery man has left bottles of non-homogenized milk. Brrr! It's freezing cold and the cream has risen to the top, jutting upward---the cylindrical frozen cream much like a present day push-up.

Just as those memories tell you something about an era, my first introduction to government was seen in the stern actions of public health officials, whose responsibility was to identify sick houses by appropriate signage. The precautions were akin to treating a plague epidemic, and I doubt that contagion was made less---if even it should have been. Oh well, it made them think they were doing something. My memory is that my father, the breadwinner, could enter and leave the house. For others, travel in and out was verboten. Ach! It was almost like having to wear a sign proclaiming, "Unclean." The public health official, probably a doctor, would tack variably colored signs to the door---warning of contagion. There was violet for varicella, red for red measles, chartreuse for chicken pox, etc.

This enforced house arrest lasted for 5-7 days. With such confinement, parents today would be candidates for the loony bin. In my childhood, however, children were so well-behaved and saintly that mothers almost welcomed those warning signs of contagion as instruments of family togetherness. Why are you grandchildren smirking? Come to think of it, what DID we do without television? Ah, Parcheesi.

Circumcision
(And I'm not even Jewish)

I suspect that circumcision or non-circumcision of male newborns in 1925 had little to do with present day medical debate about the wisdom of circumcision. The reasoning was more pragmatic than scientific and involved logic: 1) Why take precious time when it might never be necessary anyway and 2) Why introduce yet another possible complication? When I was about age 10, without consulting me, my mother and Dr. Murray Dumont secretly connived to amputate my precious prepuce. Phimosis was defined in the *Dictionary According to Ralph* as "a flimsy excuse to create humiliation in a young boy." Oh, woe! Oh, embarrassment! Did Dr. Dumont have to compound the torment by having his high school girl assistant watching?

You might think that this office procedure was the forerunner of ambulatory surgery, but the ambulation was---well, hesitant to say the least. It must have taken 30 minutes for me to walk or crawl 6 blocks to our home. Hoping to be seen by nobody, we had the misfortune to be confronted by a nosy neighbor. "My," she weaseled, "what seems to be the matter with Ralph?" Now, in 1935, subjects of sex, body elimination of wastes, and genitalia weren't topics of the day. I couldn't believe my saintly mother. Esther thought you'd go to Hell if you told a lie---but, sidestepping adroitly, she came up with an outlandish cockamamie excuse, "Oh, Ralph has had some surgery near his legs---and you can see that his legs just won't work quite right." Sometimes, a protective mother must bend the rules. The lesson? Special circumstances demand special dispensations.

First Hospitalization
(The oxygen tent capers)

In the 8th grade of my early education, tragedy struck the Hudson household. You may have heard it said, "Cleanliness is next to Godliness." I say unto you however (quoting my mother), "Cleanliness may bring you close to God, but it's really perfect attendance that brings salvation." Such maternal influence undoubtedly was a prime factor in creating an obsession within me that resulted in a surgical practice of 32 years in which I missed not one single work day due to illness. To those who either marvelled or showed disgust at such a record, I referred to:

1) Good genes, 2) Fairly good health practices, and 3) A generous dose of stupidity.

The awful truth: Perfect attendance through 7th grade was shattered by a microbial invasion---pneumonia---taking over the air spaces. I still suspect that my mother and Dr. Stengel have, through the years, deliberately inflated the magnitude of this pneumonic threat, declaring the pneumonia to be life threatening. You've heard of walking pneumonia? Well, this was a galloping pneumonia---requiring Dr. Stengel to procure an experimental drug, sulfapyridine, from the U. of Wisconsin hospitals. This drug is no longer in use because it proved to be too toxic for human use---but, in 1937, the pneumonia was vanquished by sulfapyridine and I withstood the toxicity.

A lesson: Humankind is in a never-ending battle with other organisms in the environment. On this battlefield, public health officials have been the heroes, providing us with armament and ammunition (preventive medicine, immunization).

Deaconess Hospital in Freeport, Illinois, not only was a haven for the 12 year old boy with pneumonia. It just so happened that Deaconess Hospital also was a sponsor for a school of nursing. When R.N.'s were closely involved with bedside care, even giving baths, it followed that nursing students would be giving baths. Perhaps you will find some humor in the discomfort as a young nursing student approached her assignment---yep, the same 12 year old boy. The drama unfolded slowly as the young girl washed my legs, my arms, my face, my back, my abdomen---and then abruptly said, as she retreated, "Now you can finish." There I lay with only a towel covering what were supposed to be private parts. Pondering her directions, the 12 year old boy in me hadn't the foggiest idea what she meant. However, with uncanny perception, the boy knew instinctively that the answer to her question, "Have you finished?" was a quick "Yes." Yet another lesson: Effective communication starts only when all parties are on the same page---the same side. In health care, never assume that a patient has understood what you think you have said. Patients can be devious, evasive, and inventive when asked, "Do you have any questions? Do you understand?" After all, the patient doesn't wish to come across as a dumbbell---and often wants to please the physician by being non-complaining.

A Scrambled Brain

Dancing at times is a contact sport. Football is never a contact sport. Football is a collision sport, designed to thwart another's progress by violent means. At least, this was part of my mother's justification for withholding me from the sport until my junior year in high school. Our class of 1943 received above average grades in scholastic, academic, and social achievement. In competitive athletics, we weren't at the bottom of the barrel. We weren't even in the barrel. Our football team won 1 game, lost 8; our basketball team won 1 game, lost 22. Ping-pong was our forte.

While playing the Rochelle "B" team one night, my head was mistaken for a football. Kicked in the head and seeing stars, I found myself on the other side, wandering around on the other side of the line of scrimmage in la-la land. A concerned referee asked, "Son, what's the score?" Trying so hard, groping for words, the best I could come up with was, "7 to 12 in your favor." I failed the test and was banished from the game, no longer a hero candidate. With probable cerebral edema and clinical concussion, there was no MRI. No CT scan. No hospitalization---just astute observation by Esther. Technology now has proved to be a blessing in the diagnosis and management of neurological deficits. The lesson: Even with multiple high-tech scans, the clinical sense and common sense of Esther are no less necessary.

Dog Days

Dog gone! Why do dogs have an inherent dislike for postal workers? During the Christmas rush, I was richer in the pocketbook and richer in my feeling of importance as I delivered mail for the U.S. Post Office. I intended no harm to man or beast. While on the sidewalk, not even approaching the house, I was accosted by a terrier, who chose that moment to protect his turf. Heading straight for his target, he interrupted his yipping only long enough to sink his teeth in my ankle. "Man's best friend" became a life-long threat with that one bite, completely destroying my trust of canines. Did the bite heal? Of course! My mother said it would---end of discussion. I always suspected that Esther had a little of the Christian Scientist in her.

On that same mail route, I was a disciple, a true believer of "neither rain nor sleet, neither floods nor snowstorms can keep me from my appointed task." Accordingly, I was out in freezing weather, wearing no gloves because I thought that the gloves interfered with the precision incumbent upon the dedicated postal employee. The result? This macho type of thinking resulted in a frozen hand, with black skin eventually peeling off in the form of a withered glove. Worried about the hand, I knocked hesitantly at Dr. Dumont's apartment door on a Sunday evening. Details of this encounter are vague but, in my shyness, I sensed a brusque dismissal of my concerns. Another lesson: A great physician must simply assume that a patient won't bother the great one unless the matter is deemed urgent and worrisome.

Down in the Mouth---
The Dental Dilemma

Wise parents eventually understand that their children, as they prepare to leave the nest, are influenced by many others---by friends, employers, doctors, teachers---

and ***dentists.*** In those early, non-fluoride years, Dr. Boyle had repeated opportunities to influence me because my dental enamel, more like porous limestone, required so much repair. Indeed, the total size of cavities exceeded the remaining dental mass. Dental fillings, one after another, left inner and outer walls of enamel surrounding trenches of mercury and dental cement.

I was a pioneer orthodontal patient, referred by Dr. Boyle to Dr. Cole in the Block & Kuhl Building in Rockford. Perhaps some of my classmates suffered similar treatment, but braces weren't seen as glamorous and we didn't talk about it. It appears now that a student can't receive a high school diploma without orthodontal certification.

It seems to me that dental schools must place great emphasis on: 1) The targeting of canker sores; 2) The monologue, cleverly disguised as conversation with a captive, cotton-immobilized, open-mouthed patient.

When Dr. Boyle engaged in dialogue rather than monologue, he had a certain missionary zeal about him, encouraging me to choose the path of dental study. When I demurred with a fairly weak protest that I wouldn't really care to have my hands in people's mouths, he twinkled. "Son," he said, "when I think of the places where you might have your hands if you become a physician, maybe the mouth is preferable to the rectum."

A Vision, A Dream

Although said before, it bears repeating---yes, life IS a series of new beginnings. In determining a life's vocation, a direction, this new beginning called for a declaration. The Mt. Morris Kiwanis club helped senior students to sort out their thoughts, sponsoring a vocational essay contest. Memory serves me badly as to how many students wrote about their dreams---but Gerald Deneau, Eric Mann, and I read our essays before the Kiwanis club. Excerpts reveal an innocent resolve, colored by the idealism

Quote: "The ultimate culmination---my goal is to be a successful surgeon---a help to mankind. I expect to get just as much out of my work as I put into it. In the process of helping others, I shall help myself. Those people who help others obtain the greatest true enjoyment out of life. The greatest enjoyment I can ever hope to find is to work with the human body---to see the mysteries of life and its living mechanisms---and the greatest thrill of all, to save that life." At age 76, I try to understand what the mindset might have been at age 17. Words, words, words! Idealism, not yet dented by reality, is the stuff of dreamers, indeed!

THE CONTINUATION OF A JOURNEY

U.S. Navy V-12

Is life determined arbitrarily, by chance? So much seems to depend on the year of your birth. The Japanese attack on Pearl Harbor had called forth an unprecedented national defense effort. That effort included a government resolve to preserve the professions for the armed forces---with programs to educate those qualifying for medicine, dentistry, chaplaincy, etc. In 1943, at age 17, with Mt. Morris fading in the distance, there was nothing lonelier than the wail of the Norfolk & Western train whistle---nothing more foreign than the red clay of North Carolina. Durham---Duke University, with the majestic Duke Chapel, now home for uniformed V-12 sailors---neophytes not yet dry behind the ears. Is life determined by chance? Totally unaware, and with little direction, I found myself in a pre-engineering registration line. Oh, to be on the other side, a registration line for pre-medicine. Overcoming a 17 year old's shyness, I pleaded to be on the other side---granted! In a wink, the world lost an engineer, striving for precision and perfection---and gained a physician to deal with disorder and imperfection.

There was no shirking in V-12. Early morning formations, military routine, six semesters of study compressed into two years---and, at age 19, suddenly enrolled in the U. of Illinois College of Medicine in Chicago. On one of my brief visits to Mt. Morris during those years, Dr. Stengel invited me to accompany him, introducing me to the O.R. at Deaconess Hospital in Freeport for the first time. The main event? A heavy lady was having an emergent exploratory laparotomy and appendectomy. In my surgical baptism, though I was only a spectator, the baptismal fluid was sweat---induced by a warm night and nervousness as the scalpel found its way through skin, fat, and muscle, releasing another baptismal fluid---blood! A not totally unexpected combination of palor, clamminess, rubber legs, and eyes going every which way---ushered me to a chair. Wasn't it the better part of valor to sit down before falling down? I was a wimp? At that moment, sheer survival was paramount, surpassing fear of what people would think.

This O.R. scenario, of course, was my introduction to what would later become commonplace. Many times I have reflected on that warm Summer evening. At that moment, I was most content not to be on the other side---either as patient on the O.R. table or as the one wielding the scalpel.

Medical School---
U. of Illinois at Chicago

You surmise correctly that there were those who were quite skeptical of the brevity of our pre-medical preparation. Emphasis on what comprises the best pre-medical education has had its pendulum swings. Students often have been encouraged or required to have a broad liberal arts background. Somehow, it was felt, this would ensure a supply of nobler and gentler physicians. I remain unconvinced! Length of preparation most likely is inconsequential. The compleat, kindly, compassionate, and caring physician is more likely to be the product of inherent inclination and goodness rather than the product of learned behavior, supposedly gained through a lengthy education.

In 1945, tuition for in-state students was $108/semester. Present day medical students struggle to meet school costs, amassing huge debt loads. For years, there is the struggle to repay debts, which are often in six figures. Isn't it obvious that this financial burden has to impact the cost of health care? Plunging into my medical school courses, at least I didn't have the specter of debt hovering over me. I could concentrate on the "-ologies" thrown at me---bacteriology, physiology, pharmacology, embryology---and, of course, that "non-ology"---ANATOMY!

Oh, the uncertainty of the encounter. Woe, the trepidation as fledgling students were introduced to their cadavers in the anatomy lab. In this new beginning, we were admonished to show great respect, to be almost reverent and in awe of the lifeless body---but something was missing. "IT" was still a body, an object. I recall no teacher who understood that the cadaver was the former dwelling place for a person---a person who actually had a life. In hindsight, I question the time effectiveness of months of dissection, especially before the clinical years when dissection might have been correlated with the study of disease processes. Furthermore, if these young wannabe M.D.'s truly were to benefit from what dissection would reveal, would it not have been appropriate to have some guidance in dissection techniques? Alas! There was no prior training and not even concurrent training. Let's face it! We were on our own---subject occasionally to snide, sneering comments from the trained anatomists, ridiculing our efforts. Surely, the study of anatomy could have had more promise had it not been slowed by painstaking and inept dissection. Oh, well---some things never, never change. This, of course, is said somewhat facetiously, but I have wondered. . .? Did this first year hurdle in the anatomy lab instill in the embryonic physicians a determination to keep their patients from becoming cadaverous?

Training in any pursuit may involve its humdrum repetition with an unspectacular march to completion---but punctuated by bursts of sheer passion, the feeling that you have chosen well. A wise man once said, "Choose a vocation for which you have passion and you'll never work a day in your life." After plodding through the preclinical "-ologies" and after surviving the dreaded pre-junior year comprehensive exams, the clinical years were upon us. Medicine, obstetrics, surgery, PEDIATRICS. Influenced by a stimulating faculty, with down-to-earth teaching styles, I felt the passion---the lure to be a pediatrician. How else could you explain the young medical student spending his precious Christmas vacation days working in the pediatrics outpatient clinics at the U. of Illinois Research and Educational Hospital?

INTERNSHIP
MILWAUKEE COUNTY GENERAL HOSPITAL

If you have accepted by this time that life is truly a series of new beginnings, perhaps you also can believe that great things can come from new beginnings. Does an oak tree not owe something to the lowly acorn? "Human being" really is more a verb than a noun, which speaks strongly of motion, progress, an ascending up the ladder toward success. Every ladder to success must have its bottom rung---and the bottom rung in the medical hierarchy is the lowly intern. Seen by some as merely a rite of passage toward becoming the accomplished physician, the intern is recognized by nurses as unseasoned, thought of by the resident staff as sadly lacking, but valued in an odd way by the hospital administration because who else would do the scut work?

The intern year started in July and my first assignment was at the Wisconsin Avenue Emergency Hospital---perfectly timed to meet the avalanche of July 4 trauma. Scary! Fearsome! Never have I appreciated the hierarchy so much---those residents and attending M.D.'s who were on higher rungs of the ladder. The great lesson: Teamwork is of an essence!

Farther west on Wisconsin Avenue, the evolving intern year gave further evidence of the value of teamwork---working together with nurses, valuing and respecting their contributions. There is no doubt in my mind that this appreciation of nurses stayed with me throughout my medical/surgical career. In training, the waters are sometimes choppy and the sailing not so smooth---even precarious at times. Among the many successes, there are bound to be some misfortunes. In recounting my personal journey, you'll have to hear of learning experiences which have been like bumps in the road, like the frustration of flat tires.

I think of the orthopedic ward where, long before the birth of intensive care units, critically ill patients were grouped together in a small alcove. Their condition approached the futile and, realistically, they weren't expected to live. Yet, for families, there is always hope. Picture one such patient, one such family---transfixed as they watched the slow, steady drip of an intravenous solution, which they interpreted as sustaining that small hope for life. Consider now the plight of the young student nurse, caring for this elderly patient. The I.V. solution was primarily just for hydration and, since the solution had infiltrated the tissues, the nurse was instructed to remove the I.V. catheter. The student nurse faithfully carried out the order---and wouldn't you know it? Very shortly thereafter, the patient died. Pandemomium reigned! The distraught family, grief-stricken, demanded that the student nurse be fired since she obviously had caused the death of their father by removing the I.V. catheter. A most agonizing and difficult lesson: Cause and effect in treatment outcomes aren't always crystal clear. It was obvious that communication hadn't informed this family---had failed miserably.

There certainly are rewards to relieving a patient of the fullness of bowel obstruction, but sometimes those rewards are bought with an awful price, an odious price. With clinical and x-ray evidence of bowel obstruction, it fell to the intern to explain the reasons for a naso-gastric suction tube. After explaining that decompression of the stomach and small intestine would relieve fullness and retching, it then fell to the intern to insert the dreaded tube. In this maneuver, the odious price was forthcoming. Having gained confidence in my ability to reassure the patient and to insert the tube with minimum discomfort, I was priding myself a bit prematurely. In the process of inserting a tube one evening, the very sick and nauseous patient suddenly vomited all over my white uniform---a vomitus with predictable fecal odor, causing me to retch reflexly and I almost joined the patient in vomiting. A pungent lesson: In planting a garden in which medical skills can flourish, you won't always come up smelling like a rose.

At Milwaukee County General Hospital, interns were required to take ambulance calls---to bring in obstetrical patients, to answer medical emergencies, and to respond to trauma calls. Wanna come along with me?

1. Answering an obstetrical call, a frantic father pointed to the bathroom---where a multiparous mother had birthed a baby in the toilet. Good fortune! The baby was extricated from this neonatal baptism, the umbilical cord was cut, and a relieved mother and baby were transported to the hospital---vowing never again to experience conjoined birth and baptism.

2. I guess I never did understand the Milwaukee County policy of providing transportation for mothers-to-be who were being seen in the pre-natal clinics. The role of the intern wasn't to reason why. We just went along with the system and, come to think of it, many of those families simply didn't have transportation in 1950. Arriving at an apartment in response to a near-term patient's call, there was no doubt that waters had broke and there was active labor. We decided that there was sufficient time to transport her to the hospital. The father was invited to ride along---whereupon he indicated, "I'll follow in the car." Puzzled, we were left wondering why he had-

n't just brought his wife to the hospital in the car. Then we realized that this family simply was following the instructions given to low income folks---a luxurious system of benefits, to say the least.

    3. Have you ever been lonely, felt isolated, wanted a friend? Ride now with the young intern, responding to a medical emergency---there's an apparent heart attack victim in Wauwatosa. Rushing up the steps, we were met by a distraught family surrounding a heavy-set man, who was sitting upright in a chair---very still. Skin color was deep purple, he obviously was unresponsive---and dead? Remember, while trying to do our best in 1950, there were no cell phones for consultation with the hospital, no electrocardiograms to determine asystole or wacky heart rhythm. Clinically, there was no pulse and no breathing. The man was dead---and had been dead for some time.

    Out in the real world, far removed from the halls of the medical school, you learn that you treat not just the patient, but concerned family and friends also. By this time, the family of the heart attack victim had retreated to a nearby room. The sobbing and the sounds of discontent were increasing. "Isn't the doctor going to do anything---something?" Quick! Help me move this man to the floor so we can do something. CPR, chest compressions, resuscitation---sorry, not on the standard treatment list yet. Hand me that long intracardiac needle and adrenaline. Although visual and dramatic, injecting medication when there was no circulation to transport it anywhere---well, you have now met the height of futility. What's that? A siren? I felt a wave of relief that someone was coming to share responsibility, relieve me of my loneliness. Red lights flashing, a firetruck pulled up in front of the house. As firemen entered, I did nothing more than whisper, "He's dead, fellas." With that, they turned and left with, "Thanks, Doc, we've got another call." Terribly alone again---do you feel it?

    I tried to console the family, suggesting that they call their pastor and mortician. Riding back to the hospital, spirits were low and there was a sense of failure. Rest assured that this heart attack victim had all the criteria for being genuinely dead, but what if? I anguished for that grieving family, but the haunting question, "What if?," pursued me through the night and the next day until the obituary brought a sense of being right. Lesson: Sudden death is gut-wrenching for everybody.

  4. In Milwaukee County, ambulance drivers were under intense pressure from the sheriff's office to hit their targets unerringly in the shortest time possible. As a consequence, ambulance speeds of 80-90 m.p.h. were the rule along that treacherous 3-lane highway #100. I've always felt that work stoppages---yes, strikes---in the health care field violated the caregiver's oath and promise to be there---to serve. Therefore, it was difficult to do, but all interns announced collectively that we would no longer ride the ambulances unless speeds were reduced to something approaching safety. Our reasoning?

  a) High speeds were scary and, by the time we arrived at the scene of a crash, we were basket cases, less able to care for the crash victims.

  b) We had a quaint, admittedly self-centered desire to stay alive. Hallelujah! Our concerns were heard and common sense prevailed to lower ambulance speeds. Incidentally, during that year of servitude, we lost only one intern in the course of ambulance calls---and he was a wannabe psychiatrist who, for some reason, opened the side door during full flight and stepped out.

  5. During internship, I also had a comeuppance, learning the hard way that we live in a precarious balance with our environment. Most people are blissfully unaware and pursue happiness with little concern for organisms around that can invade our bodies and impede our progress. My vulnerability was brought home to me in the 4th quarter of my internship when I began to take on the appearance of a lemon---at least in color. Jaundice! Hepatitis! "Why me?" prevailed until replaced by a more sensible "Why not me?" This poorly-timed hepatitis caused a

hiatus in my medical training, but was accompanied by a crash course in patience. The drab, dull treatment routine? Diet, vitamins, rest, tincture of TIME. A vital lesson: Since none of us is invulnerable to assault from without, it behooves us all to start each day with awe and appreciation of everybody and everything around us---savoring good health as long as we can.

U.S. NAVY---
NEWPORT, RHODE ISLAND

Early U.S. Navy years--Capt. J.J. Timmes, chief of surgery, and Dr. Hudson

It's payback time! During my internship, I had received Lt., j.g. wages with the requirement that I'd have a 3-4 year hitch in the U. S. Navy Medical Corps. Initial assignment, by way of the Portsmouth, Virginia, Naval Hospital and the Boston Naval Shipyard---the naval hospital at Newport, R. I. New vistas for a young midwestern couple, another new beginning, the Pennsylvania turnpike with its tunnels, beautiful New England, naval housing, a medical officer in the U. S. Navy. Wow! Among the highlights:

1. Disaster! An overloaded boat, piloted by an inexperienced sailor, swamped in the rough waters of Narragansett Bay while returning sailors to their destroyers anchored near Newport. 17 young men drowned that dark night and bodies (floaters) periodically popped up in the ensuing days and weeks. Bodies were brought to the naval hospital for identification and the officer of the day's burden was to communicate with the next of kin. Naval wisdom, which for once was parallel with common sense, dictated that families not view the bloated bodies. Indeli-

ble learning is best gained in close-up personal encounters. Just so! Following internship, this was my first on-my-own confrontation with deadening grief as seen in the faces of families of those young men. In life, there are tasks which are truly unwanted, but necessary. Even the recovery of a body can offer the beginning of closure.

    2. My belly was a might queasy that morning when I set out for a naval training session in Boston, Mass. By noontime, queasiness was taking over and, for 15 minutes, was mistakenly interpreted as hunger. It wasn't! With nausea and discomfort crescendoing, the homing instinct became an obsession---I just wanted to get back to Newport. Driving alone, nausea called the shots, causing the car to stop by the side of the road frequently as wretched Ralph retched and ralphed---with no relief whatsoever. My torment was compounded by a swirling New England snow storm, eliminating road markers. Finally, at last! My good fortune! A sailor hitchhiking somewhere near Fall River, Mass. "Get in, sailor, you can drive." "Sorry, sir, I don't drive." Muttering something about his bad judgment in choosing this particular car, I managed to find Newport. Ascending the steps to our apartment ever so slowly, my steps told Peggy that something was amiss. "I think I'll just lie down for a while" was followed within 10 minutes by "Maybe I should go over to the hospital." The verdict? (I mean, diagnosis?) Acute appendicitis! The treatment? Appendectomy at midnight by Capt. Joe Timmes---with spinal anesthesia. It may be difficult for you to believe, but my usually shy, reticent manner was medically transformed into garrulousness by demerol (meperidine). Rambling, incessant, but complimentary patter was stifled by anesthesiologist Mike, judiciously using I.V. pentothal. Two lessons: 1) Always think of appendicitis when a bellyache persists. 2) Divide by 10 when assessing drug-induced compliments and promises.

    3. In gaining a sober estimate of your own self worth, pride can be a burdensome impediment. During internship, I had become supremely confident of my abil-

ity to manage diabetic emergencies. Even though this confidence fell far short of cockiness, I didn't think that there was any diabetic problem that couldn't be handled. Now, a challenge---and a comeuppance! A young sailor had just been admitted to the hospital in a comatose state. With a fruity odor to the breath and an extremely high blood sugar, the diagnosis was obvious---diabetic coma and acidosis. In retrospect, I don't think we misassessed the gravity of the problem, but the acidosis had had a head start and body systems already were beginning to shut down. Lacking present-day resuscitation skills and equipment, we still acted quickly, administering I.V. fluids to correct acidosis and I.V. insulin to lower a blood sugar out of control. Even this expeditious management was to no avail. The young diabetic responded poorly, going downhill rapidly---and died. A difficult and humbling lesson, indeed: In spite of your best efforts to do good, you'll not always succeed.

    4. The feeling of being able to handle any eventuality extended also to pediatrics. How well I recall the good feeling I had in treating children and their families at the U. of Ill. Research & Educational Hospital clinic. What was hidden from my view, in those early experiences with patients, was that the pace was slow, structured to the pace of learning---and not determined by the patients. As officer of the day, I also saw outpatients. I wasn't prepared for the onslaught as sailors brought their dependents in for medical attention. All Hell broke loose with crying babies, ill-tempered children, impatient and insistent worried parents---in an understaffed department. The lesson: Decisions as to medical specialization should be made only when all the facts are in. Gee, maybe the life of a pediatrician isn't so glamorous?

    5. Rubella, roseola, varicella---MUMPS! Aren't those communicable diseases supposed to be childhood nuisances? Now, I saw nothing funny about mumps. Why, then, was there side-splitting laughter heard from onlookers on the other side? Maybe laughter is accentuated by

somebody else's torment---or could it have been the chipmunk like appearance of mumps (epidemic parotitis)? Then, too, there were the sneaky and insinuating questions about vanishing virility. It's true! Mumps in the adult male may, on occasion, leapfrog to the testicles where, as the result of uncomfortable swelling, sperm production and procreation potential may plummet. Even to this day, the content of Peggy's prayers is undisclosed.

The growing family: Peggy, Rick, Ralph

HENROTIN HOSPITAL—
CHICAGO, ILLINOIS

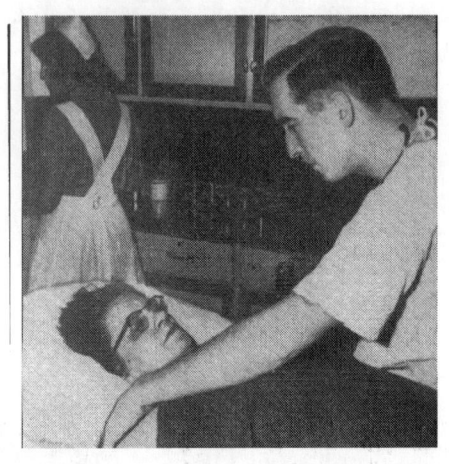

"MYSTERY WOMAN is questioned by Dr. Ralph Hudson at Henrotin Hospital after double suicide attempt." (Chicago Tribune newspaper report)

With the history of hepatitis and augmented by the good medical care we received in the U. S. Navy, it was tempting to consider a Navy career, maybe even becoming an admiral. These thoughts surely were borne out of uncertainty, but there also was that normal yearning to get back to our roots, to the Midwest. Choosing a Veterans Administration surgical residency, I was accepted with the stipulation that I'd spend the first year of residency at Henrotin Hospital. I later appreciated that this was a devious way of providing adequate medical coverage for Henrotin Hospital. Now, in the general scheme of things, I may have been a lowly first year resident in the V.A. system---but I was a head resident at Henrotin, in charge. The Henrotin Hospital E.R. was the repository for the hurting, the wounded, the zany---any poor soul the fire and police departments found in their street sweeping operations on the north side of The Loop. Sometimes known as "the knife and gun club," the Henrotin E.R. was a clearing house for alcoholics, trauma victims, and the demented. We also provided the benediction and blessing for those we pronounced dead in the police wagons---a prerequisite so that the dead could continue their journey to the county morgue. Shackled by long hours and imprisoned by a somewhat misguided sense of obligation, there was a troublesome gulf between Henrotin and our apartment in Broadview. Sometimes, we worry and would like to change the situation, but then we crash head-on into the truth. On life's treadmill, even with its regrets, it's impossible to get off, to re-live, to start over.

For some reason, the Henrotin days offered me glimpses into the lives of physicians and others who taught me something about life. You should meet them:

1. In the eyes of the house staff, our favorite mentor was Dr. Jay Cross, the young assistant to Dr. C. B. Puestow, chief of surgery. There were rumors floating around, never verified, that Jay received the princely sum of $12,OOO/year---a pittance for his performance. I mention compensation only because it was the norm that junior physicians, especially junior house staff, essentially were slave laborers. This seemed so blatantly unfair since it was obvious that the most skilled surgeon, the one who instilled confidence in the house staff, was the junior physician. The resident staff, following the patients closely, were well aware that it was Jay who protected the patients and served as a shield for the senior physician. Is it any wonder that we patterned ourselves after Jay---trying to copy his easy, unassuming, and reassuring manner with patients? The lesson: Even in the halls of medicine, follow the Jesus principle---judging not by external, suave appearance or high-priced houses and cars---but by the inner self.

2. Tom Kaveny was a marvelous nurse anesthetist. Tom Kaveny was a happy-go-lucky person. Tom Kaveny

was gay, homosexual. How difficult it is to remember growing up in a small town, but I recall no mention of homosexuality, incest, or domestic abuse---although, admittedly, these could have been lurking in some dark corner of that town. Perhaps I was raised in the straight and narrow path, shielded from what was considered sordid by righteous folk. Who knows? What I do know is that these subjects weren't comfortable topics either in Sunday school or on the playground.

At Henrotin, we heard things and were naturally curious, reconnoitering the Rush Street bars where males gathered. A revelation! A foreign land! A world previously unknown! In those days, there were far more cruel and demeaning terms for homosexuals than "gay." With all that, Tom was a jovial, forthright, and honest person, never beating around the bush. Putting people at ease, his simple comment was, "Well, some people like chocolate, some like vanilla." What we knew was that Tom was a highly competent anesthetist---a person you liked to see at the head of the O.R. table.

Tom Kaveny helped me formulate my understanding, my feelings about the homosexuality issue. Beginning with Tom and persisting to this day, with scientific evidence not specific one way or the other, it is obvious that there is an inherent predisposition in some males who have effeminate mannerisms and tone of voice---such that there should be no doubt that Tom and others didn't choose to be homosexual. The lesson: Again, judge not the book by its cover. Unbeknownst to most, Tom single-handedly provided the financial means for his three sisters to complete nursing school. Tell me. Why should a good person like Tom Kaveny be seen as some sort of a threat by heterosexuals? Methinks, through years of observation, that much of the Bible-quoting venom, the scriptural denunciations of homosexuality as sin---comes from the mouths of those who haven't been very comfortable with their own sexuality.

3. We talk a lot about role models in our lives and,

by inference, the reference is usually to the positive role models. Haven't you---I have---found that you have learned as much from bad examples as good examples? To the intern and resident house staff, attending physicians and consultants lived in another world---somewhere out there in Chicago or the suburbs. Our eyes weren't blinded and we didn't blindly worship, but these were established physicians with a glow of success. After all, they had already attained a significant position in medical circles.

In our post-operative care of patients, we had a front row seat in evaluating competency by observing the recovery and the comfort of patients. A proctologist in the Navy is the rear admiral. In civilian life, he is described as bringing up the rear, but getting to the bottom of things. The proctologist at Henrotin did many, many hemorrhoidectomies. My concern? His technique was less than gentle, he used excess catgut, and he routinely ordered hot compresses to be applied to the ano-rectal area post-operatively. There was no better way to ensure swelling of traumatized tissues---leading to inordinate pain, too many narcotics, and to inevitable urinary retention. Urinary catheters were a hot item! This surgeon's response to distraught patients? "Things sometimes have to get worse before they get better." Is it small wonder that I resolved then and there never to use hot packs, preferring cold applications to reduce swelling? Is it small wonder that I resolved to keep operative insult to a minimum? Yes, there's a lesson here, too: Indeed, although we follow the lead of those who set a good example, I submit to you that we learn also from bad examples. Haven't you ever said to yourself after witnessing some screw-up, "Deliver me from that!" A wise person has said, "He is a fool who learns not from his own mistakes. It is a mature, reasonably intelligent person who does learn from his own mistakes---but you have found a truly wise man when you meet the man who learns from the mistakes of others."

4. Why does misfortune have to come to the really

nice guy? Let me preface by telling you that the world's worst catastrophe that can befall any young obstetrician is a maternal mortality on his/her record. When we needed help handling obstetrical problems in the E.R., we knew we could always count on the young obstetrician. Building a practice, he was ready, willing, and supremely able to help. Every obstetrician knows that it is risky, even precarious, to accept a patient without prior prenatal care---tantamount to walking through a dangerous mine field. Sadly, the availability and willingness of this obstetrician tangled him in a web, saddling him with the no-no, a maternal death.

One evening, a young woman in her 9th month of gestation presented herself to the E.R., insisting that she was in labor. We were totally unaware of previous medical or psychiatric history, but her evasive mannerisms made us skeptical. She told us that she was under the care of an obstetrician elsewhere in the city, but she insisted that she needed help immediately. After determining that she, indeed, wasn't in active labor, we tried to reassure her and instructed her to contact her own obstetrician. We hadn't seen the last of this time bomb.

Three days later, our worst fears were realized when she reappeared in the E.R., bleeding like the proverbial stuck pig. We pulled out all the stops and the young obstetrician responded, not realizing that he had been dealt a losing hand. In fragments, the story unfolded that the hemorrhaging young woman was severely depressed. In desperation, not wanting the baby, she had swallowed rat poison (the same medication which is used as an anticoagulant in carefully controlled doses). Blood pressure bottomed out and, before we could gain access to veins for resuscitation---before we could even consider an emergent C-section---she bled out as we tried frantically to control an uncontrollable situation.

We couldn't evaluate the sincerity of the unwed father's grief. In catastrophic situations such as this, experience showed that the ones most critical and exhibiting the most profound grief often were witting or unwitting partners in creating the catastrophe. Due to this man's demands that more should have been done, a nerve-jarring and inconvenient grand jury hearing was held, concluding that the death was a suicide and without any misconduct on the part of the hospital or physicians in attendance. This helped only slightly to dampen the turmoil in all who witnessed this tragedy. Is there a lesson?: In retrospect, the pregnancy grabbed our attention, hiding the underlying deep depression. Persons suffering from a crushing depression, with feelings of hopelessness, don't always bubble over with their true feelings. Quite obviously, we failed to appreciate the gravity of the problem, the potential disaster, and the awful outcome.

HINES VETERANS ADMINISTRATION HOSPITAL
MAYWOOD, ILLINOIS

Presently the site of an extensive Loyola University medical complex, Hines V.A. Hospital was a throwback to military hospitals---with farflung wards on one level. In my first quarter, I drew an assignment to the anesthesia service. This may seem inappropriate for a surgical residency, but there simply was a shortage of anesthetists and the show must go on. With the experience gained in the first 3 months, each anesthesia-trained resident then gave anesthesia one morning a week for the remaining 3 years of the residency. What initially was thought to be unfair and burdensome (after all, we were surgical residents) proved to be a blessing and highly educational, instilling an understanding and appreciation of anesthesiology and the protection of the patient.

1 . The most dreaded anesthesia assignment was to be banished to the boondocks, the urology clinic. This outpost may have been only several hundred yards from the main building, but it seemed 5 miles away when emergent situations would arise and we'd like somebody there for support and hand-holding. Wonderful guys they were, but the urology residents weren't quite up to speed, literally or figuratively. From my point of view at the head of the table, they seemed oblivious of time--while I yearned to get the patient off the O.R. table and back to bed.

Dr. Max Sadove, a guru and pioneer in anesthesiology at the U. of Illinois School of Medicine, was a highly respected consultant. He happened also to have ties with a drug company, writing a research article on a new spinal anesthetic---proclaiming its safety and effectiveness. Those of us in the trenches, required to use the experimental drug, finally renamed it "Fleet-o-caine" because it's action was so fleeting. Unfortunately, patients were experiencing discomfort when the operation, timewise, was closer to the beginning than the end. You can readily see that this increased the patient's risk considerably since we had to protect the patient with supplemental sedating medications or general anesthesia. The lesson (largely learned by now): Patients should have full knowledge of the risks of experimental procedures or medications---and their consent should be informed. Granted that there still exists a significant gulf between the informed and the uninformed in health care; granted that many patients simply trust their caregivers; nevertheless, the best results are obtained when the patient and family are involved in intelligent and informed decision making.

2. Suicide is a deliberate action with exceedingly gloomy connotations. It generates deep feelings of guilt in those left behind---if only we had been able to foresee, to help. Surely, there is a common denominator in suicide---the feeling of utter hopelessness and a feeling that life just isn't worthwhile. A real concern---people contemplating suicide often keep fears to themselves. Oh, how we wish we could intervene with counselling, medications, understanding, etc. I have been forced to understand that, although a patient's feeling of hopelessness may seem to me to have little foundation---to the patient, suicide may be completely rational. Means of committing suicide are myriad---and innovative as you will see described now.

Let's now open the door to that linen closet on the psychiatric ward. Oh, no! There lies a young man, clutching a red-handled ice pick, which is imbedded in his chest. Don't! Don't touch it! Don't pull it out! With great care, he was transferred to the O.R., where the crew was preparing for a thoracotomy, to be in full control before removing the ice pick, which clearly had penetrated the heart. A startling sight! With the patient lying supine on the O.R. table, that ice pick was keeping exact time, synchronous with the heart beat. It seemed eerily surreal, like an upside down pendulum, like a demanding metronome. The patient, meanwhile, was agitated and objecting, "Why bother? Why are you doing this? I'll just do it again." Surgery was successful, the patient recovered but, as he had predicted, he was back in 6 months with yet another ice pick in his chest---and this time, the ice pick was motionless. The lesson: Never, never disregard statements of suicidal intent. A disappointing overview---not all stories have a happy ending.

3. Dr. C. B. Puestow, chief of surgery (we called him "Charlie Pus Tubes"), was a tall, stern man with an exalted national reputation---gained largely from his writings on experimental pancreatic surgery. Chronic pancreatitis results in blockage of the normal flow of pancreatic juices into the duodenum. The resulting back pressure is unusually painful. Theoretically, Dr. Puestow's idea showed promise. To relieve this awful pressure, he removed the tail of the pancreas and anastomosed (hooked up) the open pancreas to the small intestine so that there would be retrograde flow of juices into the intestine, thus improving digestion and reducing the chance of future attacks of pancreatitis.

Dr. Puestow's articles in the surgical journals reported that he was seeing no complications from the procedure---or, at least, few complications. Taken literally, that might be construed as accurate because it was we, the residents, who were seeing the complications. Alas! There were far too many instances of intra-abdominal abscesses and leakage of pancreatic juices. Needless to say, the popularity of this procedure was short-lived.

4. At the conclusion of the 3rd year of residency, residents were ranked and formally applied for their 4th year surgical service in the order of ranking. No surprise! It was mere formality for the first resident to proclaim, "I'd like your service, Dr. Puestow." Have you ever walked a tightrope? From on high, there was an edict that "moonlighting" was strictly verboten---that is, no medical work for pay could be done outside of Hines V. A. Hospital. A dilemma! What's a low-paid resident to do other

than to "moonlight" in order to pay the rent and buy some food?

I became adept at walking the tightrope, even without a safety net---performing well as head resident, but occasionally working nights elsewhere. The income for such activity was paltry by today's standards---but better than nothing. I had many hats. As track doctor at Maywood Park harness racing track (a contract with the harness drivers' association to be available should there be a spill or collision on the track), I received $20/night. I received the same princely sum of $20/night for manning the Elmhurst Memorial E.R. all night. On weekends, I would do house calls for Dr. Ferraiolo in the Des Plaines area---and suddenly felt important. After all, I was a small town boy. You can take the boy out of the small town, but you never can take the small town out of the boy. Thus, the young man emerging from the surgical training was, indeed, a general surgeon, but with a strong underlying family practice philosophy---perhaps in the spirit of Henry.

ANOTHER NEW BEGINNING---
EAU CLAIRE, WISCONSIN

Why Eau Claire? In pondering about a place to locate, a place in the real world, we didn't just throw darts at a map. On the other hand, considering the impact of the decision, we didn't have any internal or external expertise. After all, we'd never taken such a huge step before. Beginning a dual surgical practice in partnership with James Birney Dibble, we had surveyed Beaver Dam, Wisconsin Rapids, and Wausau before feeling that Eau Claire presented a significant opportunity. Wow! What a splash of color greets you in Eau Claire's autumn---muted pastels of yellow and orange contrasting beautifully with startlingly deep red maple leaves. Did we arrive in Eau Claire in autumn? No way! With the surgical residency ending in December, our arrival in Eau Claire was in January---with it's bone-chilling, teeth-chattering, sinus-closing temperatures of 30 degrees below zero Fahrenheit.

At long last, an office of my own where I could examine, treat, and counsel patients---if, indeed, there should be any patients brave enough to trust the newcomers. Our original office was in the Kappus building---hardly the Taj Mahal of medical practice. Though the outside temperature was numbing, our reception in the medical community sometimes was downright warm. Did Eau Claire really need two new surgical specialists? In those embryonic years, physicians may have been cordially competitive, but always collegial. Yes, to be sure, there could have been some resentment emanating from family physicians who were doing their own surgery---but that melted within a year or so. A special blessing on Dr. Peter Midelfort (the family name had been changed from Midelfart), who welcomed us as physicians who could raise the level of expertise in surgery. Greatly appreciated was his promise, "I can't really help you---but I most certainly won't hurt you."

As I have reminisced in writing, trying to retrieve interesting patients from the internship, Navy, and residency years, individual patients come across as a blur even though I can recall interesting problems. Then, it hit me! In those formative years of training, contact with patients didn't embrace closeness or continuity. With changes in surgical assignment, care of patients was transferred to an incoming resident. Hopefully, in this system, patients always were treated well and never considered to be just teaching tools. I'm simply acknowledging that there was less chance really to know and appreciate the patient as a person. In accepting V.A. care, I believe that patients instinctively understood the lack of lasting relationships with physicians. In returning to the hospital even within a few years, they just weren't going to see the same physician.

What a contrast! As I think back over the years of medical/surgical practice in Eau Claire, there are vivid images---persons standing out sharply in my memory. The images were formed in a climate of mutual trust and then refined, defined, and strengthened by the sense of mutual appreciation inherent in the physician/patient relationship. With a continuum of care from the start to finish, regardless of when or where that might be, the treatment scene was never haphazard or casual. In this closeness, there was the thrill of expected and unexpected recovery and, at times, the stifling disappointment when patients struggled and worsened. My hope, my purpose, my dream in highlighting some of these charismatic, unusual, and absorbing events and people is not to illuminate the world. Let somebody else do that. Neither is it my purpose to depict a standard of care which, by inference, others should follow. It would be sufficient for me---it would please me greatly ---if the reader somehow can sense in these stories and philosophies an honesty, a consistent concern for patients, and a non-financial motivation in medical care. Just by chance, there may also be an added dividend. Yes, you may even catch a glimpse of how patients have impacted my growth---and a glimpse of who I have been and who I am. That would be more than enough---and would justify the writing.

Although I'm confessing my concerns about infringing on patient confidentiality, I've still personalized some stories with names. Admittedly, when I do that, I walk through a minefield, hoping not to damage any relationship by invading confidentiality---but certainly aware of that possibility. No, I've taken no pains to contact patients or families about inclusion in these writings. First, that would have been a logistical nightmare. Second, I guess I'll just hope for their understanding and assent. Who knows? People who are mentioned might even find a sense of pride and a sense of comfort in being remembered. Perhaps, deep down, they would know that, in a way, their inclusion in my memory carries also a profound gratitude for the way in which they have added to this odyssey.

You can see that, before getting to the main meal, I have provided appetizers and salads. Perhaps you will recognize this prelude to my memoirs as another thinly-disguised foreword. The following personal observations and philosophies have helped me each day. Actually, this prelude could be an interlude or a postlude because these principles have grown and have been found to be true in experience, have been woven into the fabric of my cloth. They are timeless!

1. Physicians sometimes err in assuming that they have all the answers, even falling into the trap of being judgmental when patients fail to meet their expectations. What a pity! A generous principle treats people, insofar as possible, where they happen to be---not where you secretly think they should be. Discrimination is a part of life and there is a temptation for it to ride along with the attainment of degrees. Recognize discrimination, but keep it

in an inconspicuous place in your house, replacing it with perception and appreciation. Notably, discard it when listening to the fat or thin, the rich or poor, the high or low intellect. If you can do this, you will reap huge rewards---as the obese lady who once remarked after an office visit, "Thank you, thank you for not once telling me I'm too fat. I already know that!"

2. I think I absorbed through osmosis some of the wisdom of Henry J. Stengel, M.D. Henry, such a wise man, often told me that society would think better of the

Henry J. Stengel, M.D. with Peggy Hudson

medical profession if more physicians were to be philosophers. His implication was obvious. Society wants knowledge and technical expertise, but responds best to warmth, care, and concern---not to what might be construed as aloofness, haughtiness, or "I know what's best for you---I'm the doctor."

3. In chronic care, we deal with people who have once had a life, but find themselves trapped in a less attractive shell. Too often, frailties of the flesh have resulted in dwindling charm---at least, charm as the world sees it. In acute care, we deal with people who are more likely to be vibrant, with great promise. The common bond in treating the chronically ill or the acutely ill is the family that surrounds and supports the patient. In every situation, even while respecting the privacy needs of patients, never impose isolation of the spirit by excluding families from your thoughts.

4. Time can be an incessant, merciless taskmaster, reminding the physician of the next patient, the next, the next. Turn the tables! Treat time as servant, not taskmaster. Heed the words of Sir William Osler, the storied physician, "Listen to the patient. He/she might just tell you

what is wrong---and you may learn in the listening."

5. Life is a spiritual journey, an adventure---to be lived by FAITH---which is the evidence of those things hoped for, but not always understood.

Hanging out the shingle, a figurative declaration of the readiness to see patients, there didn't seem to be a surge of patients storming the office door to be seen. There weren't floods of referrals from family practitioners who, after all, knew nothing of the newcomer specialists. I was armed with what I thought was superb training, but without joining an established group practice, where were all the patients waiting to benefit from such training? A conundrum! Nobody wishes misfortune on another being, but the one who would practice the healing arts is as nothing unless there are those to be healed. The one who would bind up the wounded, who would make the broken whole---that one sits by the road until there are those who are wounded, broken, hurting---crying out for help.

THE COLFAX TORNADO

Opportunity presented itself when a tornado hit the town of Colfax in the Spring of 1958. 17 people died and many were injured, requiring the presence of those with medical/surgical skills---a chance to help, to prove worth. After the tornado cut its deadly swath through the Knapp hills into Colfax, emergency calls went out, urging health care teams to go to Colfax. Disaster plans were nowhere near a state of readiness---but, wisely, we were redirected to Luther Hospital, the central receiving area for triage and treatment of casualties. The pictures of two tornado victims are burned into my memory.

1. Rose J. was lying in the corridor of Luther Hospital, along with many others, when we met. In quasi-medical terms, Rose was a mess---horribly bruised and covered with mud. Perhaps fortuitously, the tornado had been preceded by torrential rainfall, converting fields into mudpits, providing a softer and safer landing place for the likes of Rose---who had been flying through the air, catapulted from her home. When I visited Rose in Colfax a month later, she was still trembling. She told me of the crushing feeling of impending doom as she realized that she might die and she recalled her wish, "Oh, how I wished I could come down."

Rose needed two blood transfusions to replace the blood lost into her tissues. Roses may be red and yellow, but black and blue will always be synonymous with Rose. Hopefully not smugly, but with a modest sense of pride in being the first surgeon to expedite a patient into the O.R., I set out to treat what appeared to be a compound fracture of the forearm. After copious washing and irrigation, the compound fracture and exposed bone turned out to be a huge piece of wood imbedded in the soft tissues near the wrist. How fortunate for Rose! Simply removing the humongous wood splinter promised her a quicker recovery than would have been the case with a potentially disastrous infection stemming from a compound fracture. While regretting the terrifying destruction and human misery, it was and still is a good feeling to have been a part of the cleanup after the storm.

    2. Tucked away in a corner of the pediatric ward lay a 9 month old baby boy---baby Lund. Triage dictated that efforts be expended for those with more apparent chance of recovery. Considering the x-ray evidence of a skull that resembled a cracked eggshell, he's still alive? Let's give him a small blood transfusion to correct severe anemia---and, of course, keep him warm in his crib with abundant oxygen. With neurological consultation unavailable in 1958---and with no obvious depression of the skull fracture---let's just keep providing good nursing care. Sometimes, an uncanny intuition leads away from injudicious intervention. Call it an example of benign neglect, if you choose. Hey! Look! Baby Lund, within 24 hours, started smiling and kicking, unaware that his father had died in the tornado. His mother later re-married and, with an appreciative note, invited me to her son's high school graduation. Baby Lund, critically injured, had survived to become a responsible young man---maybe not a giant intellectually (because of the head trauma), but surely a bit of sunshine for his mother after her terrible loss. Yes, good can rise from the ashes.

CAN THE SURGEON BE EVERYTHING TO EVERYBODY?

I believe that, for me, humility has been a stepping stone to maturity. Humility, sometimes enforced, is more experiential than inherent. Humility may even be compatible with a sense of confidence if it helps you achieve a reasonable sense of your own self worth. No matter what the public perception may be, no surgical training program can prepare a surgeon for every conceivable eventuality. To be sure, you may have heard of the stereotype of the god-like, self-assured, and cocky surgeon---exuding glamour, knowing everything, and capable of doing everything. Common sense and increasing surgical specialization have given the lie to that nonsense. Unfortunately, during the early Eau Claire years, there still existed the public assumption that surgical training conveyed blanket permission to be a jack-of-all-trades. In Eau Claire, I was keenly uncomfortable with that assumption. For completeness and with forthrightness, I invite you into my inner thoughts regarding two troubling cases.

    1. To a breadwinner, there is nothing more upsetting than a serious hand injury. Edward D., father of three, working with a band saw in his Durand place of employment, was horrified as the saw ripped through the palmar surface of his hand. Expeditiously, he was prepared for surgery where the extent of his injuries could be evaluated. With good illumination, we realized that the extent of the injury was much greater than anticipated. In my training, there had been no hand surgery per se---but I felt qualified to assess and treat, having studied hand anatomy carefully. The problem was that this hand injury was worse than anything I had ever seen. Painstakingly, I matched up and sutured severed tendons and nerves---akin

to working a puzzle. Yet, there seemed so much more to do.

In 1960, there weren't any hand surgery departments, but Dr. Lindscheid at Mayo Clinic was gaining a reputation in the Orthopedic Surgery department as having an intense interest in hand surgery. How relieved I was that Dr. Lindscheid would receive the patient in transfer to continue his care. After all, this man's hand was his livelihood. In recent years, hand surgery clinics have sprung up---with surgeons who devote their time only to hand injuries. With this specialization, reattachments of extremities and digits have become commonplace---along with other truly exotic surgeries.

2. Tonsillectomy and adenoidectomy (T.&A.) has had pendulum swings with reference to just how beneficial the operation has been in improving patient health. The fact that my training wasn't in the EENT arena mattered not to those who thought I should be able to do everything. Mrs. J. was absolutely adamant that I should perform the T.&A. on her two daughters. She couldn't imagine anybody else as the surgeon. Reluctantly, I agreed and the procedures went satisfactorily---if not smoothly. Too much trepidation! Too much ill at ease!

Never have I felt so much at peace as when I confronted myself and resolved never again to undertake procedures where I had doubts about my training level or where my comfort level wasn't the best. I think it was bad timing for me to complete residency training when the general surgeon was expected to do orthopedics, urology, ENT, even neurosurgery. My personality failed miserably to meet those expectations. As I foresaw, with the passage of time, the general surgeon no longer has had to be the do-it-all handyman. To the contrary, the pendulum swing now has general surgeons doing less and less as other surgical disciplines have developed their own specialty boards. Although there are surgical boards of certification (I was a diplomate of the American Board of Surgery) which establish high standards to protect patients, there is yet a more important quality---personal integrity. We seem to have no trouble discerning a wide range of talents in singers, artists, athletes, etc. Is it, then, such a stretch to acknowledge that surgeons, also, have greater and lesser abilities? External societal regulation in the service professions should and does impose acceptable levels of performance---which, you'll note, usually consists of minimum standards. Far more important is an internal regulation---the resolve of each surgeon to be centered on patient welfare and not on his/her own image.

THE ANNUAL DEER HUNT

To understand fully the following vignettes, you must have felt the fervor for, the camaraderie in, the male machoism of---the Wisconsin November deer hunt, co-sponsored by the D.N.R. and the Department of Tourism. Before I am corrected, I hasten to note the increasing change in the gender ratio. Just as the hunted are male and female, "male machoism " has given way to hunters being both male and female. The Wisconsin deer herd is carefully monitored and nurtured in preparation for harvest--- when 800,000 gun and bow hunters are in the woods. During this hallowed time, the rallying cry, the reason for being, the thrill of the hunt is to---"get my deer." Lacking, it has always seemed to me, is the forthrightness to admit that, "I really like to kill something." The intensity of the hunt and the potential for injury are seen vividly in these illustrations.

    1. Actually, considering the thousands of hunters in the woods, mishaps are few. Yet, in spite of the "wearing of the orange," a man was brought to the E.R. with a serious gunshot wound through the left hip and groin, tearing away the spermatic cord and testicle. Dr. Gene Kilkenny, orthopedic surgeon, and I worked collaboratively. As the incision approached the groin area, all Hell broke loose! There was blood everywhere! with the patient hemodynamically stable, we hadn't anticipated that the femoral vein had been severed. Quickly, we were able to clamp the bleeders, control the hemorrhage, and breathe a little easier. In further assessing, we were amazed that the adjacent femoral artery hadn't been severed also. If that had occurred, the hunter wouldn't be in the E.R. He would have bled out in the woods.

    Regrettably, because of the extensive loss of femoral vein, we had no option other than to tie off the vein. Predictably, this hunter developed a chronically swollen leg, but he did survive to tell the tale. As he re-lived the event, he could distinctly see the other hunter as he took aim. Across a field, he saw the gun swinging around, pointing right at him. Obviously, this was unintentional. Have you ever gone through a stop sign and realized that your mind was someplace else? Just so! In this case, a hunter was so engrossed with something he saw beyond the injured man that the "wearing of the orange" proved to be of no protection.

2. Just five days before opening day of the deer season, Tim (a senior high school student) fell and fractured his right clavicle (collar bone). With the bone fragments overriding, the preferred treatment was a simple snug figure-of-8 splint to hold the shoulders in military posture. What was his first question? You guessed it! "Can I go hunting?" As so often is the case, the question was asked almost rhetorically because the answer was already known---but just hoping, hoping. My responsibility was to point out that carrying and shooting a gun, walking and possibly tripping---these factors would pose too great a risk for comfort and safety. "Sorry, you really shouldn't."

Near tears and caring little for comfort or safety, Tim insisted that he could shoot from his left shoulder. Two weeks later, in a scheduled follow-up exam, Tim was all smiles as he uttered the magical words, "Hey, Doc, I got my deer." Admittedly, in the process, he hadn't really harmed himself. I share with you now a crucial lesson---humbling, but realistic and understandable. Very soon after completing training, physicians should heed this warning. Hear ye! Patients will not necessarily take either your pills or your advice.

IS FOOTBALL THAT IMPORTANT?

Following the previous demonstration of patient autonomy, I recall another instance in which my better judgment was overruled not only by the patient, but also by the consulting internist---surprisingly. John C. was one of those natural athletes, a standout high school quarterback in his senior year---with all-state potential. In the height of a competitive football season, John developed fever, lassitude, and striking physical findings of massive swelling of lymph nodes in the neck together with palpable enlargement of the spleen. John's father always was a little flighty. Well, he went ballistic, convinced that his son had leukemia. A simple blood test confirmed the clinical impression---infectious mononucleosis. The prescribed treatment? Nothing but vitamins, nutrition, rest, and my favorite drug---tincture of time.

With John feeling better, a predictable clamor arose from both father and son. "Rest? I'm feeling better. Why can't he/I play?" I warned about the danger of exposing an enlarged spleen to a collision sport. The spleen is actually a large and bloody lymph gland tucked up under the left rib cage. A torn spleen can be a critically and scary emergent situation. To satisfy the family and, at the same time, to share responsibility, I suggested consultation. To my surprise, the consulting internist permitted John to play in the last game of the season. A few moments of glory! The only lesson here? Obviously, we can have differing views on what is important enough to die for. Fortunately, John starred---and wasn't hurt.

GO TO JAIL! DO NOT PASS GO!
(A community responsibility?)

The reasons why I started going to jail? I can't quite bring the answer up on my computer. My cerebral synapses are jammed, blocking out some of those nights in the early 1960's. Perhaps I already was nauseated by the evidence of too much alcohol on the highway---with resulting death and injury. Perhaps I was guided by a sense of community responsibility that some physician should go to jail---when called. It certainly wasn't for monetary reward. My recollection is that going to jail and staying there for an hour netted me a check for $20.

Whatever! Law enforcement officials knew that I would respond to their call to interview and examine guests of the police department who had been apprehended on suspicion of DWI. Before the availability of precise breathalyzer determination of BAC (blood or breath alcohol concentration), the only laboratory help was a urine sample, difficult to obtain in an uncooperative suspect or one whose pants were already soaked. With concern for individual rights, I routinely informed suspects, "You don't have to talk to me." Here, I quickly learned the lesson of variable justice. Some subjects would just blurt out, "That's o.k---I'm just drunk." Others, knowing how the game was played, clammed up and got a lawyer. The latter usually belonged to the more intelligent, country club set. In my examination (wanna try it?), I'd use word and test phrases to determine impairment---phrases such as, "Around the rugged rock a ragged rascal ran." Then, I'd test coordination with heel-to-toe walking and the finger-to-nose test.

In that day, to be on the safe side, we recommended that people go to trial only when they couldn't even walk or talk without obvious impairment. In retrospect, after much experience, it's now apparent that the BAC of those going to trial was about 0.20. Frequently, as a consequence of going to jail, I'd also have to appear in court to testify for the prosecution. For your interest, I now describe two highlights of those court appearances---one, a moment of anxiety---and the other, a lasting resentment.

    1. When I testified about heel-to-toe walking, a defense attorney attempted to downplay the significance, proclaiming, "Why, a normal person couldn't do that." Then, he asked me to demonstrate the test and the judge agreed. Can you imagine what was going through my mind as I carefully walked heel-to-toe in front of the jury---hoping against hope that I wouldn't sway or stumble? I didn't!

    2. I frankly was surprised that one young floozy made it to court. When she was apprehended for DWI, she was so impaired and inebriated that she thought that her drinking companion (a Greyhound bus driver) was a policeman. Her attorney was a man whom I had considered to be a friend. In the course of his questioning of me, he strongly insinuated that my judgment would be tainted by bias. "After all," he charged, "you have this sweetheart deal with the police department to make lots of money." I didn't then---and I don't now---appreciate that slur on my integrity. The jury, quite predictably, convicted his client.

    I've never understood the charade played by attorneys, calling each other names in the courtroom and then laughing it off at lunch as just part of the game. Within a few days, my attorney "friend" called me with the hope that I hadn't taken his courtroom words personally. Did I take those words as personal? Wouldn't you? Call me thin-skinned if you wish, but I still remember.

TRI-COUNTY MEMORIAL HOSPITAL--- WHITEHALL, WISCONSIN

Arriving in Eau Claire, our bank account was as low as the temperature. We carried with us one savings bond and Union National Bank, bless them, gave us a loan without collateral. Just as in residency years with the moonlighting, the rent must be paid, the family must be clothed and fed. If there were a stage play depicting the glamour of surgery, I'd create a villain character, typifying reality, running around the stage searching for sources of income.

Ah, a beacon of light in the distance! The distance? 40 miles. The beacon? The small hospital in Whitehall, badly in need of a surgeon. The opportunity was a God-send to us. As we initiated weekly surgeries plus on-call emergency cases, we never neglected to examine patients carefully to ascertain proper indications for surgery---and to see patients post-operatively. Assisting at surgery and providing much of the care following surgery were the referring family physicians---Dr. Larry Hanley, Dr. Mark Schneider, Dr. Charles Meyer. We were comfortable and reassured by the excellent quality of the lab and x-ray departments, the dedication of the nursing and O.R. staffs. Furthermore, and very important, there was a high degree of community and patient confidence in the hospital. Travelling south to Whitehall was, in a way, a respite from Eau Claire---a place where I was "king for a day." If that weren't perk enough, there was the ever present German chocolate cake baked by Judith Steen, the O.R. supervisor, general overseer, and jack-of-all-trades.

You'll recall that, with my background in anesthesia during my residency, I gained a deep appreciation for the person at the head of the O.R. table. In Eau Claire, there was the luxury of having pioneer anesthesiologists---Drs. Thimke, Bjurstrom, and Kelley. At that time, most anesthesias in the nation were administered by well-trained nurse anesthetists---independently. Through the years, anesthesiologists and nurse anesthetists have merged their talents, working in groups together. In 1959, Esther Johnson was the nurse anesthetist in Whitehall. Trained at Chicago's Cook County Hospital, she primarily was skilled in the use of open drop ether---dripping ether onto a gauze mask held over the patient's face. Although often accompanied by post-op nausea, ether had a wide margin of safety. On the downside, ether's obnoxious odor produced resistance in children and adults alike---and post-op vomiting was the rule. Furthermore, in the O.R., ether fumes filled the air so much that there was concern that the surgeon might become sleepy. Peggy always knew when I had been called to Whitehall for an emergency. Coming home at 3:00 a.m., after performing an emergency appendectomy, I had to be especially alert and Peggy knew when I entered the house because the house soon reeked of ether.

Major elective surgical cases were usually transferred to Eau Claire. Yet, we felt confident in treating some life-threatening emergencies in Whitehall when transfer would have been difficult or a hardship for patient and family. To accomplish these more critical surgeries safely, we utilized a bizarre system of blood procurement, somehow sanctioned by the Eau Claire blood banks. When I received the call for emergent surgery---and knowing the blood type of the patient---I'd stop by our hospital lab and carry several pints of blood with me to Whitehall, where the blood would be cross-matched for compatible transfusion. I predict that you'll never hear another instance of such a practice---a practice which, of course, would be considered anathema in today's blood banks. Two cases are now recounted as examples of how the combination of surgeon and available blood was helpful in bringing patients through critical situations. Added are two more cases, involving obstetrics and orthopedics.

1. In the Whitehall area, there were many Amish farm families. Horse and buggy transportation exemplified their simple way of life---and certainly gave them identity on the highway. Can you imagine trying to stay warm in an unheated buggy in Wisconsin's freezing winter? To resist the cold winds, tight side curtains were employed in, what seemed to me, to be a futile attempt to insulate the buggy. Unfortunately, in trying to stay warm, sight lines were severely restricted. Add the element of a swirling snowstorm and, friends, we've got a problem. No, not just a problem. A disaster!

An Amish farmer, coming to town for supplies, couldn't hear or see the train and was struck by the locomotive at a crossing in downtown Whitehall. Falling blood pressure and abdominal pain strongly indicated hemorrhagic shock due to internal bleeding. Just so! Surgical exploration revealed an extensively lacerated spleen. With blood infusing, splenectomy was accomplished, stabilizing the patient. Post-operative course was more uncomfortable because of fractured ribs, but the Amish farmer made it. His buggy habits probably wouldn't change but, at least, he'd be ready for Spring planting.

2. Let us not criticize the understandable human reluctance to engage in encounters with surgeons. Let us agree, also, that the one who would lie down on the O.R. table just for the thrill of it would be adjudged to have lost something upstairs. Let us also not criticize the person who would prefer to leave this world with all body parts intact. Rational people, in general, cherish extremities and internal parts considered to be precious and meaningful. Is the soul to be found in the brain, the heart, the liver. . .?

For some Amish women, the soul was firmly imbedded in the uterus, the womb, the watery playground for those waiting to be born. Before mechanization, many farm couples desired large families out of necessity to provide a much-needed labor force. Who knows? The Amish woman also may have cherished the uterus as that which made her more attractive in giving birth to so many children. On a cold and gray January day, an Amish mother gave birth to her 12th child early in the morning---easy, spontaneous, uneventful. After all, hadn't she done this before? After expulsion or extraction of the placenta, it was the uterine responsibility to contract quickly, firming up the uterine muscle fibers to clamp down on bleeding. Maybe this uterus was just fatigued and pooped out---or just plain lazy after 12 pregnancies. Whatever the reason, uterine contraction was weak---the tired old horse wouldn't respond even though whipped and urged by medications and massage. As expected, heavy bleeding persisted.

Dr. Hanley monitored the situation carefully through the day, realizing that hysterectomy might be the only way of keeping the mother from bleeding to death. When the possibility of hysterectomy was suggested, the Amish woman was adamant---she wouldn't, she couldn't lose her uterus. Finally, by evening, with her husband's support and reassurance, she gave permission for surgery---albeit reluctantly. Having been in conversation with Dr. Hanley during the day, I wasn't surprised to receive the phone message, "Come as soon as you can---and bring blood." Surgery on the uterus, with the pelvic engorgement of pregnancy, presented risks---but the greater risk had to be faced and removed. Fortunately, the procedure went smoothly, the flabby uterus was removed, and the patient went home to care for her 12 children. In trying to understand what seems to be bizarre and irrational thinking in another, we never can really get inside that person's head. I've always wondered. Do you suppose that, in her weakening condition and with the thought of dying, her desire to have more children was overridden by the spectre of those 12 children being motherless?

3. Using the retrospectoscope, our manner of handling Cesarean sections in Whitehall now seems primitive. Even so, it still seems to me that conscionable physicians through the years have tried to do the best they could with the equipment and knowledge at hand. Today, anesthesia

for Cesarean section causes little or no sedation for the baby, uterine incisions are usually transverse through the thin lower uterine segment, and resuscitation of the newborn is an art, much more effective.

In the Whitehall O.R., with its ether anesthesia, we protected the baby by first making an incision through skin, soft tissues, fascia and muscle, right down to the peritoneum---using only local infiltration anesthetics. Then, during induction of general ether anesthesia, we were poised to quickly open the peritoneal membrane lining the abdominal cavity and, through a vertical uterine incision, the baby was delivered before any respiratory depression could occur. Although crude by today's standards, there were no complications. Mothers and babies all did well. An interesting sidelight: Many years later, while performing surgery at Sacred Heart Hospital, a young surgical tech obviously wanted to tell me something. She was tickled and bubbling over as she revealed, "Dr. Hudson, my mother tells me that you delivered me by Cesarean section 20 years ago in Whitehall." De ja vu! A good feeling!

4. Do you recall my references to orthopedic surgeons as carpenters? Do you recall my feelings of discomfort when, as a newly-trained surgeon, I was expected to do everything? Well, in Whitehall, there was a system set up for the reduction and nailing of hip fractures---and I was there. After familiarizing myself with the instrumentation and the x-ray monitoring, we actually did 5-6 hip fracture fixations. This involved placing the patient on the O.R. table with the affected leg widely abducted. Guide wires were placed across the fracture site and, with x-ray confirmation of correct placement of the guide wires and alignment of the fracture, reamers were used to bore a channel over the guide wire---through which a threaded nail could be inserted. This nail was then attached to a metal plate along the lateral aspect of the femur for solid fixation. At the time, it was something which had to be done, but soon I willingly left bones and joints to those who enjoyed jig-saw puzzles and hammering.

OSSEO AREA HOSPITAL--- OSSEO, WISCONSIN

To some readers of a certain vintage, the pseudonym, "Old Blue Eyes" would bring forth the voice and visage of Frank Sinatra. In West Central Wisconsin, "Old Blue Eyes" was the moniker for Dr. Robert Leasum, the droll and dry humorist, who just happened also to be an unusually adept family physician, loved by his community. In the early 1960's, Bob returned to Osseo after completing medical school, working with his physician father. Tragically, the elder Dr. Leasum was struck down by a massive cerebral hemorrhage and died, leaving Bob to mind the store---with the help of two physicians---brothers Brad and Dick Garber. At about that time, the Osseo community decided to build a hospital---and I was privileged to be a surgical consultant. Just as in Whitehall, I was comfortable in the Osseo O.R. because of the competent nurse anesthesia and the excellence of the ancillary lab and x-ray services. There were many, many surgical cases, but two cases stand out as unique, difficult, and testing. In the first case, you are given a glimpse of Dr. Leasum, surely a selfless and patient-centered physician.

1. How fortuitous! My schedule was clear when a call came from Osseo, describing a 70 year old man with a history of duodenal ulcer, now with marked hypotension due to sudden massive vomiting of blood. My gut instinct was, "Better transfer him to Eau Claire." The answer was quick in coming, "Don't think he could make the trip. We're taking him back to the O.R."

When I arrived on the scene, having flown down I-94, the patient had been anesthetized and an incision had been made. The clinical impression of massive bleeding from a duodenal ulcer was soon confirmed. What a pumper! Opening the duodenum, we could see the spurting artery in the middle of the ulcer. The gushing of blood was stemmed by my finger pressing firmly against the ulcer bed---the "hole-in-the-dike" maneuver. Perhaps this doesn't sound exactly elegant, but believe me---it was effective. Then, with a measure of calm restored to the O.R., a figure-of-8 silk suture was carefully placed around the open artery and the hemorrhage was controlled. The battle having been won, this was no time to attempt more extensive gastric surgery to correct the underlying ulcer problem. This was the time to be thankful that we had won this battle. The patient now could recuperate---and we could think about fighting the war some other day.

What I'm about to tell you now should surely intrigue you. My prediction is that you'll probably never hear anything approaching what happened that day in that O.R. Granted that I haven't done a computer search on the subject, but I doubt that I, likewise, will ever see the equal of what happened that day. During the routine closure of the incision, the anesthetist informed us that the patient was---well, o.k but, "He'd be a lot better with another unit of blood." Aware that the lab had no more compatible blood available, Dr. Leasum simply offered, "I have the same blood type." With that, off he went to the lab to donate a pint of blood---and then scrubbed back into the O.R. picture as if nothing had happened---while his blood was infusing into the patient. Please contact me if you've ever heard this scenario matched. What timing! What spontaneity! What unselfishness!

2. This vignette is, in some ways, in stark contrast with Dr. Leasum's unselfishness. To set the stage for the problems encountered in a cholecystectomy mishap, I must give you a glimpse into the past. There is no question that, in the present day, patients are benefitting from much less invasive laparoscopic surgery, especially that involving the gall bladder and bile ducts. This obviously is a wonderful surgical advance. Fifty years ago, we likewise were making advances in applying precision to surgery.

Over and over, it was drummed into us, "Always be able to see. Identify cystic duct, cystic artery, and common bile duct before transecting any structure in the process of removing the gall bladder." Scrupulously observing this instruction, a distinct improvement over the previous two decades, not once did I injure a common bile duct in the course of hundreds of cholecystectomies. Not once did I have to take a patient back to the O.R. to control bleeding from a cystic artery. Now, were those untoward events possible? Yes, of course---even in good hands---but I always had an inner feeling that they shouldn't happen. Look over my shoulder now as a bizarre problem unfolds, involving a serious bile duct injury. In the process, you may also share some disbelief at the quirkiness, the defensiveness, and the rationalization put forth by the surgeon responsible for the injury.

I wasn't there but, at first glance, there seemed to be nothing unusual about what was described as a fairly routine cholecystectomy on Mrs. J performed by another surgeon at the Osseo Area Hospital. Within 5 days, however, it was clear to all observers that she was in trouble, experiencing excessive bloody bile drainage. Dressings were constantly soaked and lab tests documented increasing jaundice. Without C.T. scans or other present day diagnostic techniques, there was no recourse other than to follow gut instincts---to surgically explore, define, and correct the problem.

Re-entering a recent operative area requires good lighting and exposure together with a generous dose of patience. Gradually the cause of the problem became apparent---a complete transection of the common bile duct. It would have been hazardous---yea, well nigh impossible---to attempt suturing the severed ends of the bile duct together. The reason? There was such a gap between the severed ends of the bile duct that too much tension would result on the suture line. This would have been an invitation to disaster and failure. Therefore, to restore bile flow back into the intestine, I brought up a limb of jejunum (the

2nd portion of the small intestine), suturing it to the proximal severed bile duct just underneath the liver. It's sort of complicated, but lower down, the food pathway was also reconstituted. Drainage stopped, healing was prompt, and Mrs. J. recovered nicely---a very grateful patient.

In this litiginous society, Mrs. J. eventually filed a malpractice claim against the original surgeon for severance of the common bile duct. Actually, in this type of case, the legal principle of "res ipsa loquitor " (the thing stands for itself) would prevail. I can understand the disbelief on the part of that surgeon that such a mishap could have occurred. He had been out of town when we had corrected the problem. He began to postulate the possibility of rare embryonic anatomical variations to somehow be responsible for the bile drainage. I'm not sure what he was thinking, but in depositions on the case, he involved me by suggesting that I didn't necessarily have to re-operate---that the problem would have resolved on its own.

Hearing this assertion, Mrs. J.'s attorney naturally jumped on his words, enjoining me in the suit---necessitating numerous time-consuming depositions and court appearances over the next year. I could afford to be outwardly calm because, after all, I was the one who identified the injury and corrected it---and Mrs. J. was steadfast in her belief that I had saved her life. Inwardly? Disappointed and seething! Not a happy camper! Of interest was the testimony of a plaintiff's surgical consultant---who expressed amazement that surgery of that magnitude could have been performed at Osseo. Predictably, I eventually was dropped from the suit and a settlement was made in Mrs. J.'s favor. Lest you carry bad feelings about the surgeon who created the injury, let it be known that he, with humility, came to my office to apologize personally---expressing great remorse, feeling that he had damaged a friendship by his actions and his ill-founded deposition.

AND BACK AGAIN TO EAU CLAIRE

During the 1960's the surgical practice grew gradually, but steadily, for the following reasons---not necessarily in the order of importance:

1. There was a relative shortage of physicians and hardly any new physicians were coming to Eau Claire during that decade.

2. My partner decided to do missionary work in Africa on several occasions. These sabbaticals allowed patients to become accustomed to my manner of care, my personality---with relationships which endured even after he returned to Eau Claire.

3. I chose to practice at both Luther and Sacred Heart Hospitals, leaving the choice to the patient. "You decide which hospital you prefer and I'll be there with you." Also, Midelfort Clinic surgeons sometimes were busy at Luther Hospital and reluctant to go across town to Sacred Heart Hospital. Consequently, I received numerous requests for consultation for emergent problems. Simple! I was available.

4. Without the present day specialized E.R. coverage, I wound up providing extensive coverage for the E.R. at all hours of the day or night.

Yes, the surgical volume kept escalating---resulting in some 120 hour weeks. Some of that time commitment, admittedly, was self-imposed. Perhaps I'd have to plead guilty to compulsiveness, but I was uneasy until I had seen the patients. Maybe I didn't do a good job of relegating responsibility, but to whom would I relegate? In that day, almost all patients were admitted to the hospital on the evening before surgery. This gave me opportunity to ascertain fitness for surgery, to explain procedures once again, to answer questions, perhaps to offer some verbal and pharmaceutical tranquility. In addition, I would be seeing as many as 10-20 post-op patients in the morning before surgery and again in the evening before I could go home.

Today's emphasis on fewer hospital days and more out-patient surgery is welcome and proper---influenced greatly by less invasive surgery, less anesthetic carryover, and the simple fact that 3-5 day stays, for example, for simple hernia surgery were totally unnecessary. Pendulums do swing and pendulums even can swing too far in reducing hospital days. Facetiously, but actually discussed, isn't it a little extreme to contemplate drive-through mastectomies and C-sections? As I reminisce, I have no regrets that I did twice daily rounds on patients. Apparently, unbeknownst to me, this practice wasn't common among surgeons. One evening, when I suggested to a p.m. nurse, "I suppose everybody does twice daily rounds?"---she shot back, rolling her eyes Heavenward, "You've gotta be kidding." For me, the dividends were simple. Not only was the practice beneficial to patients---I gained peace of mind. In the evening, I saw a different patient, a different set of nurses, and often I could talk to visiting family members. I slept better. It was as simple as that.

A surgeon should come across as being hopeful, careful, confident, but cautious in recommending only appropriate procedures for those who are hurting. In recommending any surgery, there should be great promise that the patient will return to a normal life. Hopefully, the surgeon will retain humility, never become hardened, and be at peace with the truism that, even with our best efforts to help, we won't always succeed. Results of surgery generally are pleasing to patients and surgeons alike. If it weren't so, the surgical vocation would be a dreary one, indeed! Unexpected complications can and do occur. Some patients, unfortunately, present with terrible insults to their bodies and are overwhelmed by their physical frailties, making survival improbable. In surgical jargon, we refer to morbidity and mortality---both of which are resisted and, hopefully, kept to a minimum.

HAPPY FACES

Now, if you were the surgeon, wouldn't you like to see happy faces, feel the gratitude of appreciative families, and delight in patients who have remarkable recoveries, with burdens lifted following surgery? There certainly are others, but let me lay out for you a few scenarios in which surgery almost inevitably gives dramatic and quick relief.

1. Hypertrophic pyloric stenosis is seen in babies, usually age 1 month to 6 months. As we search for reasons why certain conditions exist, we sometimes are left with, "These things just happen." In hypertrophic pyloric stenosis, the pyloric sphincter muscle (the outlet of the stomach into the duodenum) becomes enlarged and gristly firm, resulting in obstruction and characteristic projectile vomiting. This overgrown muscle assumes the shape of an olive---sort of like an ovoid tumor. In our training, we were advised that we should be able to palpate this enlargement in order to be sure of the diagnosis. Using your common sense, do you think it would be easy to examine the abdomen of a crying, irritable infant? Confusion about diagnosis led to delays, dehydration, and a sicker baby. Part of the problem was that radiologists and pediatricians didn't want barium swallows given for fear of regurgitation of the barium and aspiration into the tracheobronchial tree---a disaster.

With passage of time, those fears subsided and much earlier diagnoses were possible by barium x-rays done as soon as there was suspicion. What a boon! Surgery became safer as babies were going to surgery in a healthier state. In the case of the tiny daughter of Dawn, a nurse, the baby was taken directly to the O.R. from the x-ray department after clinching the diagnosis. Through a small transverse incision, the olive-shaped "tumor" was readily identified and brought up to the level of the abdominal wall. Carefully teasing and separating the gristly muscle fibers, the obstruction was no more. Within 18 hours, the baby once again was taking sugar water and formula---now without the frightening projectile vomiting. Smiles and happy faces all around---especially the mother and the surgeon.

2. When a person writhing in pain wakes up from surgery with little or no pain, there are bound to be happy faces. Sudden escape of acid stomach contents through a perforated duodenal ulcer is so irritating and shocking that any attempt to press on the abdominal wall is met by a characteristic "board-like rigidity." When recommending surgery to patients in such acute pain, the usual response is, "Please---do something."

The typical clinical picture plus unmistakable x-ray evidence of "free air" under the diaphragm (air escaping from the stomach cavity) easily confirmed the diagnosis in Gene P. and the sooner to the O.R., the better. At surgery, there still was stomach acid bubbling from the perforation. Quickly, the perforation was closed by suturing and then protected by an onlay fatty omental graft. The most important and relieving part of the operation then followed---washing out the abdominal cavity with gallons of saline solution to dilute the acid.

What a joy! Soon after the surgery, Gene was sitting up in bed, needing only minimal medication for relief of post-operative discomfort. Within 24 hours---smiles and "I feel fine." Specific plans for subsequent medical or surgical management of his ulcer disease could be made once this hurdle was passed. 30 years ago, treatment of ulcer disease revolved around, "How best can you control hyperacidity?" Recent research has identified a bacterial cause for ulcer problems, magnifying the role of medical management and greatly reducing the role of surgery.

3. Let's talk about incarcerated and potentially strangulated hernia (inguinal, femoral, abdominal). There's no need to go into a detailed discussion of anatomy, embryology, and the myriad reasons for hernia for-

mation. Suffice it to say that every hernia represents an abnormal protrusion from a body cavity through a defect in the wall of that cavity. Every hernia has a lining (hernia sac), which enlarges with time and excessive straining, whether work-related or illness-related. There are times when intestine can worm its way into the hernia sac and, if the hernia opening is small, the intestine can become incarcerated (caught) and can't be reduced or returned to the body cavity. With swelling and tightness of the hernia opening, blood supply to the herniated intestine may be compromised. Strangulation is the term applied---and intestinal gangrene may result---obviously a life-threatening situation. Friends, that's not the hand you'd like dealt to you.

In impending impairment of blood supply, every hour---yea, every minute---is crucial. For Bill H., surgery wasn't delayed. The incarcerated intestine in the hernia sac was discolored and crying for relief. After the tight hernia ring was incised to free the intestine, normal coloration returned quickly. Again, happy faces and smiles in the morning.

For Tim S., there had been delay on his part because, after all, wasn't he well aware of the hernia and hadn't it always reduced easily? Arriving at the E.R. 12 hours after the hernia was non-reducible, he was in sore distress---with unrelenting pain, fever, and elevated white blood cell count. Though surgical exploration was undertaken expeditiously, the herniated intestine was gangrenous, necessitating removal of the affected intestine. With antibiotic coverage and patience, Tim eventually recovered, but the smiles were delayed for several days.

GIRL FRIENDS

As a reflection of society, patients come in all ages, sizes, and colors---with varying intellect, temperament, and financial resources. Common sense, kindness, and just plain courtesy urge us to treat all patients where they happen to be---not where we secretly think they should be. I've encountered a few unreasonable, demanding, angrily upset patients---but the overwhelming number of patients are cooperative in their treatment and are grateful for attention. To tell the truth, some patients are far too good and non-complaining, trying to please their doctor. Who is this "good" patient we hear about? The "good patient," in my definition, is the one who, in times of trial and adversity, makes life easier for everyone around him/her.

In over 10,000 surgical adventures, you would expect that many lingering personal friendships would develop. Although this type of friendship was never intended to be buddy-buddy, it was easy and relaxed. I tried so hard to advise family medicine residents about the proper form of friendship. Indeed, my #1 admonition was, "Never enter a room as if you're somehow trying to prove that you're an authority. Hey, the patient already recognizes the authority of your training and experience. Discard any thought of haughtiness, relax, set the patient at ease, and be a friend."

I'm not now going to give you a litany of names of patients. A patient is more than a name. I can't hear a name without conjuring up a vision of uniqueness and unforgettable personality traits. At the risk of forgetting or omitting some, let me introduce you to a few "girl friends." Raise not your eyebrows. Be not dismayed as though "girl friends" might be an insult to Peggy. Actually, it was Peggy who established ironclad rules that "girl friends" had to have been operated on by me---and they had to be over age 80. As further protection against overly aggressive "girl friends," Peggy often shared our social encounters. Let no one make the mistake of categorizing such togetherness as dating.

    1. Amanda B. was a delightful, deceptively soft spoken gal who often treated me to coffee and cookies when I stopped at her house on Market St. on my way between hospitals. Rap poker was her game. People won't necessarily tell you everything about themselves initially---and that's probably good. Gradual disclosure is more the rule---and more comfortable. Beneath Amanda's sweetness and light, there was to be seen a feisty old lady. She had lived through the Depression years with her bootlegger husband in LaCrosse. Beneath that superficial calm lay a coarse interior, capable of calling forth 4-letter expletives when she was upset. An example of her fierceness was seen in this tale told me by her nephew. As owner of a small diner in LaCrosse, she gladly gave soup to those out of work in those lean years. One day, one of her "soup people" made a mistake, appropriating something she hadn't given him. What a spectacle! Picture the justifiably terrified man fleeing down the alley with Amanda in hot pursuit, wielding a huge kitchen knife. Let's just say that Amanda was determined in protecting her turf.

    You might also say that Amanda enjoyed her spiritus fermenti. Over the phone, she was ordering bottles of hard liquor from a Water St. establishment---and they were delivering to her without my prescription. In that year, Luther Hospital had instituted a personal protection plan for older people living alone---requiring each person to call the hospital each morning. Well, one Sunday morning, the hospital informed me that Amanda was a "no contact."

    Stopping by her house, I met an Amanda roadblock. Typical of many older people, she had that little house impenetrable---tightly bolted and shuttered, with shades drawn. Fortunately, I knew where to find a key, but the screen door was latched. There was nothing else to do! I had a trusty screwdriver and, with a police officer present, I removed the screen door, entered the house, and found Amanda lying on the kitchen floor. "Amanda, are you all right? What happened? What are you doing there?" Never losing her sharp wit, she rather gleefully said, "I've been waiting for you." Amanda, playing the heroine queen to the hilt, was placed on the ambulance stretcher and transported to the hospital. In the intake history, a nurse naturally inquired about the events that led to hospitalization. Amanda was up to it, playing her part like an actress. "I got up during the night and fell on the floor---couldn't get up. My doctor came, took off the screen door, and found me." "My," said the nurse, "that was awfully nice of him." Without missing a beat, Amanda countered, "Well, he'd better put the door back."

Amanda was a fun person, wrinkled as she was. Coming back to me are the times Amanda, Peggy, and I would go out to eat at Stafne's late at night---Amanda liked the good life. So many times, Amanda and I drove to Augusta to visit her sister in the nursing home, each visit ritualistically preceded by a stop at the local restaurant for a dish of ice cream, which Amanda would dutifully feed to her sister, Selma.

The deliveries of booze to Amanda from the Water St. liquor store had been unbeknownst to me. Then, the revelation! It struck home that Amanda liked the bubbly stuff. I was incensed when I found that her source, that liquor store on Water St. was delivering the drug to her. Problem: In falling, Amanda broke a small bone in her neck. By the time I personally confronted the store owner for his part in supplying drugs without a prescription, you may be sure that the injury had grown in magnitude to a "broken neck." Repentant, indeed, was the store owner, promising to cease deliveries. The ultimate problem: Amanda finally had to be transferred to a nursing home, no longer able to care for herself. When she put up a fuss with her most indignant pout, I had to remind her, "Hey, I don't like this any more than you do, but you're so weak you can't even shuffle the cards." Amanda died within two weeks of entering the nursing home. Lessons? People who don't want to go to nursing homes sometimes lose the will to live. Also, alcohol problems aren't limited to the young.

2. Lillian A. was a heavy woman with flat facial expression---and she most certainly wouldn't be seen as an Einstein. Her conversation was, to say the least, inappropriate. She never seemed to understand---she just didn't get it! Yet, there was something appealing about Lillian's simplicity and her loyalty. Our office staff treated Lillian where she was and I'm sure that she felt like a queen, probably never having been treated so graciously. There was a slight problem: Lillian's interpretation of our attention was occasionally misguided and resulted in plaintive phone calls from the Idle-A-While bar to our home---even at midnight---wanting to know why I wasn't there. Ah, Lillian. I now share with you a story which, at first glance, might seem funny. Well, bizarre, perhaps---but not funny. Try sad or pathetic.

I had never met Lillian's family until one morning at Luther Hospital when Lillian's husband was admitted as an urgent patient. The family picture was complete with her son and daughter also there. After a tentative and cursory exam, it was obvious that Mr. A. was desperately sick. He had huge masses of matted lymph nodes in the neck, strongly suspicious of malignancy---probably lymphoma. It was apparent that Mr. A., formerly a Uniroyal worker, was a reluctant man---reluctant to consult a physician (never had), reluctant to take a bath (rarely had), and reluctant to change clothing. O.K. It's agreed that many men resist the changing of clothes, a trait considered untenable by wives, justifying spousal onslaught---but, do you know anybody who has worn the same clothes, including socks and shoes, for months without removing them?

I held out little hope, but thought that, if we could peel off the outer layers of clothes and dirt, we might be able to biopsy a lymph node with the outside hope that the illness might be treatable. It wasn't meant to be. The aides, assigned to the task of removing the clothes and dirt, had the difficult task of informing me that Mr. A. had abruptly died. In a family conference, I think I spoke gently, but spelled out to them in plain words that their father and husband had died. Son and daughter clearly understood, crying quietly. The always impassable, impenetrable, and inappropriate Lillian could only say, "Well, is it bad?"

A lesson: In your best efforts to communicate clearly, there may be obstacles and you may fail. Friends, Lillian functioned up to the level that her intellect would carry her. I think my favorite memory of Lillian will be the picture when, as a resident of The Clairemont nursing home, she was elected as queen. Her crown a little atilt, nevertheless she posed with the king, wearing her simple, oblivious smile. It gives you hope! You, too, can be a king or a queen for a day or a lifetime if your subjects will allow it and you can find a robe.

3. Clara S.: Girl friends are sort of like children and grandchildren. You love and cherish each one of them for being special in their own way, but let's be honest. Each one of them has individual appeal and unique charm, which may set them apart from the others and make them just a little more special---at least for the moment. I can recall writing or whispering to each grandchild in some way, "You know, you really are the most speshulest of all."

This sneaky maneuver wouldn't have a ghost of a chance of flim-flamming children. After all, they already are convinced that parents are ruthlessly inconsistent and show favoritism. Grandchildren, on the other hand, will simply believe---and, above all, would never think of telling the others that they've been singled out as "the most speshulest of all" In this vein, Clara was extra special, a favorite girl friend.

An immutable fact of life is that girl friends over age 80 may not last long. They die! When Clara died, there was a deep sense of sadness and we still miss her. She was much like a family member and, most important, she was the most speshulest of all.

The "most speshulest of all"--- Clara Simonson with Ralph and Peggy's granddaughters Erin and Kelly

Peggy and I used to have coffee and cake in Clara's kitchen each Sunday. On days when our family tagged along, hospitality was ratcheted up a notch. Clara would then usher us into the dining room. Always busy, she'd be bustling around with an occasional comment, "Here---let me get that crap off the table." Our daughter, Diane, later would challenge her mother, "Mother, you never let us say things like that." That was vintage Clara---always forthright. Clara was a storyteller---a repetitive storyteller. We could recite by heart her recounting of her girlhood days, playing golf on a girls' team. Many were the times we were told the secrets of proper preparation of lutefisk. Here I interject to caution you. The older person, delighting in telling stories again and again---that person needs understanding and patience. The plea seems to be, "If you've heard this before, just let me tell it again."

Clara, at age 88, consumed two pots of coffee (the hard stuff) by 10:00 a.m and she smoked cigarettes, defying the odds, caring little about statistics. In her compulsive preparation for Christmas, she would complain, "Why, oh why was I ever born Norwegian?"---but she'd still dutifully perform the time-honored ritual of producing lefse, rosettes, and cookies---capped off by the lutefisk dinner for the family.

Approaching midnight one fateful evening, Clara's neighbor, Dennis, called me with a worried tone and an instinctive concern because Clara was incommunicado. Once upon a time (that's how fairy tales start), I was more agile than fragile---so, with Dennis boosting me up to a window, I opened it and squeezed into the house. Good and bad news! Good news that Clara was alive and we found her. Bad news that she was lying on the bathroom floor in filth. Details are vague---they escape me---but eventually she needed major surgery for bowel obstruction and abdominal herniation. Life's treadmill is made more slippery by these insults, no matter how necessary the surgery might be. The elderly, weak, and fragile may lose hold and slip off the treadmill precipitously. Clara's sense of humor, often pointed at herself, persisted even as death was just around the corner. At The Clairemont nursing home, Clara was agitated and demented, sometimes screaming for her mother. When aides would calm her and remind her, "Clara, you're screaming again," the perky, white-haired pixie would apologetically ask, "I'm doing that again?" Favoritism? Let's just say that it's more difficult to bid farewell to the most speshulest of all.

  4. Pauline D.: Specialization in medicine has almost always led to overall improved care of injured patients. With a sigh of relief, we have welcomed the springing up of regional burn centers. Thermal burn injuries, in my opinion, are one of the cruelest insults ever to befall an individual. With the advent of burn centers, survival rates have increased, disfiguring scarring has been lessened, and mobility has been preserved. The treatment of major burns is so arduous, time consuming, and frustrating that it used to be said in jest, "Send the burn patient to your worst enemy."

  Before transfer to regional burn centers was the norm, we WERE the burn center. Somebody simply had to care for burn victims and, actually, the careful and competent general surgeon was quite capable of treating burn emergencies and performing skin grafting procedures. I know of no other aspect of medicine/surgery in which teamwork is so vital as in the treatment of burn victims---

as in the care of Pauline.

Pauline was a 76 year old retired school teacher, residing in Rice Lake, Wisconsin. Pauline, by her own description, had become a tad reclusive and self-centered. It's hard to realize this could happen, but she slipped down into a bathtub of scalding water. The thermal burns she sustained were intensified by the length of exposure to the overheated water. She wasn't able to attract any attention for assistance in getting out of that burn trap. Getting weaker by the minute, she finally summoned up enough strength to extricate herself from the bathtub before losing consciousness.

When examined at Luther Hospital, she had full thickness burns over 45% of her body surface. The areas affected presented a fearsome challenge in treatment---her back, lower extremities, perineum, and buttocks, barely sparing the anal area. Initial treatment of major burns involves pain relief and judicious I.V. fluids for treatment of burn shock. When stabilized in 24-48 hours, inspection and debridement of burned tissues could be accomplished under anesthesia. Over the course of Pauline's treatment, there must have been 15-20 anesthetics.

With no burn unit, the problem was managed on the orthopedic ward---with teamwork involving surgeon, nurses, aides, physiotherapists, lab techs, anesthesiologists, and others. Can you imagine the unusual caution and skill necessary in nursing care? Just picture the problem posed by a bowel movement when so much skin was missing around the anus. Indeed, there were times when we seriously considered creating a sigmoid colostomy (bowel diversion) to help both the patient and the beleaguered nurses. Management of feces would have been easier and more accessible with a colostomy--- and there would have been less danger of contamination of burned areas. Because of the excellency of nursing care and the use of a Stryker frame, we were able to forestall the colostomy. The Stryker frame (Pauline's bed) was a God-send for her, allowing her to be turned prone and supine while strapped to the frame. How would you like a bed like that for weeks and weeks?

Miraculously, skin grafts taken from Pauline's upper back and abdomen "took "---they were successful when transferred to the burn sites. Grafts were taken with an electric dermatome set extremely thin so that donor sites would re-grow promptly. The taking of grafts always struck me as akin to the harvesting of sod to satisfy our worship of green lawns.

During her trials and tribulations, we witnessed a conversion of spirit in Pauline. She became more outgoing and resolved, insofar as possible, to give to others that which she had received. It seemed to be such a natural continuum of the hospital teamwork as those involved in Pauline's care formed the WLP (We Love Pauline) committee. Pauline's sister gladly would bring Pauline to one of our homes for lunch, celebration, and reminiscence. Pauline lived her final days in Rice Lake and she was so pleased when we would visit her in her final nursing home days. It was such a small thing to do---just to keep her in our thoughts. Would you have done less?

5. Florence S.: Florence was a quiet soul, age 85, appearing at least 10 years younger because she wore an attractive wig. Undoubtedly, she was more concerned about personal appearance, perhaps more vain than other "girl friends." Florence just had that prideful human quality of trying to do as much as she could with what she had been given. You'd think she was a sales rep. for Oil of Olay lotions---and she yearned to be told that Oil of Olay was working magic with her skin. If you were to visit her, you'd soon discover a slight chink in her armor. Rather than waiting for compliments, she was outlandishly bold in asking for them. "Do you think my skin is soft?" was thrown into every conversation. If you were there with me, you would have known instinctively that the only answer was, "Florence, you have the softest skin, the skin of a woman 30 years younger."

Florence was a prolific poet, writing about everyday subjects and posing interesting questions. In some of her verses on the pills she was taking, she wondered, "Now, how does the heart pill know just where the heart is and how does the kidney pill know how to find the kidney?" Perhaps her most pleading and poignant poem conveyed her joy in receiving a letter, a card, a phone call, but---"the greatest thrill of all is to see YOU---coming up the walk."

One visit with Florence and you'd perceive her correctly as a little possessive and persistent. No matter how long the visit, I would hear as I reached for my coat, "Do you have to go?" Finally, I invented an answer which somehow soothed her, "Florence, do you want me to come back to see you?" When she answered, "Oh, yes---please," I could give the clincher, "Then, how can I come back until I go away?"

Since we don't always understand our own family dynamics, I don't even presume to understand what caused the estrangement of Florence and her son, whom I never met. This son, obviously a strange, misguided, and unconcerned person, living in Chicago, would send his mother a Mother's Day card with $10 enclosed---but he'd never come to visit her. If he came to Eau Claire for his mother's funeral, I think that I, a non-violent person, might have hit him---at least verbally. He didn't come.

Florence, the gentle soul, should have been granted a more gracious way to exit this world. At the Center of Care, she developed a rapidly growing sarcomatous malignant mass in the soft tissues around the left axilla. We tried to excise the mass, but the effort was futile. Alas! Her surgical wound became infected. Although I felt that infection control could have been handled easily with simple hand washing and use of gloves, the medical director placed her in a private room with total cap and gown isolation---without my knowledge. I was furious---well, at least mildly disturbed. It mattered not. It seemed a natural consequence that Florence turned her face to the wall, wouldn't eat---and died. A simple observation: If somebody, though she be age 88, will write you poetry and say she loves you---just accept it.

6. Lillian O.: One of the deadliest and most evasive malignancies is ovarian cancer. Because of the location of the ovaries deep in the pelvis, rarely is the problem detected until the horse is out of the barn, when possibility of cure is nil. It was just so with Lillian, a widow with 4 grown children, trying to eke out an existence, working as a waitress. Exploratory laparotomy, before the advent of less invasive laparoscopic surgery, was just that---exploratory only. With malignant implants seeded over every square centimeter of peritoneum, omentum, and intestinal surfaces, there was that inevitable feeling of hopelessness. Chemotherapy, at that time, wasn't an option---not available. Perhaps the art of medicine is seen best in the telling of bad news---while not destroying all hope. Lillian was a proud person, accepting her diagnosis and prognosis with class. During our conversations, I absorbed some of her feelings and became acquainted with her disappointment in two of her children who, for some reason, had never been very good to their mother.

It happens so often that it's predictable. Those scallywags, who never seemed to care very much from a distance, immediately became overbearing as they arrived from California. Expressing great love for their mother, they wondered loudly why more hadn't been done to help her. When Lil died, her very caring daughter in Eau Claire came to me with an unusual request, "Will you say a few words at my mother's funeral?" Since she didn't define what I should say or what "a few words" meant, I agreed.

It was a first for me---and a last---to speak conversationally from the pulpit in First Lutheran church. Keeping eye contact with Lil's children, especially the black sheep, I offered these thoughts: "You know, your mother's death causes me to remember the deaths of my mother and father. Now, when I was growing up, I didn't tell my parents everything. What surprised me, listening to others, is that they obviously hadn't told me everything either. Now, you sons and daughters of Lil are probably no different than I was---you didn't tell your mother everything. After what you've heard of my experience, is it then such a wonder that Lil may not have told you everything? Let me share with you a few things Lil told me in these last few months...." Judging from their eyes, it was a fitting introduction to remarks which, hopefully, proved to be helpful in obtaining closure.

7. Mae H.: Except for some catastrophic personality change, which may occur post-stroke, the personality of older folks is usually just an extension of their younger selves. The sweet and kind little old lady, the smiling and charming person, has been just like that throughout her life. The helpful and accommodating elderly gentleman probably was always a friend to others. Then there was Mae---in a ball park of her own. If there were a contest to determine the meanest woman in the world, Mae would be right up there, vying for top spot. You question her inclusion in my list of "girl friends?" Now, where did you ever get the idea that "girl friends" have to be agreeable? My interest in Mae stemmed largely from my admiration for her husband, perhaps for his resilience. When Walter died, what seemed on the surface to be, at best, a tolerable marriage suddenly blossomed, in Mae's telling, as the idyllic romance of the century. Whenever I visited Mae, I was honoring Walter.

Mae's most appealing qualities? She was spiteful, jealous, angry, selfish, and combative. While living at the Mt. Washington residence, she wielded her cane effectively to establish ownership of her place at the table, to claim her right to a solo elevator ride. She had a penchant for things of the church---you can see that she was a good Christian---so I would read scriptures with her, sing hymns, and reminisce about 1st Baptist Church. Then came the beginning of the end of our relationship. One fateful day, the Mt. Washington staff informed me that Mae had overstepped the bounds of reason and had injured another resident with her cane. Their best judgment?

With my approval, Mae was placed in semi-confinement behind Dutch doors.

When I arrived later that day, Mae questioned why I had done such a dastardly thing to her. With her best petulant and gravelly tone, she whined, "Dr. Hudson, how could you?" "Well," I countered, "Mae, the nurses tell me that you've been mean to people, hitting them with your cane." Immediately, she issued the expected denial, "Now, how could they say such a thing?" Then she stretched her 5-foot-2 frame and pronounced the benediction on our friendship. "Dr. Hudson, we've been friends for a long time, but it's all over." She shed no tears---I shed no tears. Come to think of it, in looking back, I can't recall much in the way of tears or laughter in Mae's life.

There must be a lesson here somewhere: Not all relationships are made in Heaven---and not all relationships have a "they lived happily ever after" ending.

8. Cordelia G.: Cordelia was an absolutely intriguing person and a visit with Cordelia always was challenging. She grew up in a small Iowa town, the daughter of a pioneering physician and surgeon. Pioneering? This man performed the first c-section ever performed in that town's Catholic hospital. Cordelia was soon recognized as a brain and her father saw to it that she had a college education, unusual for that time. Who really can put numbers on intellect? Is intellect to be defined in I.Q.? By ancient standards, when she graduated from a school of journalism, her. I.Q. may have been about 175. Cordelia raised eyebrows in her family, probably infuriating some, when she married Albert, an ordinary man with little education except in the school of hard knocks.

Albert had a natural business sense and, when he wished to start a mortuary business, Cordelia had the brains to breeze through mortuary school, becoming the mortician. Cordelia had life-long running battles with many members of her family, but she was fiercely loyal to her husband and to her granddaughter, Ellen, who lived with them much as an adopted daughter. Ellen had a severe dyslexic learning disorder and had been stigmatized by her own father as being a dummy, shunned---and sort of disowned. Guess what? With Cordelia's insistent support and guidance, Ellen graduated from college. It was a genuine symbiotic relationship, Ellen living with her Grandma right up to Cordelia's death.

Cordelia was also fiercely loyal to me. I now admit that some patients thought I could walk on water, but Cordelia thought that I was in a class way above Jesus---and could do no wrong. This is, of course, open to dispute, according to Peggy.

By definition, most "girl friends" came into being through major surgeries. However, my years with Cordelia started with something I thought to be inconsequential. I simply treated a dogbite on her forearm, bringing skin edges neatly into their pre-dogbite alignment. A contributing factor to her loyalty arose, also, when she was hospitalized for tests. After 2-3 days, I finally confronted her, "Mrs. G., you've been here for 2 days and I haven't had a chance to say a word." Instead of getting huffy and dismissing me, she announced that she'd never leave someone so honest. The story of the dogbite was resurrected through the years ---and amplified with each telling.

An unfortunate incident, with Albert as principal player, surely tested Cordelia's unshakable loyalty. Albert wasn't one to consult a physician but, with Cordelia's proddings and threats, Albert consented to observation and testing for heavy chest pain. This was prior to the concept of coronary care units. With nothing pinned down to explain Albert's discomfort, I had a cardiologist consult---with no benefit except for reassurance. Abruptly, Albert walked out of the hospital. A man can stand only so much. One day later, while I was seeing patients in my office, Cordelia called, "Albert is having bad chest pain again and difficulty in breathing. What should I do?" With some exasperation because of Albert's obstreporousness, I sighed, "I really don't know. I guess you'll have to take him back to the hospital. I'll be there." I'll clue you. One "code" patient in the E.R. causes excitement and an uproar. Two or more "code" patients amounts to disaster! What I had no way of knowing was that, as Cordelia and Albert arrived at the E.R. door in a taxi, everybody in the E.R. was involved in the treatment of a "code" emergency inside the E.R. Resourceful Cordelia, with no help from the busy E.R. staff, commandeered a cart and somehow managed to wheel Albert inside the door. At the same moment, I arrived from a different direction. Heading for the E.R., I saw a man being wheeled from the E.R. onto an elevator. It is a dangerous exercise---jumping to conclusions. It was easy to assume that this patient was Albert. Asking the nurse about his condition, she indicated thumbs-up. Only after I communicated this good news to Cordelia did I discover the horrendous error. Albert was lying in the E.R dead. Even with this regrettable mixup, Cordelia was unflappable, strong, and convinced that I'd done everything I could---and certainly nothing wrong.

Approaching my retirement, I painstakingly tried to match each patient's personality and problems with an appropriate physician so that there would be no interruption of care. This proved to be well nigh impossible with Cordelia, who still felt that nobody could take my place. During the next decade, Cordelia used an accelerated revolving door for physicians. Initially I had selected a young woman physician for her only to find that Cordelia thought that a physician should be a male. After all, her father and I were males. To tell the truth, only the most patient M.D. could mesh with Cordelia, who was a real threat to any office schedule she encountered because of her rambling conversation. Complicating this, a hint of paranoia hung over her like a cloud as she grumbled that physicians didn't really care nor did they listen. Thus, in retirement, I was the port in the storm, summoned on occasions to explain, to placate, to comfort---an art, indeed, without a license or prescription power. Toward the end of her life---she was age 99 when she died---she just wanted to go down by the riverside and jump in. On alternating days, she then would plead, "Just push me out into traffic." This wasn't just attention-getting or idle conversation. She was so lacking in mobility, so weak, so dependent. I do think that she appreciated my support in those days preceding death because she knew I welcomed death for her and didn't say, as many families do, "Oh, don't talk like that."

What are the precious memories of Cordelia? 1. Her loyalty. 2. Her insistence that she didn't have anybody on her side---only me. This, of course, wasn't true---but it was payment enough for services rendered.

9. Dorothy B.: Society has never really understood mental illness. Society has struggled, but never come to grips with an acceptance that mental illness is just that---an illness---an illness without known causation or consistently effective treatment. The societal reaction is all too predictable. Too often, differences in people's mannerisms provokes caution---perhaps even fear, which translates into disdain, ridicule, alarm, and restriction. Look back at your own communities. Every community, in common parlance, has known who its odd balls or "crazies" were---those who aroused a disquieting discomfort. If harmless, they were tolerated as a humorous aberration even if not accepted. If aggressive or violent, they were subjected to some form of institutionalization, warehousing. Insane asylums with drugged, incompetent, straight-jacketed zombies were the rule. Even county poor farms were repositories for "strange" people whom society preferred to keep at a distance.

Though there is some light on the horizon, mental illness and mental health still are subjects given short shrift by medical schools, insurance companies, and governmental budgets. Is there progress? Absolutely! Will mental illness eventually be given carte blanche by insurance companies? Probably not! Unfortunately, even as this nation prides itself on its constitutional rights and individual freedoms, it still isn't really o.k. to be different. The movie, "A Beautiful Mind" is a forward step in helping people to understand mental illness, but the comfort zone is still small. While viewing the movie, we noticed that the most tittering in the audience was prompted by scenes really not so funny---when students were mocking professor Nash's strange gait and behaviour.

As I recall, and my recollections aren't necessarily to be trusted for their accuracy these days, there was only passing reference to mental illness in medical school. For whatever reason, we were given only brief glimpses of those mentally ill. The whole process seemed so remote from the mainstream of medicine/surgery, where there was more precise cause and effect---and treatment more often alleviated problems. Our attitudes were even shaped by observing the students who, predictably, leaned toward psychiatry. There is an outmoded adage, "You don't actually have to be nuts to be a psychiatrist, but it helps."

Even with this clouded and incomplete picture, I came to appreciate those who devoted their lives to the care of the mentally ill. If only from a practical standpoint, somebody in society had to lend a helping hand. Reflecting the low level of importance given to mental illness in the health care arena, insurance company policies usually have severe restrictions on compensation and number of visits allowed. From an actuarial standpoint, this has been justified on the basis that much of mental illness is chronic and recurring---and total coverage would break the bank. If only there were some bright light pointing to causation. Is it a matter of genes? Is it some chemical imbalance in the brain? To show how bankrupt our notions of mental illness have been, it was once postulated as a societal myth that masturbation would lead to mental illness. Hey! There wouldn't be any sane people.

Sadly, some people born with lesser intellect were mistakenly interpreted as mentally ill and were warehoused in institutions. Other unfortunates became brain-cooked zombies, the result of chronic ethyl alcohol abuse and also were "put away." Dorothy was mentally ill.

Dorothy functioned on a limited level in a nursing home. Dorothy shared something with the other residents of that nursing home---she had once had a meaningful life.

She had been married and had a son. Now, a person may be mentally ill and still crave and appreciate company. Our office staff recalls the day when Dorothy walked away from the nursing home and was found in a nearby motel bar, apparently with the hope that she might meet somebody.

Perhaps, in a small way, our treatment of Dorothy, our simple friendship, helped to forestall a major psychiatric conflagration. Every week or so, I would take Dorothy to lunch on Saturday. What a picture! She thoroughly enjoyed those lunches and was oblivious that her mascara was dripping, her lipstick was dripping, and her food was dripping. Yet, this lady, inappropriate in many ways, had a certain graciousness about her, a sense of appreciation. It's my humble opinion that this graciousness and appreciation isn't always seen in those who supposedly are mentally healthy or normal---whatever that is.

10. Donna A.: Technically, following Peggy's parameters, Donna didn't quite qualify as a "girl friend." However, she was one of my favorite people of all time---perhaps because of her simplicity, which bordered on charm. By some people, Donna would be considered to be a genetic mistake, a discard. She, her sister, and her mother all functioned to the best of their abilities with I.Q.'s below 80. Completing the family picture were a "normal" sister and a father, who was a skilled farm implement mechanic, receiving good wages.

Donna and her sister were born in an era when part of their care at the Chippewa Falls Northern Colony included state-mandated sterilization, considered to be a preventive measure. Donna and her family were members of our church, sitting in their accustomed place each Sunday---just the way the "normal" people do even now. I was bemused, intrigued as I noted "good" Christians casting non-approving glances at these three ladies---perhaps not so stylishly dressed and with hair unkempt. What really tickled me was the subtle wish of some of the church faithful that Donna's family be somehow transplanted to another part of God's pastures. What those righteous ones didn't know was that this family was way up at the top in giving to the church treasury.

You would have just naturally liked Donna. She was simple, but honest and with good manners; no C.P.A., but blessed with human emotion, falling in love and marrying a man with an I.Q. that matched hers. When Donna would come by the office, we could smile. Oh, that everybody would be as malleable, as non-demanding, as grateful as Donna.

A conversation:
"Hi, Donna, what's the problem?"
"Hi, Rawlf. I twisted my knee bad."
"Let's examine that knee. It seems stable, Donna. You know, with an Ace bandage and taking it easy on walking, I'll bet you'll be a lot better in a week."
"Thank you, Rawlf."
That's all there was---that's all Donna needed. A simple exchange between two human beings--and something perhaps that I needed, too.

A DIGRESSION ON GAS

Sometimes, a thought which has been begging for expression will be overlooked because of cerebral overload. That which has been stifled or lost may surface because current events give it importance. Having given space to "girl friends," thoughts now go to my real live girl friend, Peggy, who is facing intestinal resection to rid her of obstructive and, hopefully, localized Crohn's disease. Perhaps you will understand a little better why this digression is inserted here.

Intestinal surgery exposes every patient to the possibility of having a naso-gastric suction tube---a noxious thing, but a potential blessing if it works and an abomination if it doesn't. Through the years, patient safety has improved with the use of the suction tube. The purpose of the naso-gastric or small bowel decompression tube is to treat intestinal obstruction (sometimes forestalling surgery) or to keep the temporarily inactive bowel from distending (gassing up) following surgery.

The introduction of these tubes in the awake patient is an art form, requiring experience and skill in converting the reluctant or fearful person into the accepting and patient patient. More often, at the time of surgery, the anesthetist will insert the tube through the nose, down the esophagus, and into the stomach---before emergence from anesthesia. It's oh, so important that the naso-gastric tube be patent and functioning properly because, as noted above, it's so helpful when working properly and such a curse when it's plugged or in improper position. When asking patients what they remember about their surgery, the spontaneous reply often is, "That tube!"

Greater than any Christmas or birthday is the day on which the naso-gastric tube can be removed, having served its purpose---but how to know when it can be removed? For some decisions in surgery, answers are found in charts, numbers, high-tech analysis. In gastro-intestinal surgery, the various senses (especially common sense) prevail. It's what you see, hear, feel, and smell. It's absolutely vital that the intestine regain its peristaltic activity, that bowel sounds can be heard gurgling or rumbling with or without the stethoscope. Above all, it is a Hallelujah day when gas is passed rectally. Patients are soon aware of the obsession of surgeons and nurses in their persistent questioning, "Have you passed gas?" In social circles, even mention of such activity may raise eyebrows or noses---but not on surgical wards, where socially objectionable noises and odors are indicators of recovery and are cause for celebration. Just as the tulip is the harbinger of Spring, flatus is the invitation to a banquet. Flatus, gas, or fart! What's in a name? Even in Boston, genteel ladies will pronounce it "fart" as long as you spell it p-h-a-r-t.

THE ANNUAL NATIONAL GUESSING GAME: INFLUENZA VACCINATION

Let not your heart be troubled. Above all, fear not that I have abandoned all reason and public health principles when I express reservations about programs which have become sacred. As a member of the Eau Claire City-County Board of Health, I've always been impressed that basic public health practices---immunizations, clean water, clean air---are greater than technology in increasing life expectancy. In addition, I have faithfully subscribed to the germ theories laid down by Louis Pasteur. Let's just say that I believe there should always be room to criticize what seems sacrosanct and holy. Contributing to some of my irreverence for influenza vaccination is that I was raised in a generation which had an acceptance that influenza might even be the friend of the elderly.

Only those totally without a lively immune system need live in a bubble. Otherwise, out in the real world, avoidance of all germ contacts is unrealistic. Obviously, the O.R. isn't in the real world---and germs aren't welcome there. Those of us raised in the snotty nose generation benefitted by gaining immunity to foreign invaders. Although mothers routinely sterilized baby bottles, babies then crawled on floors which weren't exactly germ free and guess what? Baby instincts brought some of that stuff into their mouths.

Immunization is a precious public health principle, especially in infancy and childhood, when potential invading organisms are discouraged. Such organisms have been precisely identified---diphtheria, tetanus, measles, whooping cough, etc. On the contrary, the influenza vaccination program hasn't been built on such precise identification. The problem? With exotic testing, we now know what influenza viral strains have assailed us last year, but next year? Who knows? It's worse than predicting the weather a year in advance. Will the viral strains about to pass through be Asian, Caucasian, Maylaysian , Eurasian? It's a guessing game!

Another problem of imprecise definition is that everybody with chills, fever, and aching is said to have "the flu"---which may be true or untrue. Nursing homes, with hundreds of elderly residents, dutifully give flu vaccinations. I've always had a funny hunch that the nursing home concern, though genuine, is equally divided between concern for the residents and concern for the nursing home---that it not be overwhelmed by a sick population amid understaffing. Based on my view that I need not be immunized against some unidentified threat, I have never submitted to influenza vaccination---except ONCE!

It was in the days of President Gerald Ford, a man caught in the middle of what threatened to be a swine flu epidemic. He was in that uncomfortable position of "you're damned if you do and you're damned if you don't." With the best information available, I sided with President Ford. Great concerns were raised when a soldier at Fort Dix, N.J., died of influenza, the viral strain called the swine flu strain. What caused a national concern was that this swine flu strain was very similar to the influenza virus which devastated this nation and the world during World War I days.

All of this was alarming enough for me, but more troubling was that I was unfamiliar with what happened in 1918, 1919---with young people becoming sick one day, dying the next. I don't have the numbers, but thousands, perhaps millions of people died around the world---and I didn't know it. I felt cheated that, in medical school training, nobody had ever mentioned that influenza outbreak---a catastrophe. Perhaps I shouldn't have been surprised because the public health budget in medical school was at the bottom of the totem pole---and public health offices were in the basement. Quite wary now, I began to ask my elderly patients what they recalled about the great influenza epidemic. One after another, they confirmed the awful truth! That influenza was in no way the friend of the elderly. It was the executioner of the young.

With the Board of Health, I joined in supporting President Ford, who had made the difficult decision to implement a swine flu oral immunization program. I spoke to church groups, service clubs, anybody who would listen. With the specter of 1918-1919 in my mind, I encouraged---almost pleaded---that others take the vaccine. Yes, I swallowed the oral vaccine. I never regretted acting on solid information in an attempt to avert tragedy. Nothing is to be gained by second guessing---but only death might have been worse than the flu symptoms I developed as a result of that vaccine. Much more than those teeth-chattering chills, it was my skepticism outlined heretofore that has kept the flu vaccine from entering my body, even to this day.

SOME RAMBLING THOUGHTS
ABOUT THE O.R.

By general acceptance, everybody conjures up pictures of a sterile, perhaps eerie environment when they hear "O.R." On the surface, the term means little. Room for operating? You'd think that something more descriptive could be used to distinguish and identify that mysterious place. Just what manner of operation is this? As in other corners of our lives, we simply accept that which has been passed down. So be it!

Any repetition of my thoughts of appreciation to fellow workers only intensifies those thoughts. In retirement, I cherish the memories of nurses, lab and x-ray technicians, pastoral ministers, aides, and physicians working collaboratively to make lives better. For the surgeon, it's obvious that much of this effort centered around the O.R. Whether I even knew it at the time, I know it now from bits of conversation with former colleagues. The atmosphere in my O.R. was subdued, always educational, sometimes swirling and tense---but, for the most part, relaxed. Surgeons run the gamut of temperament, no doubt reflecting society in general. Whenever a surgeon's conduct in the O.R. was reported as rude, profane, or childish, I was sad and embarrassed---for our profession. Alas! There's something in human nature that prevents the transgressor from recognizing his/her own transgressions. The phrase is so applicable, "If only we could see ourselves as others see us." Inappropriate, rude, and childish behaviour, profane language---these are seen by others as revealing a lack of good manners, obvious immaturity, and probably a lack of confidence. What other message could there be when a surgeon swears or throws instruments?

I understand it better now than I did then, but I apparently was capable, just by my presence in the O.R., of modifying the behaviour of some of the worst actors, the show-off types---whether I was assisting at surgery or simply observing. Nurses would whisper to me, "We were so glad you were here---he was so different because you were here." Why? Why could a coarse surgeon act crudely and demean others---but not in my presence? I always valued the friendship and colleaguery of fellow practitioners, but there are limits and sometimes decisions have to be made. One orthopedic surgeon, especially known for his red-faced tirades, profane outbursts, and throwing of instruments, wasn't dissuaded even by my presence. I finally resolved, "I'll never, never again assist him." What a feeling of relief. Actually, he wasn't really a very competent surgeon. Don't rush to the happy conclusion that my decision changed him. It didn't---but I was more at peace.

During my surgical tenure, it was customary to have an assistant surgeon---sometimes my partner, sometimes the referring physician. Almost to a person, these referring physicians were revered by their patients---and their presence at the O.R. table, therefore, was comforting and reassuring to their patients and families. Their contribution at surgery was dependent upon ability, which varied considerably. One referring M.D. from Colfax invariably added some humor to the O.R. with his humming and singing as we worked. He was a barbershopper but, unfortunately, his part wasn't always the melody. After our major goals had been reached and we were in the process of closure, much to the delight of the nurses (and only when the patient was asleep), the two of us would harmonize. One day, during the closure of the incision, Dr. E. was tying knots as we closed the fascia. Once---twice---a third time---the suture would break. Showing restraint, I was bordering on interjecting, "Here, just let me tie the knots," when he coined a phrase which is unforgettable. He sang out, "Do you know why these ties keep breaking? It's not the suture---it's the jerk on the end of the string."

Absolutely essential to tranquility in the O.R. was-

--and is---the presence of expert anesthesia care. How fortunate I was! How fortunate were the patients! My contention is that our anesthesia care was the best in Wisconsin---even the nation. I recall no operative mishaps---no O.R. deaths---traceable to anesthesia. What a comfort---the freedom accorded the surgeon to do his/her work, knowing that the patient was in good hands. Were there some deaths in the O.R.? Yes, but these often were inextricable situations following horrible trauma in which the victim was rushed to the O.R. as a last gasp measure.

Serious minded we were in the O.R., but there were times, there had to be times of light-heartedness. As backdrop, I pass on to you the philosophy of one mentor at the Hines V.A. Hospital. During the routine closure of a case, he suddenly stopped and said, "You know, people, it's good to laugh a little. As a matter of fact, sometimes things are so serious that if we didn't laugh, we might cry." Some of this playfulness even extended to the somber anesthesiologist---as shown here. One day, when I was feeling the spirit and waxing a little quirkily about Peggy, I was lecturing the O.R. crew on the cost effectiveness of dating, marriage, and gift giving. "It's surely a wise man whose wedding day is close to Christmas (our wedding day Dec. 27) so that one gift is sufficient. Furthermore, that same wise man will choose a mate whose birthday is close to Valentine's Day (Peggy's birthday is Feb. 11)---thus again saving on gifts." Dr. Bjurstrom, the anesthesiologist and my former medical school roommate, couldn't stand it any longer and leaned over the anesthesia screen, uttering only one word, "cheap!"

Surgeons would be floundering without their surgical equipment armamentarium---especially the orthopedists and neurosurgeons. Historically, before my time, each surgeon had to own his/her own set of instruments. Logistically, you can see what a nightmare that would have been had it continued. Common sense prevailed and the hospital became the owner of instruments and equipment, both surgeons and patients benefitting immeasurably. Every year, there have been innovations, wonderful improvements in equipment---improving safety and reducing O.R. time---all of which combine to reduce morbidity and mortality. I can't give a complete, exhaustive list---but here are a few of the breakthroughs in general surgery:

    1. Metal skin staplers to approximate skin edges---primarily time savers. However, there still is nothing so neat and cosmetic as a hand-sewn subcuticular closure.

    2. Specially designed long forceps with metal clips (liga-clips) to replace laborious, time consuming, and potentially dangerous ligating of blood vessels with catgut or silk. These vessel clips were especially helpful in gall bladder surgery and in surgeries deep in the pelvis---such as hysterectomy and abdominal-perineal resection of the rectum.

    3. What a boon when metal stapling machines were introduced, making rapid and snug gastro-intestinal anastomoses possible. These machines, strange as it may seem, had their birth in Russia. They revolutionized much of our surgery, sometimes reducing surgical time as much as 30-60 minutes. Introduced as an alternative to the tiresome two-layer anastomoses of catgut and inverting silk sutures, they didn't replace the hand-sewn technique entirely, but there certainly were fewer complications.

    4. New inert mesh material, hypo-allergenic, became invaluable in accomplishing difficult hernia repairs by offering strength without tension.

    5. Electric dermatomes, exquisitely precise in depth measurement, to harvest skin grafts (remember Pauline D.?). These marvelous machines, easy to use, replaced cumbersome and not so predictable hand controlled dermatomes.

    6. Innovative retraction equipment, attached to the O.R. table, to provide the necessary surgical exposure. Our training was insistent, over and over, "See what you're doing." The retraction devices not only gave us a relaxed and consistent exposure, but relieved the O.R.

crew of holding retractors almost to the point of exhaustion. With this equipment, upper abdominal surgery (gall bladder, bile duct, splenic, and gastric) was approached with more calm.

7. With our mentors drumming into us the necessity of adequate exposure, incisions often had to be extended. Whenever I received the question, "Why is my incision so large?", I would truthfully answer, "The better to see you, my dear." Then came the blessing of fiberoptic lighting and laparoscopic equipment---a boon to patients, accomplished through smaller and more comfortable incisions. This patient-pleasing advent came just at the close of my surgical practice. If I had been 5 years younger, I would have blended with change and pursued training to do laparoscopy, especially gall bladder procedures. In retirement, I can only rejoice for any advance which improves patient comfort.

8. Although perhaps not involving equipment, it would be remiss not to mention the contribution to safety in surgery with the advent of TPN (total parenteral nutrition). Especially in complicated problems, essentially with little or no nutrition for the patient for weeks, a negative nitrogen balance would weigh upon the patient, greatly increasing morbidity and mortality In plain words, how can you heal without the building blocks of nutrition, especially protein? TPN provides precious carbohydrate and protein to sustain a patient through difficult times. On a personal note, Peggy was fortunate to have TPN for 8 days when she had absolutely no nutrition by mouth for 14 days.

Now that you've digested these examples of newer surgical armamentarium, with the understanding that the list doesn't approach completeness, go back to #1 for a lesson in marketing techniques, gullibility, and humility. In addition to skin staplers, there also was touted a "revolutionary" fascial stapler, providing large metal staples to approximate the tough layer above the abdominal muscles. I smile, in retrospect, at my human gullibility when, at a trade convention in Chicago, a salesman included in his sales pitch the appeal to vanity. "Wouldn't you like to the FIRST surgeon in Eau Claire to use the fascial stapler?" Jumping at the bait, I went along with, "You bet I would," envisioning the awe of the O.R. staff, the envy of other surgeons.

Whereas I smile at my gullibility, I'm sure that some family members are smiling at my compulsiveness, the ease with which I fell victim to Madison Avenue bally-hoo. At that point, I was turned over to a young and smilingly attractive young lady who took me by the arm, escorting me to the sales desk, where I signed on the dotted line. When the new fascial stapler arrived in the mail, I couldn't wait to demonstrate it. Oh, woe! Oh, disappointment! Oh, reality! Real live fascia didn't respond like styrofoam or whatever material had been used in the Chicago sales pitch. Now, I hasten to assure you that there was no hurt to the patient. We just completed the closure in the time-honored way---perhaps less spectacular, but safer and surer. That very afternoon, the fascial stapler was packaged and returned unceremoniously---without tears, accept for those tears of chagrin. In the real life world of the O.R , my conclusion proved to be prophetic---that stapler never caught on. The lesson? It takes more than glitzy trinkets to make the Christmas tree meaningful.

A SOFTER SIDE OF THE O.R---
DAUGHTER STATUS

Later, I'll tell you a related tale of "bearing" and caring with memories of hospital "days of caring." Now, I show you the softer side of the O.R. and the easy and unpretentious manner in which we worked together. There simply wasn't a caste system in our O.R. The O.R. conversation included concerns about children, families, illnesses, etc. There even were occasional social get-togethers. There was no need for rules prohibiting fraternization because we all were confident of our own roles, our own contribution, so that we could dispense with aloofness or haughtiness.

There wasn't anything unusual about the morning. I had finished two cases and, preparing to visit some patients out on the ward, I put my suit coat on over my green scrub suit. As I passed through the surgical lounge, where several O.R. techs were taking a break, I suggested that I might be some sort of a fashion statement. "How do you think I look?" Playing the game, most of the girls said, "It's absolutely stunning," but Jill S. gave a smirking denial, "It's not color coordinated---and it's just awful!" Recovering from this cruel blow, I announced, "Spoken like a daughter. Jill, you now have achieved daughter status." From that time forth, Jill retained the daughter status and subsequently was joined by a few others who satisfied the following stringent criteria:

    1. Should carry a sort of benign irreverence for the father.

    2. Should simply accept weirdness and display a casual and calm coexistence with it.

    3. Regardless of the supposed or real insult, should present a non-complaining face to the world regarding the

woes of genetic transference.

 4. Should have the forthrightness to admonish the father ever so gently about his failings and shortcomings --while putting up with the same.

 5. Should forever honor the father by treating the mother kindly---taking her to dinner, on vacations, etc.

 6. Lastly, and most importantly, must pray that the father precedes the mother in leaving this world---for his own good.

 Occasionally, in the absence of a physician surgical assistant, one of the surgical techs, already scrubbed in, would serve as assistant across the table. Yes, it was part of their job, but I'd give a voucher in appreciation so that the tech could take spouse or friend to dinner at Stafne's or Fran's. The gratitude response was a characteristic, "But, that's not necessary." In some instance of your own, hearing that same phrase, you might like to appropriate my response, "You're probably right. It isn't necessary, but doesn't that make it a little more special---for that very reason?"

AN EVOLUTION---
CHANGES IN SURGICAL PHILOSOPHY

The one constant in our life is CHANGE. Now, change isn't always progress, but change is a reality. A real problem arises when change engenders fear and uncertainty in those who are wedded to the status quo. Most of us appreciate tradition. We like the familiar, preferring to wallow in the comfort zone. Widely accepted societal change happens slowly, but can be compelled when there is obvious benefit to the majority. Change in surgical philosophy meets a parallel resistance---there's an entrenchment of the old guard---"we've always done it this way." The possibility of necessary change has the best chance when somehow, the focus of healers is "what's good for the patient."

You'll no doubt notice that these thoughts on changes in surgery will piggyback on those fantastic improvements I've spoken about in the creation of change in surgical armamentarium, dressings, and sterility guarantees. I offer you, with some hesitation, my own theory for resistance to change in any field. There is an appropriate adage, "When a man has only a hammer as a tool, that man will tend to think that the hammer is the solution to every problem." Is it such a stretch to see that the surgeon---with the scalpel as his/her tool---has often tilted toward surgery as the solution to health problems? Understanding this mindset, you can understand the surgical tendency to think that everything should be cut out. In cancer surgery, this philosophy translates into, "Get beyond that very last cancer cell." Indeed, this concept was so widely disseminated that patients' and families' questions centered around, "Did you get it all?"

With the scalpel as the only tool, the assumption,

when cancers would recur, naturally was that not enough tissue had been removed. That kind of thinking was akin to a snowball getting larger and larger as it rolls downhill out of control. It's like sinking in quicksand and getting deeper and deeper by thrashing around. With what we know now about cancer, how foolish! I began to be scared by the blind following of a shaky major premise that, if cure escapes the first time, the answer is to remove more and more tissue.

Great questions should arise if the weight of the resected surgical specimen going to the laboratory for analysis is greater than the weight of the patient going back to the ward. You can readily see that I was among those welcoming alternatives to extensive, radical surgery. "Lesser surgery" became a catch word, the cry of progressive revelation, based on sound research studies. Let's now talk about some changes in surgical approach, examples of lesser surgery---for the good of the patient.

1. As mentioned heretofore, the control of duodenal ulcer disease was predicated on the assumption that excess gastric acid was the villain. A natural surgical corollary was the reduction of acid by removing extensive numbers of acid-producing stomach cells and/or inhibiting the formation of acid by cutting the vagus nerves. Surgery, to be sure, was a last resort when medical means of controlling excess acid had failed. Surgery was indicated primarily for:

a) Pyloric obstruction---a condition in which the stomach simply couldn't empty because of scarring secondary to inflammatory ulcer disease.

b) Repeated dangerous bleeding episodes, sometimes requiring emergency surgery.

c) Uncontrollable chronic, recurring pain.

d) Perforation of duodenal ulcer.

Just as in cancer surgery, when ulcer disease would recur in spite of surgery, some surgeons were advocating more and more stomach to be removed---even 75-80%. Horrors! Too predictably, post-operative diarrhea and eating distress were all too common. Weight gain was difficult and patients could become "surgical cripples." Early on, it was my judgment and experience that hemigastrectomy plus vagotomy was not only adequate to control the ulcer problem. It was superior and carried with it much less post-operative discomfort.

In the last decade of my surgical journey, the need for gastric resections became few and far between. The reasons? Research had revealed that excess acid production, although still a factor, was secondary to infection as a cause of ulcer---a bacterial organism had been incriminated that could be treated effectively by good medical management. At the same time, with the advent of fiberoptic endoscopy, better visualization and definition of the problem greatly aided medical management.

2. Cancer of the esophagus used to be a prime target of extensive surgical resection, sometimes with added radiation therapy. With cure rates practically zilch---and with patient's lives made abysmal by extensive resections, it was only natural that other modes of treatment would be considered. Again, lesser surgery! Now, more emphasis on focused radiation and chemotherapy---with a little more hope.

3. Cancer of the head of the pancreas too often was detected very late, only after the tumor had obstructed the common bile duct, producing a troublesome, itching jaundice. The big name surgeons were performing radical pancreatico-duodenectomy in hopes of cure. Unfortunately, just as in the esophagus, cure was almost nil and the postoperative complications of bile and pancreatic leakage were very upsetting, resulting in some prolonged hospitalizations. No surgeon away from the major medical centers could hope to do enough of these procedures to remain competent and proficient. As a principle of conscience, I refused to attempt such a procedure. First, I didn't feel qualified and, second, I thought the procedure was futile. Of note, the procedure is done infrequently now and, even then, only after targeted radiation and chemotherapy.

4. Have you noticed that there are some awfully heavy people in this nation? When weight tips the scales at 300-400# and plus, we refer to obesity as morbid obesity. Now, probably, all these people should have gone on the Subway diet, but they didn't. In general, they didn't like themselves and they were desperate---for somebody else to help them lose weight. Enter again the surgical philosophy that there's nothing that can't be cured by cutting it out. Two procedures, with excellent research and supporting articles in surgical journals, began to be applied in the battle against morbid obesisty---intestinal bypass and gastric exclusion.

a) As named, intestinal bypass effectively bypassed almost the entire absorptive surface of the small bowel. The technique wasn't difficult, utilizing standard intestinal anstomoses. Weight loss was a natural accompaniment of non-absorption of nutrients, but with diarrhea as a troubling consequence.

b) Gastric exclusion utilized a stapling machine to reduce the size of the gastric pouch to about 5% of its normal capacity. Weight loss, then, would depend upon enforced inability to eat very much at any one time. The technical difficulty of this procedure and its potential complications dictated, at least in my mind, that the procedure belonged in centers which were doing hundreds of cases. It seems impossible, but there are recorded instances in which dedicated eaters could out-eat the gastric exclusion and not lose significant weight. With reputable surgical journals supporting these procedures, we did 10-12 intestinal bypass procedures without mortality. Our criteria for suitability of candidates were strict and most patients weighed over 300#. One lady weighed 475#. Incisions were transverse and extended flank to flank. Obviously, it was time-consuming just to traverse all that adipose tissue in order to gain access to the abdominal cavity. Assessing results objectively, most patients seemed pleased at first because of weight loss, but weight loss was sporadic, variable, and sometimes less than expected. The forewarned diarrhea was troublesome and often confining. Most damaging were liver problems and potassium deficits which, on occasion, demanded reversal of the bypass. Using the retrospectoscope, the rationale was adequate, but the total experience wasn't happy and the procedure was abandoned. My understanding is that gastric pouch reduction procedures are still being performed.

A side note: It's still an open question as to whether all obesity is due only to overeating. There's no doubt that when "calories in" exceeds "calories out," you're going to put on weight. Yet, I've heard some obese people complain, "I just smell food and I gain weight." Even with the certainty of weight gain with excess calories, there may be genetic, metabolic, hormonal, or unknown factors which weigh in on the weight problem.

Our morbidly obese surgical patients were cooperative and grateful even as they were willing to have someone else solve their problem. Post-operatively, we tried to involve them in a self-help program by changing eating habits and, especially, by changing grocery shopping habits. After all, it all starts in the grocery store. You eat what you buy! Excessive weight is a burden, not just on the feet, but also on the mind. We hear over and over that obesity is an invitation to hypertension, diabetes, and stroke---sort of a ticking time bomb. Even as I subscribe to the truth of that worry, I still used to see numbers of elderly overweight people. Perhaps there is something we don't understand that allows some to adapt to their overweight, even outliving their doctor.

We always treated the morbidly obese patients with respect. Even so, you couldn't stifle a little smile and chuckle when seeing Juanita and her husband, both morbidly obese, tooling up to the office in their Volkswagen.

5. I have already referred to the avalanche of laparoscopic surgical procedures, welcomed as patient-pleasing less invasive "lesser surgery." I now amplify the subject with commentary on possible dangers and inappropriate laparoscopic procedures. With exultation and

enthusiasm, remember that pendulums sometimes can swing too rapidly and too far. Remember---surgeons tend to want to extend the frontiers and sometimes going too far results in some skirmishes with the Indians---complications will increase, in other words.

No surgeon will tell you that laparoscopy is the answer to every problem. For instance, when facing a laparoscopic cholecystectomy, you will be informed that, if complications occur or the anatomy is distorted, an open operation may be necessary.

Perhaps I shouldn't introduce cost into the equation because most people don't care about cost if a procedure is more beneficial. Nonetheless, it seems to me to be an unwise use of the health care dollar to extend laparoscopy, a more expensive procedure when preceded by CT scans, to appendectomy. Nothing should be referred to as "simple," but I recall how quickly (15-20 minutes) we could remove an inflamed appendix. Through a small transverse cosmetic incision, I could gain generous exposure to assess and treat very complicated appendiceal perforations. What ever happened to common sense and clinical sense? With our safety and accuracy record in treating appendicitis, it seems ridiculous to employ a more expensive, more time-consuming technique to accomplish appendectomy. Then, there's the matter of safety. Just a few years ago in a nearby town, a surgeon, while performing a laparoscopic appendectomy, punctured the abdominal aorta of a 13 year old girl, leading to massive hemorrhage and death. Of course, there were lots of hindsight "what if's", questioning the management---why wasn't an immediate large incision made to control bleeding? What remains after all the suppositions is that the young girl died due to a laparoscopic error---a girl who would have been completely safe in my hands.

ANOTHER DIGRESSION ---
PROFESSIONAL DISAGREEMENT

As I reflect on the changes in surgery from my perch in the sheltered tree of retirement, and perhaps with a belated sense of satisfaction that I wasn't frozen by tradition---it strikes me that the medical/surgical world is oh, so human and reacts to change and competition with human responses. In a sense, we all share a resistance to change. Haven't you become accustomed and comfortable with your way of life---and haven't you become a little upset with changes you can't escape?

Although not stifled by tradition, I haven't strayed completely from the mainstream of medicine---heeding that old adage, "Be not the first by which the new is tried nor yet the last to lay the old aside."

Surgeons as human? What a quaint thought! Those human qualities of envy, competitiveness, one-upsmanship, and headline seeking were alive and flourishing not only in competing surgeons, but also in their institutions. This usually unspoken, unwritten competitive atmosphere sometimes found expression out in the open at surgical conferences when there might be heated discussions about choices of treatment.

Though probably much less now, it was no secret here in the Midwest that there wasn't any love lost between prominent physicians in Minneapolis-St. Paul hospitals and the Mayo Clinic at Rochester, Minnesota. I'm not setting it forth as rampant, but it was there. You may think of it as jealousy, but that depends on the camp where your tent is pitched.

Amazingly, difference in surgical style and management even emerged during my stomach churning oral American Board of Surgery exam in 1960 (I passed). The exam was held at the Mayo Clinic. Not feeling very confident after two days of probing tests, I found myself one afternoon in a one-on-one session with Dr. R., a well known surgeon from St. Paul. He was quizzing me about surgical knowledge, but also he seemed to be exploring attitudes.

Out of the blue, he gave me a hypothetical case in this manner. "Right now, upstairs in the O.R., they've a young patient on the table, trying to identify the cause of repeated low blood sugar episodes (hypoglycemia). They've searched and searched for an islet cell adenoma of the pancreas and haven't located it. What do you think the surgeons are going to do now?" I disliked oral exams, I trembled, but the only reasonable path was to give honest answers, not trying to guess where Dr. R. might be going with the question. My answer, "I would predict that they're proceeding to remove about 2/3 of the pancreas in the hopes that the hypoglycemia will be corrected." Quickly, he snapped, "Would you do that?" Now, remember that pancreatic resections of that sort at that time were fraught with complications and I didn't feel qualified for that kind of battle. Therefore, my answer was a simple, "No, I wouldn't!" Smiling, Dr. R. said, "Good!" At that very moment, I knew that I had passed the exam in his eyes---and he had let come to the surface a not so subtle disagreement between institutions.

GREAT CHANGES IN SURGICAL MANAGEMENT OF BREAST PROBLEMS

As a subset of the evolution in surgical management, an entire section is now devoted to problems of the breast, especially breast malignancy. I deem this most fitting because, of all surgical diseases I encountered, I spent considerably more time with breast malignancy treatment. At a time when I can now have the luxury of looking at myself objectively, coupled with commentary of patients I have treated---I think that I excelled in the communication so necessary in this emotionally charged illness.

The mammary gland, the breast, a nutritional lifeline of mother's milk for babies---increasingly has become a visible sexual symbol in our culture. It isn't that this hasn't always been so---to some degree, but we are now victims of advertisers, bombarding us with sexual symbols. We're inundated with the picture of the "body beautiful" in movies, magazines, TV, and beauty contests. There seems to be an insatiable appetite for measurements, the life blood of plastic surgeons. Is it any wonder, then, that an adolescent girl, in comparing her development to a Miss America or Miss World might attach more importance to breast than to heart, kidney, uterus, or brain? Looking in the mirror, the wonder is, "How do I measure up?" It matters not what age we are, any growth on the surface, visible to others---be it adolescent acne or senile keratosis---may assume an emotional importance beyond reason! A not easily consoled frustration and concern about breast development is now more understandable---in our culture.

With hormonal urging at puberty, breast enlargement occurs in both sexes. To be sure, enlargement is variable because we're individuals and we develop according to a specified gene plan. Our daughters have insisted that they inherited their father's breast genes. You know, parents have to have a strong back, weak mind, and thick skin to withstand all the criticism and complaint thrown at them. Children may dislike the names assigned to them by parents. Children may not be satisfied with the anatomy bequeathed them by parents. Whatever! In both boys and girls, there may be real concerns about "too much" or "too little." The emotional importance of the breast is real and never can be discounted.

Let's not dismiss idly the reality that breast problems also can affect men and boys, but in much less numbers than in the female. Although much less in numbers, the significance to the individual can be shattering. Statistics can be thrown about willy-nilly, but they mean very little to the individual. If you try to quote statistics that a certain problem doesn't occur very often, I assure you that the person afflicted with the problem will shoot right back at you, "Well, it may not be very common, but with me---it's 100%."

1. Malignancy of the male breast is very rare, but it does occur. I never hesitated to biopsy lumps in the male breast for reassurance, but I not once treated a breast malignancy in the male.

2. Shyness hasn't been completely eliminated from the social development process. Shyness is everpresent, to some degree, in the showering with others. What if? What if the young adolescent male, taking a gym shower, has enlargement of the breasts, technically termed gynecomastia? Why? Oh, why? Is it inherent or learned behavior that causes or allows people to be so cruel to others who seem different? Because of teasing, ribbing, or downright ridicule, some boys with breast enlargement were embarrassed to shower, didn't even want to go to school because of the cruel taunting, "Hey, girlie, get a bra." Some physicians advocated forestalling surgery, but they weren't attending the same schools. Subcutaneous removal of breast tissue was a boon to the boy---and perhaps salvation for social and scholastic performance.

Much more space will now be given to the breast problems of girls and women. Somehow, I think that I was always aware that women patients might be more comfortable being examined by a female physician. Occasionally, I would challenge my male colleagues, "Tell me, who would you prefer examining your genitalia---a male or female physician?" In the present years, it's a welcome addition to have more young women joining the medical profession. By and large, women are more compassionate and caring---by nature. At the U. of Illinois College of Medicine, we had 20 female students in a class of 150. However, there were no female physicians in Eau Claire in 1960. It hit me! Women really had little choice---they were seeing me because they had no other options. Whether I was ultra-sensitive to this fact, I don't know. What I do know is that, after seeing thousands of women for breast problems, I had heard it said that I was approachable and capable of sympathetic understanding. Indeed, one outspoken woman even verbalized her feelings, "Dr., you really seem to understand these problems pretty well---for a man." Another woman said spontaneously, after a discussion of her options in treating a malignancy, "Well, you surely are different," to which I naturally responded, "Thank you," intuitively realizing that my manner of approach had been recognized and appreciated.

Because of my intense interest and because I just couldn't buy all of the practices in vogue at the time (practices, incidentally, that had been established by men), I was tuned to modify and improve techniques which might be more patient-pleasing. I have no inflated feeling that I had any impact nationally, but at least in Eau Claire, I am confident that I was on the cutting edge of change. Let me now lay before you some examples of how change was promoted---sometimes even before the national literature suggested change.

1. Extent of surgery and choice of incision: In my training, breast surgery was approached just as malignancy in other organs---with radical, aggressive surgery to

"get every last cancer cell." The radical mastectomy, as opposed to the simple removal of the breast, consisted of wide removal of the breast together with removal of the pectoral muscles from the chest wall---in addition to axillary lymph node dissection. In some centers, so much skin was removed that skin grafts were necessary for coverage of the chest wall. In New York, one pompous and bold surgeon even extended the "radical" to the "super-radical." How gross! How foolish! He certainly didn't increase cure rates. In the light of present knowledge of cancer biology, the radical philosophy just didn't hold water.

  To accomplish the radical mastectomy, a long longitudinal incision was the standard. Alas, this incision was unsightly and certainly was a painful reminder for any woman looking in the mirror. I found that a transverse incision was neater, equally effective, more aesthetic, and healed better than the longitudinal incision. Furthermore, with the transverse incision, a woman could wear a dress with a low neck line. Was I out of step? Sit with me at a post-graduate conference, watching surgery at Cook County Hospital in Chicago. Heading up this session was a renowned surgeon from Oak Park, waxing eloquent about the procedure we were watching in the surgical amphitheater. When I asked a simple question, "Would you ever consider a transverse incision?" the great one almost seemed insulted as he rather disdainfully proclaimed, "The incision will be up and down." In the surgical pecking order of the day, those who were the top guns, the ones who were speakers at conferences---these surgeons protected what was traditional. All I knew was that common sense dictated that, in an already unfortunate and scary circumstance, the transverse incision was more pleasing and gave a small measure of comfort to the woman patient.

  2. Was there no place for individual assessment? Long before the advent of outpatient same-day surgery, every woman would be admitted to the hospital the evening before surgery---the surgery to be performed under general anesthesia. For no other reason than that it had

always been done that way, she was asked to sign a consent form, authorizing the removal of the lump and then, if the lump proved to be malignant by immediate microscopic frozen section, also authorizing a mastectomy. The only rationale I can find to support that practice was the desire to avoid another hospitalization. Would it be possible that we might put ourselves in her place---terrified of the possibility that she might wake up without a breast? A great problem with this practice was twofold: a) It completely violated the medical conscience to treat people as individuals, not as a group, and b) in many of the women, there wasn't very much suspicion of malignancy.

When I reflected on the fact that, of 100 lump excisions, only 5-10 proved to be malignant, I began to rebel against this traditional approach. Furthermore, in women under age 40, the possibility of malignancy was even less. Quite obviously, most lumps, especially in young women, were benign cysts or fibroadenomas. Especially since my experience and clinical senses allowed me to predict fairly accurately whether a lump was benign or malignant, I ventured out on a new path. I started talking to patients in a more reassuring tone, testing the waters in this manner, "Yes, we really need to know what the nature of this lump is---if nothing else, just to get the worry behind us. However, since I have such an overwhelming feeling that it's benign, wouldn't you like to know going into the procedure that, on awakening, you'll have both breasts---and not even think of the possibility of mastectomy right now? If, on the way outside chance that there should be a malignancy, we could deal with it then." The response was one of indescribable relief especially in young women because they had heard of other women who had had to sign that possible mastectomy consent form. I can't recall ever being wrong in my preoperative impression. This welcome change, so natural and filled with common sense, has been followed by more change in the latter years of my practice---with more outpatient surgery, more local anesthesia with I.V. sedation.

3. A special way of treating breast cysts: with experience, it was possible to develop a good clinical hunch whether a lump was a benign solid tumor (usually fibroadenoma) or a fluid-filled cyst. As every woman knows, the breast responds to cyclical, up-and-down hormonal changes---with pre-menstrual engorgement of the breast, accompanied by variable tenderness and fibrocystic changes. With care, I could insert a needle into the cyst, without discomfort, by pinioning the suspected cyst between two outstretched fingers of my left hand. The sensation of needle entering cyst was unmistakable and, after withdrawing the cystic fluid, the cyst was no longer palpable. Initially, I sent the fluid to the lab for Pap smear but, after 100 or so negative results, I was confident in foregoing even that test---with its attendant cost. The emotional results were dramatic and relieving---as illustrated in the following incident in which a young woman's terrifying anxiety gave way to exultation.

Miss C. had visited another clinic for examination of a newly discovered tender breast lump. Her anxiety completely immobilized her when she was told that the lump was most likely malignant and would require surgery---now! Actually her history of sudden tenderness, which prompted the finding of the lump, tilted the scales away from malignancy. Never forget! The mere mention of the "C" word can strike terror and create fear. Our wonderful office nurses and receptionist were trained to treat breast anxiety as urgent, sometimes even emergent. Therefore, Miss C. was seen on that same day at the end of our office schedule. My impression, after history taking and clinical exam, was that we were dealing with a benign cyst. However, with the "C" word having been implanted (rather carelessly, I thought), it had to be replaced by the "R" word---reassurance. With no surprise to me, the needling and aspiration of the cystic lump brought forth fluid and collapsed the cyst. Behold! No lump!

For effect, I would then instruct the patient, "Would you place your hand on your breast and show me where the lump is?" I wish you could have seen the loosening of the facial skin, the relief---and heard the exclamation, "It's not there! It's gone!"

4. Could it be possible? Could there be cure of breast malignancy outside of the realm of radical mastectomy? Now, as you read these thoughts, reflecting on changes in the time frame, 1958-1990, isn't it clear to you that evolution is continuing even now---always against the backdrop of "What's best for the patient."? Sometimes I thought that changes in treatment and diagnostic procedures were at a snail's pace in those decades. Just keep in mind that the only constant in our lives is change---so expect further change.

Dr. George Crile, of the Cleveland Clinic, was a brave and pioneering surgeon. At a time, in 1960, when it was almost anathema to suggest that there could be any treatment for breast malignancy other than radical mastectomy, Dr. Crile was suggesting that simple removal of the malignant lump plus post-operative radiation might be as effective and certainly more pleasing to women. Dr. Crile was once considered to be a non-scientific maverick or kook by some. In some surgical centers, he was treated as a pariah for his non-traditional views. Although he often received a cool reception at surgical meetings, he has gone down in history as a prophet because of his thoughts, encouraging lesser surgery in treating breast and thyroid malignancy.

Guess what? No surprise! Gradually with the support of appreciative women, more attention has been given to breast preservation procedures. Yes, of course, the primary goal of any treatment should be the eradication of the problem---total cure. Indeed, in my experience, most women identified as having breast malignancy had as their primary concern, "Will I be o.k.? Will I live? Will I be able to be a mother to my children?" The secondary concern, of course, couldn't be avoided, "How will I look after surgery?"

Sound clinical studies gradually emerged, proving

that breast preservation procedures were just as effective in effecting cure as the more radical procedures. Prime candidates for the lesser procedures were those breast malignancies in which the prognosis of cure was very high. For instance, some types of breast malignancy, which were localized, in situ, and not infiltrating, were prime candidates for lesser procedures, knowing in advance that the cure rate would approach 100%. Yes, all cancers, and especially breast cancers, shouldn't be perceived as just one animal. Some cancers are like terrifying predators while others have to be treated with caution, but are more like frisky pussy-cats.

Dr. Crile's removal of the breast lump, followed by radiation, quickly got into the surgical literature as "lumpectomy." In my precise mind, the term is a throwback and not truly descriptive. I never liked the term, greatly preferring, "partial cosmetic resection of malignant breast tissue with breast preservation." O.K.! Maybe it was just semantics, but it was more anatomically accurate and descriptive of what was being done.

5. The role of prosthesis following mastectomy: As openers, in a nutshell, prostheses can be external or internal. External prostheses---that is, outside the skin surface---are synthetic. Internal prostheses---beneath the skin surface---can be synthetic or fashioned from the woman's own tissues in a reconstruction procedure done simultaneously or following mastectomy. The goal of any prosthesis is to help each woman through a terribly difficult time by making her appear normal to the world---even though she may never feel normal.

Routinely, I spent considerable time, trying to explain how a prosthesis might effect cosmesis and increase emotional well-being. I've never understood whether the response I received from women in my practice had to do with my manner of presentation or with an unusual mindset ingrained in women in this geographical area, especially in the age 50 group---or older. Maybe I was seeing some lingering pioneer spirit, maybe some fatalism, perhaps some religious stoicism. Whatever the motivation, most of my patients in this age group opted for external prostheses---or nothing. By nothing, I mean that they simply chose to stuff the bra with soft facial tissues, cloth, or whatever. The general feeling I heard was, "I just want to know that I'll be o.k. I can cope with the appearance later." The external prosthesis, filled with a gel, was amazingly normal to palpation. Trained, empathetic prosthetists were invaluable in fitting the woman with proper size of prosthesis, which was slipped into the bra. Nobody! Nobody should be so foolish or stupid as to suggest that the mastectomized woman would feel normal---but, at least, she seemed normal when facing the world. A drawback to the external prosthesis was that it restricted the woman's options for physical activities such as swimming or tennis. Rest assured that, once I made such a statement, some brave soul would delight in proving me wrong.

The choice of internal prosthesis was affected by the amount of skin and soft tissue available to work with. Actually, I preferred that women who wished the internal prosthesis would wait 3-4 weeks to have this performed as a separate procedure. My reasoning was that I felt it was enough to worry about just to get through the mastectomy. However, I'm sympathetic to women who would like to have substance on the chest wall immediately, not later. Also, there may be less and less worry about complications as the procedure is improved.

In a practical sense, I have seen the gamut. There are those who seem to forge through tragedy by proclaiming by word or manner, "I could care less." More commonly, there is the rush to be normal---especially to be that glamorous person portrayed on television. Unfortunately, in the rush to be normal, these philosophical or common sense thoughts are easily crowded out:

a) Normalcy is more subjective than objective---more from within than from without. Perfection, after all, is just an idea---and the quest for wholeness in life rarely is to be found in the clamor and insistence on perfection.

Indeed, what is normal?

b) After ANY injury, whether it be an ankle sprain or mastectomy, nobody really ever returns to the pre-injury state. Therefore, a mastectomy patient must come to grips emotionally with the obvious loss of a part of her anatomy---regardless of the prosthetic or breast reconstruction option pursued. It has been driven home to me---haven't you thought about it?---that we're oh, so human and, as such, vary widely in our ability to cope with loss and adversity. Fortunately, there are wonderful examples of those who will always be survivors---come what may. Undaunted, these survivors sing the song, "We Shall Overcome," with special meaning.

If only you could have seen Mrs. W. on one of her post-mastectomy visits. With a well-healed cosmetic incision, she flung open her gown and proclaimed to the world, "Hey, look at me! Sure, I've lost something, but just look at all I have left." A true survivor! A person who typifies those who will meet the mystery of death without flinching!

In wading through the psycho-sexual post-mastectomy waters, some women will come close to drowning and there are others who won't even know it's raining. Nonetheless, all can benefit from helping or being helped in positive support groups. How often have we seen this recurring theme---no man or woman is an island? The male of the species isn't always comfortable with expressing soft feelings, but I witnessed a truly supportive scene in my office---wish you could have heard it. When I was discussing various options post-mastectomy with a woman and her husband, he said very feelingly to her, "Hey, hon, you've lost a breast---true! But that's not why I married you."

6. Breast Self-examination: Ideally, every malignancy should be diagnosed and treated as early as possible before spread (metastasis) has occurred. With that as the goal, it became popular to promote breast self-examination as a means, theoretically, of finding breast

lumps earlier and thus increase the chance of cure. I have no problem with the concept and the goal. My problem, as I talked with women, was that this, essentially, transferred much of the responsibility and burden onto patients. You can see the basis for my concerns in the following observations:

    a) Accuracy of detecting a breast lump on palpation is far from 100% even in the hands of the most skilled and experienced physicians and nurse practitioners.

    b) Accuracy is further affected adversely when examining a very large breast.

    c) Fibrocystic changes, with fluid-filled cysts and firm fibrous tissue, can be so confusing as to make a woman complain, "I have absolutely no idea what I'm feeling."

    d) Growth rate of a breast malignancy, from inception to the size of a palpable lump, is known to be slow---maybe two or three years. Therefore, with early detection as the goal, self-examination may fall far short of the goal anyway. Thinking this way, other diagnostic modes, such as mammography, should have more emphasis.

    e) Self-examination has the potential for increasing anxiety and over-concern in the very person who needs reassurance. Too often, I've heard confessions, "I'm afraid I'm doing it all wrong. What if I'm missing something?"

    f) Yet, a relaxed self-examination, interpreted as just one part of the total plan for taking good care of yourself, can be a good reference point in interpreting future exams.

    Having examined with you some of the changes in management of breast problems, I'd like now to turn to some pertinent issues that never change. The need for communication is ever present in medicine. The best communication is that which puts patients at ease and doesn't increase concerns. Listen now to a horror story.

BAD COMMUNICATION CAN WREAK HAVOC

In recent decades, I've been so pleased to meet wonderfully well trained health educators in elementary and secondary schools. Sadly, it hasn't always been so. Grandpas and grandmas will appreciate that discussion of sexuality wasn't always handled well in their youth---if at all. If the subject was introduced, there was an attendant embarrassment, snickering, an ill at ease. For some hidden reason, touchy topics often were assigned to gym teachers. Why? These teachers had little training and may have had as many hangups about sexuality as the students. Maybe it was hoped that gym teachers would have better rapport in those unclothed moments.

In the 1960's, I witnessed the harm a teacher can inflict with ill-chosen words. I first met Sandra, a 16 year old girl, when her mother brought her to the office. Sandra expressed an unusual fear that she had breast lumps and cancer. Any shyness or embarrassment that this young girl might have had at seeing a male physician was overridden by her concern. Naively, I thought that reassurance would be a snap with my easy manner. I made a huge mistake in thinking that she would go away happy, hearing me tell her that she need not worry.

I should have been less smug about decreasing worry in Sandra. I knew that reassurance can be very short lived or well nigh impossible if the patient is a dedicated worrier. For this reason, I had almost removed that phrase, "Don't worry," from my vocabulary.

With Sandra, the worry was deep-seated. Within two months, she was still concerned about breast cancer, the concern intensified to the point of tears. Again, the exam was normal and I was groping, realizing I wasn't helping her. There was no family history of breast cancer, but she had no peace of mind. I certainly wasn't going to recommend a mammogram at her age.

At last, came the light! Sandra's mother had uncovered the crucial information from the mother of another girl in Sandra's gym class. Apparently, a female gym teacher had gathered her brood around her to instruct them in breast self-examination. Don't even ask. I have absolutely no clue why the subject was even approached at that grade level. In addition, I had no knowledge of how well the teacher was liked or what kind of a role model she provided. What I did know was that, in any group instruction involving a sensitive subject , there are going to be some in the group more vulnerable to harmful misinterpretations than others. All Sandra had to hear was the teacher introducing the session with, "O.K., girls. Gather 'round. You're going to learn how to examine your breasts to prevent cancer (horribly non-factual and misleading anyway). After all, you don't want to lose one of your boobs." Eventually, and hopefully, Sandra felt better after another visit in which we could hit head-on the underlying cause of her distress. I hammered home the perspective of age incidence and that I had NEVER seen or heard of a female under age 20 with breast cancer. What a price Sandra paid for inappropriate words.

THE IMPACT OF AGE
ON BREAST MALIGNANCY OUTCOME

How natural---to slide into the subject of age incidence after hearing of Sandra's emotional turmoil. It's common sense and common knowledge that breast malignancy, as with most malignancies, is more common after age 60. It's often said of the male curse, those bothersome prostate problems, that if all men lived to be 120 years of age, every man would develop prostate cancer. Perhaps to a lesser extent, the same might be said of the chances of women developing breast cancer---if they live long enough. There is an ominous truth that the younger the patient, however, the gloomier the prognosis. Perhaps some of that gloom has lifted ever so slightly by more intensive adjunctive measures such as radiation, chemotherapy, and bone marrow transplants in selected cases. It's just a gut feeling that, at a young age, every legitimate attempt to preserve life seems justified. At any age, though, extreme measures to prolong life are welcome and desirable---as long as we're prolonging life and not just prolonging the time of dying.

It really wasn't just laziness. I never bothered to keep statistics on numbers and categories of cases, etc. There simply wasn't the time or inclination to do so because statistics were woefully hollow when treating each person as an individual. You've heard the clarion call of patients I've already described, "Thanks for informing me about statistics, but for me---it's 100%." Although I can't come up with the exact number of breast problems treated, my guesstimate would be several thousand. In all that experience, I recall only 5 young women in their 20' s who had breast malignancy---and, sadly, not one of them survived. Let me introduce you to two of these young women---their faces etched in my memory even to this day. Regardless of the forces aligned against us, our human personalities will display our uniqueness, our hope or despair. With the same diagnosis and prognosis, you'll now see sharply contrasting temperaments.

1. Betty, age 27, had undergone mastectomy at St. Elsewhere Hospital. With dismal prognosis, her token chemotherapy protocol was prescribed by an oncologist at the U. of Minnesota Hospitals. For some reason, her family physician didn't want to be involved and asked that we assume responsibility for administering her I.V. chemotherapy injections between her visits to the U. of Minnesota.

Because we hadn't treated Betty from the inception of her malignancy and, therefore, hadn't been able to support her through those terrible times, we were somewhat at a disadvantage. She most likely thought of our office as foreign territory and, equating it with her malignancy, she probably saw it as a Hell hole---and we were the ones wielding the pitchforks. Understandably, she was bitter and angry. Try to imagine how you'd feel if you knew you were leaving three daughters heartbroken and motherless?

One day, while I was preparing the I.V. chemotherapy solutions, the emotional dam broke. Amidst a cascade of tears, she sobbed, "Why am I even taking this shit? It's just poison and I'm going to die anyway---with it or without it." As gently as I could after the sobbing quieted, I reminded her, "Nobody knows what the future brings. What I do know is that you are very important every day to your friends and family---and HOPE is still more than a four-letter word. Yet, your wishes should be respected and, at any time, you can just decide not to take these medications. If so, I'll do the best I can and, together, we'll do the best we can---for as long as we can."

Immediately, more tears---and she shot back, "You know I can't do that! My husband won't let me. My family won't let me." Oh, how right she was! Families often, in their own misery and despair, urge the patient to fight, to hang in there. At times, even in futile situations, families may insist, "You've gotta eat." The problem: That may be exactly what the terminally ill patient doesn't want to do.

    2. Jackie, age 28, a single mom with a 10 year old son, living east of Eau Claire, was diagnosed with breast malignancy and was referred to me for mastectomy. Unfortunately, 15 axillary lymph nodes were involved with metastatic malignancy. In spite of post-op radiation, the prognosis was glim and glum. Within a year, not surprisingly, she exhibited body-wide metastases. In retrospect, I knew deep in my gut that the radiation therapy was next to useless. Yet, there's something about continuing down a path, following established recommendations---and following this path actually may give a measure of hope.

    Treatment from that time on was purely symptomatic. During this journey through the valley, Jackie never lost her smiling face and a plaintive, naive hope that, "I think I'm getting a little better." Deep down, I'm sure that she knew the truth---that she'd soon be leaving her son, her mother, her sister. In spite of all this, she not once complained. Of all the patients I've known, Jackie best fit my own definition of the "good patient"--- the one who has a generous spirit in the face of adversity and, in the face of impending death, makes life easier, more bearable for all those who wait and watch.

THE INFLUENCE OF FAMILY HISTORY ON INCIDENCE OF BREAST MALIGNANCY

What are your chances of developing breast malignancy? In predicting the possibility and the course of breast malignancy, there are significant markers. Age of the patient and the type of tumor are very important in predicting the course, but there is nothing more important in predicting possibility than family history. It's a mother/daughter thing. For instance, the fact that my 84 year old mother had breast cancer has no bearing on our daughters' risk status. Although a strong family history of breast malignancy is worrisome, a woman need not walk through life as if carrying a ticking time bomb. Instead, heed this message: Enjoy life , but be more aware and vigilant, taking advantage of all means of early detection.

So true! Out-of-bounds worry and anxiety can imprison a person. If we chase life frantically and pursue good health fiercely with a vengeance, we shall have no more chance of finding it than are our chances of catching a fluttering butterfly by running after it. Behold! If we are patient, calm, and appear unconcerned---the butterfly may light on our shoulders. You say that this is the ideal emotional state, but a dream which is difficult to capture? You're right, of course, but there IS truth there. In reality, all women will feel vulnerable if family history is bursting at the seams---with breast cancer in grandmother, mother, an aunt, and a sister.

A PERSONALIZATION OF FAMILY HISTORY

Meet Joanie, a young woman I had known from the time she was a high school girl, working at a grocery store checkout counter. Later in life, Joanie remembered our conversations and chose to see me in consultation because of some worrisome findings on breast self-examination. Included in her history was a grandmother with breast malignancy. Alas! She also had the misfortune to have a breast structure which easily created confusion and ultra-concern in both patient and physician.

You may recall, in my discussion of breast self-examination, that extreme fibrocystic changes make a meaningful exam next to impossible. Hard fibrous tissue and fluid-filled cysts, akin to a rocky road, make accuracy of clinical exam extremely chancy. Therefore, for reassurance, Joanie was seen more frequently than other patients. On the fibrocystic scale from 1 to 10, she was a 22! Mammography was employed at least annually and cysts often were aspirated to reduce the sensation of lumpiness. All biopsies revealed benign microscopic findings.

At my retirement, Joanie's care was accepted by a conservative and competent surgeon. One day, after my retirement, Joanie called with an uncharacteristic plaintive voice---almost pleading, "Will you come see me?" Not knowing, even with a thought that she might want to talk about a marital problem, I was stunned by what I heard. Even though Joanie had a very supportive husband and two daughters, she felt that the world was caving in around her. Try to imagine her shock, grief, and disbelief when she was the one who discovered her mother, a suicide death. Fortunately, in this instance an autopsy was done. Lo and behold, her mother had been hiding a far advanced breast cancer. It's impossible to understand suicidal intent fully, but it would appear that the breast cancer was so terrifying that suicide seemed to be the only option.

Joanie now had the recurring nightmare of her mother's suicide and the knowledge that both her mother and her grandmother had breast cancer. At this same time, her most recent mammogram was reported as showing a "suspicious" area. I'm not sure why, but her problem was to be handled at the Mayo Clinic---perhaps because of the complexity of the problem. She was so scared! Hoping to reduce her anxiety level, I accompanied her and her husband at their request. Based on family history, aggravated anxiety, and the troublesome breast tissue (although not malignant), the decision was to do a subcutaneous mastectomy together with insertion of a synthetic prosthesis. An extension of the plan, at a six month interval, was to do a similar procedure on the opposite breast. Without identifying myself, I listened (as a family member would) to the plastic surgeon's post-op report. My perception was that he was skilled, but somewhat perfunctory and cool.

You think that the saga was over? No way! Once again, Joanie needed somebody to talk to because she was having what she described as "awful, shooting pain" in the operative site. It's no secret that pain is perceived differently in a wide range of patients. To me, recognizing this variability, it's a mark of the good physician simply to believe the patient. Not to do so is totally counterproductive. To impart the feeling to the patient that he/she isn't believed will evoke the lament, "You mean it's all in my head?" In a way, all pain actually IS perceived in the head---which receives messages from peripheral pain receptors. It just makes good sense to realize that ALL pain is real---to the patient.

The perfunctory and cool plastic surgeon now did the ultimate no-no. In a post-op visit, dealing with a tearful and upset patient, he announced that he had wondered from the start whether he should have accepted Joanie as a patient. Why? Maybe he didn't handle frustration well,

Mabe he was a tad miffed because his talent wasn't being appreciated.

Because of unrelenting pain, the prosthesis was finally removed. Rather than agonize over an impending six months decision, that opposite breast was removed also. Guess what? She immediately became pain free, malignancy free, and a happy wife and mother. Some subsequent findings about synthetic materials strongly suggest that her pain was related to the synthetic prosthesis.

A PLACE FOR PROPHYLACTIC MASTECTOMY?

For years, it was unthinkable! Even to consider surgically removing tissue where no clear evidence of disease could be demonstrated---well, this was anathema. Money often was a clinching factor because insurance companies wouldn't pay for prophylactic mastectomy. Fortunately, patients and families have more and more weighed in on decision making. The arrogant days aren't gone completely, but there's much less of the God-like physician blustering, "I'm the doctor and I know what's best for you."

Decision making should be balanced with full disclosure. Neither patient nor physician should be dominant.

Yes, this balance sometimes can be imbalance if a patient or family becomes too demanding. Don't fear! There are protections. No physician ever is compelled to prescribe or do any procedure which would be contrary to his/her conscience and good judgment. Yes, I've heard demands such as, "Hey, Doc, gimme a shot of penicillin!" The wise and confident physician need not react with umbrage at the demand/request. Rather, the tone should be, "Let's sit and talk first to see what is right and best for both of us."

Common sense, combined with what's best for the patient, finally has had its ascendancy. Especially in the woman with suspicious breast tissue and a horrific family history of breast malignancy, her request for prophylactic mastectomy with reconstruction is totally legitimate. In addition, when malignancy has been found in one breast, there is an increased probability of malignancy in the other breast. Should purists get their noses out of joint just because that breast doesn't show malignancy---YET? Don't interpret this as tantamount to a recommendation to do the prophylactic mastectomy. Yet, wouldn't it be humane to present it as an option?

What changes we have seen in the diagnosis and management of breast problems in the past four decades! However the dream persists---the finding of a vaccine, gene therapy, or medication which could dull the sword of breast malignancy.

THE ART OF COMMUNICATION, THE CORNERSTONE OF THE PHYSICIAN/PATIENT RELATIONSHIP

We often do not see things as they are---we see them as we are. We often do not see people as they are---we see them as we would like them to be. We often do not hear what is said---we hear, sometimes distracted by illness or numbed by fear, only that which we would like to hear. We are truly blessed with fantastic senses, designed to help us appreciate everything and everybody around us---in awe and admiration. However, our senses sometimes fall short of perfection. They fall short of precision. If you would aspire to be that good and sympathetic communicator, you must face the reality that all of us, at times, have jaded and imperfect senses which don't receive or process the written or spoken word as it is intended by the sender.

This section is written because our health is too important not to communicate with those who care for us. Now, naturally, that should be a two-way street. Listening, according to Dr. William Osler, is the oldest and perhaps the most powerful tool of healing. Dr. Osler, a widely quoted and most wise physician, admonished us well, "Listen to the patient. He/she may actually tell you what is wrong and lead you to the diagnosis." Sadly, studies have shown that, in interviewing a patient (taking a history), the patient is interrupted after only 17 seconds. Along this line, current medical clinic guidelines, with an eye to the bottom-line dollar, are restrictive in time allotments with patients. It's a little uncomfortable to think of communication with the stopwatch ticking

Communication: "To make known, to impart, to spread to others---to express myself in a way that is readily and clearly understood by others."

Well and good, but real life experience shows that, in our best efforts to communicate well, we don't always succeed--we fall short. On the two-way street of communication, physicians must be tuned in and perceptive to patients' needs. Too often, we (I use the plural, because I surely have fallen short, also---even when I wasn't aware) fail because the words we use are confusing. Sometimes, we forget that what we say doesn't "take" on the first utterance---it needs repetition. It's even possible that we don't know the patient as well as we should, or as well as we thought we did. Perhaps we rely too heavily on printed pamphlets (someone else's words) to explain tests and treatments. Overly trusting the printed pamphlet denies the obvious---that pamphlets are capable of raising more questions than of providing answers.

Turning to the other side of the two-way street, patients also may not be tuned to the right station, distracted for whatever reason. Who among us hasn't had the humbling experience, after what we thought was a clear and erudite discussion, of overhearing two people trying to recapture the substance of the discussion, as follows: "So Dr. Hudson says that I have two left feet." "No, silly, he didn't say that at all---he said two right feet." This stark disparity in interpretation of what was said occurs especially when dealing with serious and emotional issues, especially cancer diagnosis and treatment.

On the two-way street of communication, I've had an uncomfortable feeling that patients have a distinct disadvantage from the get-go. Come to think of it, rapport and communication is an elusive prize considering that physicians and patients alike come in various sizes, shapes, ages and gender---and are variably endowed with intelligence and ability to comprehend, variably blessed with perception. Unfortunately for patients, their side of the two-way street can be filled with roadblocks and potholes, which are hindrances to communication. Believe me! I've personally perceived or had reported to me each of the following roadblocks---and I fully understand that this is a partial list.

1. I'm on somebody else's turf and on their timetable. I'd feel easier in a more familiar home setting.

2. I clam up when I get nervous---and I'm always so nervous in the doctor's office.

3. They're so smart and they'll think I'm so dumb.

4. I'm really worried about money---what will it cost?

5. I can't concentrate on what they're saying when I have pain, a full bladder, or diarrhea.

6. My background, my bringing up, makes me uncomfortable about topics such as sexual activity or bowel movements.

7. I'd feel more at ease seeing a female physician---or a male physician.

8. They probably won't believe me. They'll think it's all in my head.

9. I forget so easily. I forgot to ask about a mammogram or about that mole on my back.

10. I can't understand what they're saying because my hearing is bad---but I'm too embarrassed to admit it.

11. I'm so tired of waiting that I'm in a bad mood.

12. They take me down when they say, "Why didn't you come sooner?" "Didn't you know better?"

13. I'm afraid to ask about charges I don't understand because I don't want to be labelled a complainer or a hypochondriac.

You've perhaps heard the phrases, "the art of medicine" and "bedside manner." You should now have perceived my belief that communication is at the heart of "the art of medicine." My original definition of "a good bedside manner" is found in the willingness to listen---and not only to listen, but to hear what is said---and not only to hear what is said, but to hear what is trying to be said. When communication goes astray and there is unintended anxiety, we fall far short of our primary goal---of helping the patient. Following are a few examples of missed communication. Oh, how words can be a two-edged sword.

1. Patients sometimes are confused by all those people coming in and out of their room. There are nurses, aides, cleaning ladies, clergy, physicians, lab techs, respiratory therapists, etc. Generally, it is assumed that all these people have the training requisite to be there. Nevertheless, an already troubled patient may be alarmed by an unfamiliar person entering the room.

As introduction for this scenario, I remind you that training programs are a necessity for both physicians and nurses. These programs, in some way, embody efforts to hone technical and communication skills by interacting with real live patients. There may be recent attempts to erase the inequity, but communication training lags sadly behind the technical training. Why this inequity?

a) A lot of wannabe surgeons and nurses are attracted to working with hands more than with heads. At the end of a day, it seems more rewarding to say, "I started an I.V., I inserted an N.G. tube, I sutured a laceration," than to say, "I talked to a patient."

b) Curricula are increasingly crowded with factual materials and technical know-how, leaving less time for improvement in communication skills. This, then, is the birthplace of a saying I've heard, a comment that makes me shudder, "My doctor is really good---he just doesn't talk to me very much."

c) It comes down from the top! If an instructor isn't comfortable around patients, there is a void in the role model department. Then, too, instructors in the age of procedural orientation may find it much easier to teach students how to work with their hands than how to work with their feelings.

I recall a nursing class---this was a real horror story---in which members of the class were assigned to talk for 15-30 minutes with a patient on the ward, exploring the patient's understanding of his/her illness and the reaction to that illness. This, of course, was designed as a learning experience for the student---a student, through no fault of her own, unfamiliar with the patient, unfamiliar with the ramifications of cancer. You'll recall that most patients feel that there's a purpose for each person entering the room. Trying to cope with a new cancer diagnosis, this patient mistakenly assumed that the young nursing student was a part of the team, an authority figure.

As she probed his feelings about his illness, including his thoughts about end stage possibilities, he became convinced that she had been sent in to tell him that he was going to die. The setback in his progress, as he began to imagine the worst, wasn't just unfortunate. It was disastrous! Yes, the art of communication is difficult to teach. More and more, I'm convinced that the art is more inherent than learned.

2. Do you recall the near hysteria foisted on a young woman who was mistakenly told that her breast lump was probably cancer? This story is somewhat similar, revolving around a poor choice of words. A middle-aged healthy woman, facing a cholecystectomy, simply asked the surgeon, "Is this a serious operation?" In all fairness, the surgeon was only trying to treat the question lightly in an offhanded manner. However, what he said absolutely bombed because of poor choice of words and poor timing. He led off casually with, "Well, you could die." In a way, what he said was the truth because, after all, anything can happen. To his distress, with this blunder he didn't have another chance.

Startled and terrified, the woman was in our office on the same afternoon, asking me the same question. When facing questions about seriousness, my training and instincts were to be forthright, not implying that any surgery is simple and akin to kid's stuff---yet answering in a reassuring manner. The patient really is asking, "will I be o.k.?" My words? "Yes, it's serious, but it's unusually safe. You can go into this procedure calmly, knowing that all of my patients have done well. Your anesthesia care will be the best and you'll be impressed by the many people around to help you after surgery. I have every confidence that we'll get through this together very nicely."

3. What's in a word, a phrase? Is it just semantics? Perhaps a phrase signifies deeper meaning.

Ah, the strange twist of words in communication. An elderly man had been hospitalized on several occasions for treatment of chronic relapsing pancreatitis. He had been in the hospital for so many days that a few days or a few weeks must have seemed an eternity to him. At last, his progress had been sufficient on Thursday and Friday that plans were made to cut his umbilical cord to the hospital, sending him to the comfort of his home on Saturday.

While making rounds on Saturday morning, it seemed to me that the elderly gentleman was squirming a trifle, not very comfortable---but his bags were all packed. Inquiring as to his condition, I perhaps could have probed a little deeper, but I settled for, "Are you having any pain today?" There's no question in my mind that he was hurting more than a little, but he was going home come Hell or high water. Literally, he was worried about the consequences of speaking of pain at that moment because he feared we might suggest he stay a few more days. His words were precise, accurate, and meaningful, "None to speak of"---indeed!

4. Have you ever succumbed to the siren song of complacency? The siren is that temptation to think of ourselves as better than we are---again with the focus on communication. Perhaps all of us occasionally need a comeuppance.

Yes, complacency can cause us to stumble. If there was anything I was sure of, it was my ability to be complete in history taking. You would have liked the thick, gutteral German accent of Hans. This 70 year old single man was living alone in Florida when he was diagnosed with a rectal malignancy. When his niece, living in Eau Claire, became aware of the gravity of the situation, she insisted that he come to Eau Claire for his surgery.

An abdominal-perineal resection of the rectum with creation of a sigmoid colostomy is a daunting procedure, especially for a person with no previous surgical experience. Yet, Hans seemed in good health based on physical exam and blood tests. Of course, we tried to put him at ease, being positive about his prognosis---and generally using upbeat reassurance. Now, picture yourself in Hans's shoes. Would you be perfectly at ease?

The surgery proceeded smoothly---with every expectation of cure. Two days post-surgery, storm clouds appeared on the horizon. Hans became agitated, sweaty, and delirious. We were fearful of electrolyte disturbance or cerebral disaster. In spite of thorough investigation with every test imaginable, something was badly out of whack, but we couldn't put a finger on it. Then a relative came forth with vital information---better than any CT scan. This old German liked his hops---was accustomed to drinking lots of beer. Indeed, because of his anxiety at being transplanted into an unfamiliar garden, he had consumed a case of beer just the day before surgery. Everything now fell into place---he was experiencing alcohol withdrawal with the agitation and shakiness of delirium tremens. Things were touch and go for several days, even with fear for his survival, but Hans apparently wanted more beer and sauerkraut---and tenaciously hung in there with a good recovery.

Shortly before leaving the hospital, Hans was the one who initiated this conversation. "Vell, doctor, I guess I caused you a little trouble." To myself I muttered, "More than a little." Warming up, he added, "Vell, I guess there vas lots you didn't know about me." I couldn't help nodding my head in agreement, "You can say that again." Then came the clincher, the lesson for all physicians to learn, "Yes, there vas lots you didn't know about me---but, you see, there vas lots I didn't know about you." Summed up in that one sentence is a lesson all of us can take to heart. Pride precedes every fall from the pedestal, but humility is there at the bottom, ready to pick us up.

5. Informed consent---a field sewn with land mines. Communication should calm the troubled waters---not increase the turbulence.

The practice of obtaining informed consent for surgical procedures has been shown to be legally necessary, defensively helpful, responsible, ethical, and hopefully educational. Fortunate we are that the days of the autocratic surgeon are largely a thing of the past. Fading into oblivion are the surgeons who, by word or manner, would pronounce, "It's not yours to question. After all, I'm the doctor and I know what's best for you."

Patients have the absolute right to be informed as to what's in store for them. The great question: Just how informed? Yes, informed consent can be a two-edged sword. In trying to provide information, there can be treacherous and unnerving overkill. I fear that, sometimes, so much information can be given that it becomes counterproductive, resulting in a worried and scared patient. "You mean those awful things could happen to me?"

Hasn't everyone been alarmed at some time by exhaustive printed drug warnings? If you read that fine print carefully, you'll wind up wary about taking even an aspirin. Personally, I have felt that part of the surgical art was to bring patients to the O.R. composed, relaxed, and unafraid. Accordingly, I was hesitant to overwhelm patients with unnecessary information. For instance, after hundreds of cholecystectomies, I had not one instance of an injury to bile ducts or cystic artery. Not once did I have to take a patient back to the O.R. to control post-op bleeding. With that record, then, should a patient have to hear about every conceivable mishap that might occur?

Simple observation, using our common sense, shows us that some people are better singers than others, some better golfers, some better carpenters, etc. Is it such a stretch, then, to accept that there might be better surgeons or communicators? I have always felt that there are straightforward, simple ways to say things, even in giving bad news, which won't create alarm or feelings of hopelessness. It's not the words as much as the ways in which those words come across. Here's an account of a surgeon who created undue concern, bordering on hysteria, while trying to fulfill what he saw as his requirement to give informed consent.

Sometimes, we attempt to modify our description of incompetence in an individual by adding, "well-meaning." I'm not sure whether it applies. A surgeon was explaining a thyroid procedure to a young woman on the evening before surgery. Do you see any problem in his words? "Well, I guess I have to tell you these things. There's a possibility that you could hemorrhage and bleed to death. . ." That evening, I was called to see the patient in consultation and subsequently to do the surgery. As I arrived on the ward, the nurses prepared me for the worst. Yes, it took 30-40 minutes to calm that young lady, to put risk and benefit in proper perspective---to reassure her about safety. A sadness!

Medical school training, internship, and residency place precious little emphasis on communication. An uplifting note! There are increasing efforts to impart communication skills, but these efforts face stiff competition from crowded curricula. Isn't it paradoxical that, while the information bank is overflowing, the ability to transmit that information hasn't covered the bottom of the glass? By now, you're hearing it like a broken record , "The perceptiveness, the ability to understand what's on the other side---it's more inherent than learned."

6. Potpourri---Let the Pearls of Wisdom Fall On the Floor.

In this closing comment on communication, it's a given that this subject is open-ended and can't be finalized. In everything that has thus far been recorded in these musings, on everything that yet will come, there IS a common thread---with a clear revelation that healing is facilitated by putting the patient at ease.

A simple word of advice to physicians: Try to avoid the superficial, the mundane, the expected, the customary question, "How are you?" This cultural, mostly rhetorical greeting on the street is answered perfunctorily and predictably by, "Just fine. How are you?" Along with this cultural disinclination to give any detailed, truthful answer there is something insidious I've had to learn. There is almost a yearning within some patients to please their doctor. Therefore, when making rounds, if you just ask, "How are you?," the response may be a quick, "Just fine"---without revealing anything. Later on, of course, the nurses will get the brunt of the patients' questions about symptoms and why they're not getting better.

Trying to avoid the tired, worn out phrases, I would, with openness, simply ask, "Tell me, what kind of a night did you have?" Truly, the healing of suffering is to be found more in compassion than in expertise---and compassion is rarely seen in, "How are you?" An added thought: When talking to those who have lost a spouse, refrain from the overused, "How are you doing?" Instead, try interjecting a little feeling by your simple, "Tell me---how's your personal loneliness?" The personal loneliness is there for years after and that person will be grateful that you recognize that.

AM I PRETTY? AM I HANDSOME?

My gut feeling, which hardly qualifies as scientific certainty, is that these following observations are close to universal acceptance.

1. Extremely rare is the person, young or old, who is completely satisfied with his/her inherited outward appearance.

2. Worth in our culture is perceived by measurements and images---images portrayed as "perfection" on T.V. and in movies.

3. The desire to improve on or at least to do the best we can with what we've been given is seen by our culture as admirable.

4. Our culture, though proclaimed by man as Christian, has assigned second fiddle to the Jesus message that who we are on the inside, how we treat others---is more important than who we are on the outside.

Think not that I am overly critical of efforts to enhance appearance. Indeed, as a high school boy, a teacher impressed upon me that I would look better if I would stand up straighter. This was a teacher who didn't realized that round-shouldered slouchiness can be anatomical. Like many other adolescents under similar assault, I survived. Now, however, in the twilight of life with shrinking stature, multiplying chins, and a wrinkled dermis---it's time to relax and say with resignation, "What's the use?"

Let us together dismiss the myth that plastic surgeons can transform us to be the likes of Marilyn Monroe or Clark Gable. Let us also be grateful for love---that love which is blind and sees no flaw or imperfection. Beauty, indeed, is in the eye of the beholder. Cultural efforts to improve who we are on the outside, whether in smell or in appearance, involve deodorants, foot powders, creams, cosmetics, and jewelry adornments. It is no small wonder, actually by design, that cosmetics counters are the gateway to every major department store.

Going beyond skin applications and jewelry are some legitimate desires to change what have become anatomical hindrances to social acceptance. Perfection may be only an idea, interpreted variably by different ethnic cultures, but some anatomical mishaps are bothersome and cry out for correction because of personality-stunting ridicule and taunting. Examples:

1. Flapping elephant ears.
2. The oversized Romanesque nose.
3. Breast enlargement (gynecomastia) in the adolescent male.

"I don't like the way I look" and "I'm so ugly" may be real or imagined pleas to justify change. I performed surgical correction of flapping ears and gynecomastia, but I was overjoyed to let the plastic surgeons diddle with tummy-tucks, face lifts, female breast enhancement or reduction, liposuction, removal or addition of hair, etc., etc., ad infinitum. Ah, to be forever young in appearance.

Non-judgmentally, I would respect personal decisions to alter appearance---that is, if the impetus comes from the person who is to be altered. Beware! Think twice if the impetus to alter appearance comes from another. Invariably, tummy tucks or breast enhancement, done primarily at the urging or insistence of another, will only confirm that person to be an egocentric, self-centered, "please-me" type of guy.

Body piercing isn't new. In other cultures, noses have been pierced. Haven't ears been pierced for centuries? It isn't that it's new---it's just that body piercing has been intensified and extended to both genders. The acceptable age for piercing has bottomed out---with babies coming out of the nursery with earrings. To the consternation and amazement of older generations, body piercing has assumed weird and imaginative expressions---seeking out strange and wonderful parts of the body, heretofore considered inviolate. Friends, it's a given that efforts to change who we are on the outside are undertaken with the knowledge that others will notice---and be attracted.

A paradox! Those who exhibit bizarre body piercings realize that others will notice, but strangely seem annoyed or insulted at disapproving words or glances. Hey, you can't have it both ways. Hopefully, all those who seek to alter who they are on the outside will simultaneously give thought to improving who they are on the inside---in this way becoming truly pretty or handsome.

AMPUTATION

Amputation of extremities has always been at the bottom of my list of favorite operations. Even when clearly indicated, the amputation somehow seemed more destructive than surgery involving removal of other tissues or organs. Amputations inevitably conjured up visions of civil war days and the barbarism of amputations without anesthesia, except for a bottle of whiskey. Amputation of the wrong extremity has occurred in this nation and never should occur, of course, with proper safeguards and identification procedures. Nonetheless, the worst nightmare I have ever suffered involved removing the wrong leg. I assure you that I awoke in a cold sweat.

Amputation often is seen as the option of last resort. Reasons for amputation include overwhelming infection, loss of arterial blood supply leading to gangrene, and devastating trauma. With great improvements in vascular surgery technique, some amputations can be forestalled by skillful vascular surgery procedures to improve blood flow. Coming on the scene has been the boon of intensive I.V. antibiotic therapy to extinguish the fire of infection. Amazingly, something which I once thought impossible has come to pass. Pioneering re-implantation procedures can reattach fingers, hands, arms, and legs following trauma. Truly amazing!

With these comments, you can see that amputation never was recommended lightly. When absolutely necessary, the amputation had to be crafted carefully---with an eye to the future. If possible, a below-knee amputation was markedly superior to an above-knee amputation, carrying with it the hope and promise of better function and mobility. Especially in the loss and potential despair following an amputation, I marvelled at the number of people surrounding the patient for support. The captain of the ship, the surgeon, gets a lot of the kudos, but it's the crew that really provides the steady course.

In post-op rehabilitation, the amputee has greater recovery potential in body, mind, and spirit because of the emergence of companies devoted solely to manufacturing and fitting prostheses. The saving of life may deserve praise---but the accolades really should go to those who help the patient to walk again---to face the world, to appear normal to the world.

1. Children sometimes are constrained by the hidebound wishes of their parents---directives such as, "never put me in a nursing home." Parents obviously don't realize the stress they impose on a son or daughter if dementia creeps in. How well I remember and sympathize with the son of a lady who developed a smelly, gangrenous foot. He struggled mightily with the recommendation for amputation because his mother, when she had her senses, had insisted, "I want to go to my grave with all my parts intact."

Decisions! Decisions! Decisions are awfully gut-wrenching for those who try to speak for those who cannot speak. The turning factor in this son's decision was when I reminded him that his prim and proud mother, even with her prior declaration, would be mortified if she knew that the odor in her room was so bad that nurses and aides didn't even want to go into the room. I sincerely think that the son finally did what the mother would have wanted had she known---and life was much easier following the amputation.

2. In the last decade or so, there have been improvements in farm safety. However, in the 1960's and 1970's, tragic trauma was all too frequent when clothing of workers was caught in the blades and tines of farm machinery. Time being of an essence in a long work day, safety could take a back seat, a casualty in the race to beat the setting sun. Too often, the farmer would inspect jammed machinery without turning off the motor. Loose

jackets too easily were caught in rotating blades.

Many of these tragedies ended up as fatalities in the field, but one young farmer made it to the E.R. after being shredded by a corn shredder. Dale arrived in the E.R. with multiple wounds and shock due to blood loss. The number of bones not broken seemed to be outnumbered by those which were broken--- the clavicles, both arms, both legs, ribs, and facial bones. Soft tissue injuries were extensive and contaminated. A worrisome priority was a partial avulsion of the left arm at the shoulder.

If only that arm would retain vitality, but it wasn't to be. Within a day, color changes indicated that this young farmer was lying in bed with a useless and lifeless arm lying in bed beside him. With no other recourse, a forequarter amputation was performed, leaving a sloping shoulder. Bravery is described with various words--- fortitude, guts, persistence, even plain stubbornness. Dale had all these---and more, surviving the potentially fatal trauma and then redirecting his life. In his leisure time from his job as an auto salesman, Dale became a sports junkie. He liked nothing better than to report to me his bowling scores---averaging well over 200. As we ponder how some people just have the strength to survive, we have the irrefutable proof that each of us heals in our own way.

3. Diabetes mellitus, with its inevitable compromise of arterial blood supply, can wreak havoc with eyes, kidneys, and lower extremities. Open wounds on the feet are frightfully ominous, too often leading to galloping infection and gangrene. Such problems beset the mother of our friend, Harris, who lived in that remote land of California. Distance was an ever present handicap as our friend tried to keep in touch with his aging mother. Our friendship blossomed during Harris's visits to his mother during her nursing home years. In a sense, I became a surrogate son while he was away.

Selma was a far cry from her vibrancy as a young woman. She was that old soul I had in mind when I would caution long term care workers, "Always keep in mind that each person in our care has, at one time, had a life." Aging isn't always graceful. You surely know something about the grief which accompanies loss. What isn't always appreciated is that loss can precede death as a spouse or parent no longer is the same person we have known.

Selma was incompetent and had a frustrating habit of eating drapes or any cloth she could get near her mouth. Most of us acknowledge that her existence could hardly be called "living"---but society refuses to count it as "death." Some of the most awful choices, therefore, confront us when we are required to make decisions for those who clearly would be better off escaping this world.

Selma was another of many who developed a rapidly spreading infection on the foot, creating an unbearable odor. With her dementia, you might say, "Just let her go." Philosophically, I'd be in that camp, but her stubborn and sturdy heart wouldn't let her go. In conversation with Harris, the only option for comfort for his mother was amputation. Strangely, following the surgical procedure, this old lady brightened quickly and suddenly seemed more with the world. From her hospital room, I could phone Harris to inform him that his mother was doing well--- and, what's more, was smiling at the flowers he had sent. Flowers are a visible expression of concern and compassion. Here again we have proof that the healing of suffering consists more of compassion than of expertise .

4. Who among us knows what our response to adversity will be unless we have to go through the valley. Responses to travail vary greatly, to be sure. There are those whose spirit crumbles when they are knocked down by amputation. There are those who cannot rise out of depression, feeling that life has no meaning. On the other hand, there are those with a tenacity toward life, which endures and persists, undiminished, until the moment of death.

As crippling to the spirit as a single amputation

can be, would any of you be overjoyed at being a bilateral amputee---especially if you had lived the life of an active coach, beloved by students? Of course not! In retirement years, I am delighted when people remind me, "You operated on me, you know." I'm careful not to blurt out, "No, I don't remember," thus exposing my incipient dementia. Instead, we just reminisce in a comfortable manner while I admit to myself privately how good it feels to know another person who made it through surgery---and is grateful.

Peggy and I meet interesting people as we deliver "Meals On Wheels." One day, out of the blue, we came to Glenn's door. Glenn was that bilateral amputee, the beloved ex-coach. He was practically bubbling as he announced, "You took off my leg 20 years ago." What an example of tenacity! This coach had never been forgotten by his players, students, and fans. Why? Because he imparted to them the real meaning of the game, on and off the field. In his apartment complex, Glenn probably had more visitors than anybody else---and the little old ladies kept him supplied with cookies. When you see Glenn in his wheelchair, a happy man in spite of having no lower legs, it may gradually seep in. For those who have difficulty comprehending Glenn's peace of mind, you may have forgotten that we often don't see things as they are. We see them as we are.

5. This vignette is included not so much because of an amputation, but because of the mystery of our marvelous living organism. In this story, you will behold a resilience of spirit and a wealth of human resources, resources which never can be amputated. The trials of Ruth started with a necessary above knee amputation. In the immediate post-op period, a horrible event occurred, a complication which threatened her life---a massive cerebral hemorrhage. Every consultant thought she would die---some even implying that she should die. She didn't die!

Transferred to a nursing home, she was totally aphasic---couldn't speak. Yet, her eyes showed some comprehension and recognition. Gradually and painstakingly, she regained some abilities. With great patience on the part of aides, she could manage to feed herself and even could help with dressing herself---but never could speak.

It so happened that, at times, I would visit patients in nursing homes, playing the piano for them. Think not that this was any big deal! My repertoire was simple, limited to familiar hymns and melodic ditties, which hopefully were recognizable, even if not played very well. One thing for sure! You don't have to be a concert pianist to impress nursing home residents---they're appreciative just because you're there.

If only you could have been there. One day, with Ruth sitting in her wheelchair by the piano, I was playing with some feeling. Swinging into "Battle Hymn Of The Republic," I glanced over at Ruth and I was dumbfounded. As we reached the refrain, "Glory, glory, hallelujah,"---Ruth was singing. Fortunately, there were nurses nearby to substantiate this seeming miracle. With the spotlight on her, Ruth suddenly retreated---became reticent, shy, and embarrassed. Did she ever sing again? Yes!

This is the stuff of music therapy. What I had stumbled upon by happenstance, what I saw as a miracle, actually was predictable. Have you ever seen a miracle? Isn't a miracle really that which occurs beyond our understanding? What a magnificent brain we have---more sophisticated, complicated, and wonderful than any computer. In that maze of neural pathways and cerebral synapses, there are rational explanations why an aphasic lady, post-stroke, could sing. For me, I'm content to think that I was a small part of a miracle.

QUIRKS OF BIRTH

My early inclination to be a pediatrician didn't completely evaporate. In little dribbles, it carried over as I switched allegiance to a general surgical residency. Pediatric surgical problems were intriguing and I found myself practically memorizing pediatric surgical textbooks and articles on neonates in Surgical Clinics of North America, a monthly publication. There were fascinating descriptions (not so fascinating to parents, I'm sure) of birth defects and anomalies. Somewhere along the embryologic trail, arrested development can inexplicably occur, resulting in a baby who is seen as not quite perfect---by a society which anticipates the "perfect" baby---by a society which isn't all that "perfect" itself. Causation of birth defects and anomalies is difficult to pin down. Often cited as causative are drugs taken during pregnancy, infections such as rubella, trauma with blood loss and low oxygen levels, etc. Sometimes, we're left with the term "ideopathic"---which, loosely translated, means, "We haven't the foggiest idea why it happened."

Society worships the beautiful baby, the normal baby, the Ivory soap or the Gerber baby, the baby with the promise of being a winner throughout life. TV, with its everpresent TV advertising, has programmed us well to cheer for winners, thus becoming winners ourselves---vicariously. Birth defects are myriad and rarely are seen as winners. Some obviously are incompatible with life. Some are surgically correctable. Some are compatible with meaningful life, but with impaired or different function. Down through the ages, humans have turned to religion for meaning in disaster or imperfection and have found comfort in birth imperfection as a blessing, generating a spirit of love and caring. The following list is far from comprehensive and is presented primarily as illustrative of what can occur.

    1. Agenesis---lack of brain, lack of one or both paired organs, lack of an extremity.
    2. Low intellect---genetically specific such as Down's syndrome.
    3. Genetically transmitted syndromes, involving a wide array of blood disorders, tissue malfunction, or neurologic deficits.
    4. Failure to close, to cover the tube---resulting in spina bifida with paraplegia.
    5. Failure to achieve midline closure in any area---such as cleft lip, cleft palate, open urinary bladder.
    6. Failure to establish an open tube---atresias of esophagus, intestine, bile ducts, imperforate anus.
    7. Hernias, which can be abdominal, umbilical, inguinal---sometimes huge.
    8. Misplaced tissues or "rests"---found in places where they're not supposed to be---such as pancreatic rests.
    9. Cosmetic disappointments---flapping elephant ears.

    It isn't unusual or wrong if parents should express disappointment when a baby exhibits embryologic deficits. Often, there is a momentary feeling of grief, compounded by guilt, thinking that there is a genetic transference. The worst possible scenario is when parents or those who just stand by try to assign genetic responsibility to one side of the family or the other.
    I've always been a firm believer in natural law---whether it be divinely ordained or just happenstance. Regardless of the point of view anybody may hold regarding creation, all of us can share an awe, which especially is called forth as we contemplate the miracle of gestation and birth. In the same sense, we can thrill at every evidence of healing, by whatever means it may occur. Of a

certainty, healing can be mystical and unexpected. Indeed, nobody has a patent on just how and why healing occurs.

Some folk have insisted, within a religious framework, that God is inseparably linked with every part of our lives, especially seen in birth and healing. I get an eerie feeling that this is a puppeteer God, who has strings attached to every human being. Well and good! It's a free world and people will believe what they will, but those who espouse this view can't escape the obvious corollary---that God must be involved in creating perfection and imperfection alike---and not all those who are hurting are healed. In the present religious flap over homosexuality, fundamentalist religion refuses even the possibility that homosexual tendencies are more inherent than learned. Acknowledging the many genetic mishaps we have seen, is it really such a stretch to accept that perfection in our sexual makeup (heterosexuality, of course) may not always occur?

Great strides have been made in caring for birth defects and, for best results, pediatric and children's centers have evolved. Unheard of and unthought of even 30 years ago, exciting interventions have arrived on the scene. Who would have dreamed of intra-uterine surgery when ultra-sound exams have diagnosed defects requiring urgent attention even before birth? Life can be oh, so precarious when operating on a newborn or a baby within the first few months of life. Most worrisome---o.k., scary---is the fragile little one under anesthesia. Over and over, I've felt blessed that we had the finest anesthesia care. Read along now as I present a few examples of embryologic problems needing surgical relief. In helping to treat the least of these, I never lost sight of the obvious---we were also treating anxious parents and grandparents of the little bundles of joy.

1. It's easy to report successes. It's terrible and gut-wrenching to report failures, always wondering if we could have done better, if anybody could have done better. Working many years ago before the advent of exotic diag-

nostic imaging procedures, we encountered a rarity. A baby was born with omphalocele---much of the abdominal contents outside the abdominal wall in a thin membranous sac. We had no time to waste and our only recourse was to try to replace the abdominal contents and somehow create skin coverage. If successful, the imperfect abdominal wall could be worked on later. Alas! It seemed predestined that we were doomed to failure. Who knows---was the baby just physiologically bankrupt? There also could have been other serious defects, including cardiac defects, since embryologic mishaps often come in bunches. Regardless, it matters only that, when not being able to restore normalcy, there is a lingering sense of sadness and inadequacy.

2. Representing a rare problem of bizarre tissue rests (misplaced tissues embryologically), this little girl's problems, for some hidden reason, didn't surface to the level of "something has to be done" until her 3rd birthday. It's almost as if she didn't get a fair shake. On closer questioning, her mother commented that the little girl always had been a much fussier baby than her other children---and she seemed unusually uncomfortable when urinating.

She finally arrived at "something has to be done" when the discomfort worsened to persistent crying, screaming, while grabbing her lower abdomen. With parents pleading for help, many x-rays and extensive urologic investigation had been accomplished by the time I saw her in consultation. CT scan today surely would have shown an abnormal "growth" near the dome of the urinary bladder. Examining a 3 year old, much less an uncomfortable and squirming 3 year old, is a challenge. Nonetheless, I had a hunch, a feeling that there was an abnormal firmness in the lower abdomen---enough to recommend surgical exploration.

After surgical excision of the "tumor," teasing it carefully off the dome of the bladder, I considered reporting the case in a surgical journal because exhaustive search of the surgical literature revealed only 10 other similar cases. On microscopic exam, the "growth" proved to be a strange conglomerate of pancreatic and duodenal cell rests. The problem is that these cells had simply been performing their assigned task---giving off secretions which aid in the digestion of food stuffs. Even in their abnormal location, they were just doing what they were born to do. The injured tissues surrounding the cell rests naturally became inflamed, indurated, and progressively painful. Since this inflammatory mass was attached to the dome of the bladder, every deflation of the bladder pulled on the mass, resulting in a terribly cranky and unhappy little girl, who naturally resisted urination. Wouldn't you?

Everybody rejoices with a winner---and this little girl was a winner when released from the prison of incapacitating pain. The part in us that feels suffering is the same as the part that feels joy. The real trick is to find the key that will open the door to joy.

3. Is there a tired mother, or occasionally a father, who hasn't sniffed and sighed, "Again? Another smelly, dirty diaper?" It's part of life that what goes in must come out---but there has to be an opening to accomplish this necessary task. I can think of many diagnoses which can be missed, overlooked or misassessed---but who could miss an imperforate anus? The lack of meconium staining or no dirty diapers would demand a look-see. What's this? There's no opening---just a skin dimple where the anus should be.

X-rays of the baby held upside down quickly demonstrated a rectal air shadow. The distance between that rectal air shadow and a metal marker placed on the skin dimple was a crucial determinant of the surgical treatment to be offered. If the gas shadow was immediately adjacent to the skin, a surgical procedure could quickly create an opening. However, if the gas shadow was too distant, the safest option was to create a cutaneous colostomy for fecal evacuation. After about a year's growth, corrective surgery then could be done, closing the colostomy and allowing the little one to be one of the regulars. Imagine! We now have a mother overjoyed to be changing a dirty diaper! In this instance, an appropriate colostomy gave a pause, a time for growth, a chance to survive, a chance to come back and fight another day.

4. Whenever I think of this vignette about Evan, I'm tempted to laugh. It's not that I'm treating Evan's problem lightly. It's just that the reaction of Evan's playmates to his surgery was hilarious---as you will see.

Evan had a congenital umbilical hernia, a huge umbilical hernia. Parents often are ultra-concerned about umbilical or groin hernias because the hernia is most evident when the baby is crying and straining. Their concern is understandable. The parental fear is that, obviously to them, the hernia must be the cause for the crying. In reality, the reverse is true, the hernia simply being more noticeable and distended when the baby is crying.

Parents can also be reassured that often these navel hernias will close spontaneously as the abdominal wall grows. Although a large hernia looks sort of gross, there really is very little danger of bowel becoming entrapped in these large hernia sacs. By age 4, it wasn't a secret that this humongous hernia wouldn't close without surgery. Adults would all agree that this hernia wasn't normal and was unsightly. Children don't necessarily think that way---at least, until they get to school age and develop bad habits toward those who are different in some way. In his small group of friends, Evan was a celebrity because the hernia stuck out in front of him like a sausage or a phallus. It was time for surgery!

In the case of Evan, we sometimes are smug and think that we've done a great service for mankind---or childkind, if you will. Then we get our comeuppance. Repeat with me again, "We often don't see things as they are---we see things as we are." Differences stand out to us based on how we've been taught to see the world. Smaller children just naturally accept differences more easily than do adults. Oh, to be sure, anatomical differences in children lead to curiosity, investigation and sometimes "playing doctor." Prior to surgery, Evan's huge umbilical hernia was sort of a prideful thing---it was Evan.

Children do share with adults the comfort zone of the familiar, the clinging to the accustomed. Evan's hernia belonged to the familiar category. Following surgical repair, it was amusing to see the perplexed look of Evan's playmates when they first saw him without his identifying hernia. "What happened to you, Evan?" With advancing years, humans are so capable of cruelty to others in their attitudes and remarks about differences---whether it be clothing, skin color, or intelligence. As such, it was predictable that Evan, by the time he reached 4th grade, would have suffered taunts about his strange hernia. If only we could recapture the simplicity of being a small child. In this fast-paced, high-tech, competitive world, what IS all this clamor and insistence that we have to grow up?

THE DARKER DAYS

If said before, it bears saying again. "In our best efforts to do good in medicine and surgery, we CAN do harm." In 10,000 surgeries, there were bound to have been some results which, for whatever reason, fell short of that which had been hoped for. There have even arisen bumper stickers which allude to the truism that bad things sometimes just happen. Common terms in surgical parlance are "morbidity and mortality," terms denoting complications and deaths which, regrettably, can occur incident to surgery. The goal of every surgeon naturally is to keep complication at a minimum---not just for the sake of good reputation, but for peace of mind and a good night's rest.

In political debates about health care costs, much is heard these days about the increasingly litiginous climate in the U.S.A. For every untoward result or injury, our society seems to be focused recently on the blame game. On the other hand, I firmly believe that any wronged person has the absolute right to be compensated in some way for errors, lack of consent, abandonment, or any practice not commensurate with prevailing standards of acceptable medical practice.

Wow! Pendulums really do swing. During the early years of my surgical practice, before the great surge in technology, the physician often was limited and sometimes could do little more than hold a hand. At those times, patients seemed appreciative and supportive as they said, "Doctor, you did your best." Conversely, along with the great advances in technology and surgical skills, there has arisen an accompanying expectation that nothing can go wrong. The "blame game" has been born and is flourishing. Let me hasten to add that litiginous woes apply even more so to product liability problems.

In continuing medical education sessions, it was common to hear surgeons glowing and crowing about good results. Strangely, there was little reference to less than good results. Hey! Maybe surgeons actually are human, after all. As a matter of honesty, come along with me through some of the dark days. Bring your own flashlight.

1. Having just come to the Eau Claire community and trying to build a winsome reputation, the worst horror story would be any incident which might suggest carelessness worthy of a lawsuit. In the early 1960's, I was engrossed with an abdominal surgery on Mrs. T. when, to our surprise, we encountered a suspicious ovarian cyst in addition to the primary reason for her surgery. While we were awaiting a pathology report on the resected ovarian cyst, I turned attention back to the original surgery. During that time, gauze laparotomy pads were used to pack bowel away from the ovarian site.

Before the closure of any incision, there MUST be a correct tally of sponges and instruments, specifically to be sure that no foreign object is left in the abdomen. Receiving a correct count from the circulating nurse, routine closure of the incision was accomplished. In her post-op office visits, Mrs. T. just didn't improve as I would have expected. There were too many unexplained symptoms---poor appetite, abdominal cramping, abdominal distention. We were dealing with an easy-going, non-complaining, and reliable patient---so her symptoms were all the more a concern. An X-ray of the abdomen was ordered. Oh, no! The radiologist called me in the office and, in a whisper, informed me that the X-ray revealed a foreign object---a retained laparotomy pad.

There was never a question in my mind but that full disclosure was the honest approach. Any other approach would have been unconscionable, but I deemed it wise first that we re-operate to relieve her symptoms. The retained laparotomy pad was removed and she was able to resume her normal routines. While she was in the hospital, I explained the surgical error to the patient and her husband. To her credit, the circulating nurse who was responsible for the sponge count was chagrined, sheepish, and close to tears. However, the surgeon is captain of the ship in the O.R. and must take the ultimate responsibility.

This untoward incident was just what a fledgling surgeon didn't need. In this type of case, there is a legal term---"res ipsa loquitor"---which literally means, "The thing stands for itself." Therefore, there was no doubt in my mind that Mrs. T. deserved some compensation for her discomfort, the re-operation, and time expended. Our medical liability insurance company approached the patient and worked out an agreement with a settlement of about $2,500. Can you imagine what that settlement figure would be today? Capping this regrettable incident on a lighter note, I had a chance meeting with Mrs. T. at a P.T.A. gathering. What a gracious lady! I, of course, was apologetic for her inconvenience. Would you believe it? She simply smiled and offered, "For that much money, I'd go through it again."

2. This next case of surgical error also involves the "res ipsa loquitor" concept. Patients are aware that, in any surgery, there can be unexpected complications such as uncontrollable bleeding, injured organs, return to the O.R---but I've always had the feeling that these events shouldn't happen. While I experienced no complications in biliary tract surgery, I have to tell you of one glaring mishap during a hysterectomy.

When I first saw Mrs. J., she was experiencing pain and troublesome vaginal bleeding from a most unusual uterine cervix. On exam, this cervix was the largest I'd ever seen---enlarged grossly perhaps 5 times normal size and oozing blood. At her age, and with my belief that her discomfort and bleeding wouldn't subside with observation, abdominal hysterectomy was advised. The size of that uterine cervix immediately presented a problem, with bleeding in the process of freeing up the cervix. The worry in this area is the proximity of the ureter in its path from the kidney to the urinary bladder. Usually, by hugging the cervix in dissection, the ureter is avoided and there is no problem. After the uterus was removed, I felt that Mrs. J. should have an uneventful recovery, but that huge cervix had resulted in placing the ureter in a jeopardous position too close to the cervix.

Coming back from a weekend off call, I found that Mrs. J. had been discovered to have a blocked ureter, blocked by a catgut ligature, utilized in controlling bleeding along the enlarged cervix. The complication had been corrected by my urologist colleague, who had to re-implant the ureter into the urinary bladder. She then made an uneventful recovery.

Here again, I was forthright with Mrs. J. and her family---even suggesting that she be compensated. With legal advice, she also accepted a settlement of about $5,000--the amount so small because the injury is recognized as an undesired complication of hysterectomy. Needless to say, the surgeon in this case was probably the most devastated.

3. We now come to the darkest of days---a malpractice suit. In the previous two cases, an obvious error had been committed. In the case now to be discussed, I feel that I did nothing wrong. However, no matter how I might try to rationalize it, the naked truth was that, in a malpractice suit, somebody was saying that I was a bad doctor--and that's hurtful.

The narrative centers around Josie, a diminutive lady not quite 5 feet tall. Historically, this tiny woman had always been terrified to see a physician---to the nth degree. Several years prior to the awful dilemma resulting in lawsuit, I had carefully coaxed Josie through an emergent surgery for an incarcerated femoral hernia. Encouraged by the success of that surgery, it was natural that she would be more comfortable with me as surgeon when she was discovered to be harboring a cancer of the rectum.

In retrospect, I have gone over and over in my mind what might have been done differently. At that time, the only recommendation for cure was an abdominal-perineal resection of the rectum with formation of a sigmoid colostomy. Yes, that's a massive procedure not to be undertaken lightly---but my experience in over 100 such procedures had been without complications.

There seemed no problems at surgery---with adequate exposure because she was such a tiny, thin woman. The only potential problem was that, during the perineal part of the operation, the small intestine was seen cascading downward into the pelvis. Following the guidance of the Cleveland Clinic on these matters, and with my previous experience, the small intestine was allowed to rest in the pelvis. Unfortunately, while I was on a scheduled vacation (it wasn't relaxing because I worried about Josie), my partner had to return Josie to the O.R. to correct a small bowel obstruction---a complication occurring in 1-2% of cases.

Nothing seemed to go right. One problem led to another. She developed an acidosis which, on consultation, was thought to be related more to respiratory problems than to infection. Because of x-ray evidence of possible abscess in the pelvis, I attempted to aspirate without encountering pus. With newer imaging techniques, interventional radiologists now could drain such a fluid collection. Sadly, Josie died in the intensive care unit at 4:00 a.m. The fact that I had never experienced a death following abdominal-perineal resection of the rectum rang hollowly. Once again, I can quote you statistics, which may demonstrate care and competence over the long haul---but for Josie and her family, the statistic was 100%.

I was with the family at the time of Josie's death, an autopsy was authorized, and there seemed no ill will or dissatisfaction---just a profound mutual sadness. How wrong! An attorney from Menomonie filed a malpractice suit on behalf of the husband. At that time, such charges were initially reviewed by a panel, consisting of a surgeon, an attorney, and a lay person. Testimony was under oath just as in a court trial. The very prompt opinion of the panel not only was that there was no wrongdoing---but that medical practice had been exemplary with an unfortunate mortality.

Still disappointed and not sleeping well, we didn't realize that we weren't free of accusation (my partner also was included in the suit). Just one week before the statute of limitations ran out, the attorney filed suit in circuit court and the stage was set for an ordeal, a testing time.

Regardless of the outcome of the trial, I wanted Josie's family not to feel badly toward me. It may be difficult to understand but, during some of the legal depositions, I had relatively pleasant conversations with Josie's daughter, expressing my concern and sadness. As the trial date neared, I perhaps made a mistake. I'm not sure, in retrospect, who I was trying to protect, but I absolutely didn't want my family in that courtroom, possibly hearing unkind things said about me. The awful truth is that jury trials can be highly unpredictable and I, therefore, was numbed by any thought of a guilty verdict. How could I face my family? How could I face my colleagues in the doctors' lounge?

Jury selection was intriguing because it would have been almost impossible to have a jury pool that wasn't aware of my good reputation. For some reason, without objection by the plaintiff's attorney, two jurors were seated---individuals who thought I walked on water. Actually, I didn't want a favorable verdict to depend on bias or my good reputation. I simply wanted it said that my surgical practice was one of high standards.

The plaintiff's case seemed to rest on the testimony of the surgical chief at a Chicago V.A. Hospital, with testimony that he felt we had missed a window of opportunity to correct acidosis during the last few days of Josie's life. Our attorney skillfully and effectively rebutted his testimony, noting the extensive consultation we brought to bear on the problem, trying to help the patient. I will forever be thankful for our most effective expert witness, a nationally renowned gastro-intestinal surgeon from the Mayo Clinic, a surgeon who had published hundreds of articles in surgical journals. This generous man didn't just give video-taped testimony. He took the time to appear personally in the Eau Claire courtroom, testifying that our care of Josie had been proper throughout. The verdict was 11-1 that we had done no wrong and that no damages were justified. I wondered, wouldn't you, about that one dissenting vote? Was it a matter of a personal dislike for physicians in general, perhaps sympathy for the family? I'll never know.

In the doctors' lounge at Luther and Sacred Heart Hospitals, there was the predictable congratulatory tone. Congratulations? We won the fearsome contest? Even to this day, I can't forget my gut feeling, "No, nobody won." To this day, I have resentment toward the plaintiff's attorney, who knowingly disregarded the initial panel review with its quick, unanimous verdict of "no wrong."

Before describing an interesting sidelight to this bizarre, almost crippling series of events culminating in the courtroom, you should have vital background information. The plaintiff's attorney had brought in an expert (?) witness to testify before the initial review panel. This surgeon, from Kentucky, was the "hired gun" type of expert witness---"have brief case, will travel---for money." His testimony was so full of holes that I think the plaintiff's attorney badly wanted an expert witness with more credibility.

The Chicago V.A. surgeon apparently filled that niche for him. I noted, with interest, that the biographical sketch of the Chicago surgeon revealed that he was a member of the Christian Medical Society, an organization composed primarily of quite conservative religious evangelicals. For what reason did this surgeon consent to testify on a case, giving hindsight opinions? I can't prove this, but I think he was contacted at the recommendation of a cadre of Menomonie physicians, who were also members of the Christian Medical Society. Coincidental? Speculation? Probably so---but it makes sense! It was only natural for the Menomonie attorney to seek names from physicians in his community.

To his credit, the Chicago surgeon wasn't the hired gun type of witness with dollar signs in his eyes. As a matter of fact, much of his testimony, on clever cross examination by our attorney, completely refuted the testimony of the Kentucky hired gun, testimony which was read into the record. You could almost call it incompetence on the part of the plaintiff's attorney---he had two surgeons testifying for him with conflicting messages. Obviously, the jury was well aware of this.

Am I compulsive? I plead guilty. Am I like a stubborn bulldog with a bone, fiercely pursuing the right, especially when I thought the right was on our side? Wouldn't you be? Furthermore, in each of us, there is a yearning to be understood---really understood. Therefore, in the days following the trial, I did what is most natural for me---I wrote a letter to the Chicago surgeon, trying to give him the picture of a competent, caring surgeon. I furnished my record of low morbidity and mortality. Deliberately, and carefully worded, I also asked him if he perhaps regretted testifying without even once having had conversation with me about the unfortunate case. I slipped into the letter a question of how he felt about testimony in hindsight without having had to treat the patient himself.

I then let him know, even more delicately and not in an accusing manner, that I had noted his affiliation with the Christian Medical Society. My inference was obvious as I encouraged him to reflect on whether he may have been advised badly, being asked to testify in a court trial without knowing everything about the case. I also thanked him for those parts of his testimony that effectively damaged the testimony of the Kentucky "hired gun" My letter proved to be effective. I would have appreciated a letter or a face-to-face meeting, but he did phone me a month later. Asking me if I remembered him, he then went on essentially to apologize for his part in the court travail. What came through as a little lame was his contention that, if we didn't meet here on Earth, we'd surely meet in Heaven.

It is said that bitterness can destroy a person. That may be so, but I don't feel done in or destroyed yet---and I'm still bitter toward the attorney who turned a mortality into an inquisition. Yes, his job was to represent his client in the best manner he could---but he gave bad advice and he carried the matter far beyond what would be considered prudent and reasonable.

HERNIA CONCEPTS

A hernia is really nothing more than an abnormal protrusion from a hollow space. A typical hernia from the abdominal cavity consists of a protruding peritoneal membranous sac, finding its way through a weakness or opening in the abdominal wall. Potentially, such a hernia sac can be filled with intestine. Very often, causation of this type of hernia, especially in the groin area, is found in a basic defect present since birth. Another common hernia is an incisional hernia, which results from poor healing of an abdominal incision---the poor healing stemming from tension or infection.

Years ago, before surgical repair became more refined and anesthesia became recognized as safer, hernia treatment consisted of a truss---a sometimes cumbersome appliance placed snugly against the hernia opening. A problem! Patients quickly tired of the encumbrance, were annoyed by restriction of activity. Furthermore, trusses which didn't fit snugly could lead to dangerous complications if intestine should sneak past the truss.

The most common hernia, especially in childhood, is the inguinal (groin) hernia. Surgical correction of these hernias became known as "bread and butter" surgery. A necessary part of the surgery, in addition to doing away with the hernia sac, was the closure of the hernia opening. Wouldn't common sense tell you that closing the opening with tension (pulling and suturing the edges together) could invite discomfort, poor healing, and greater chance of hernia recurrence? Therefore, based on conferences at large centers, which specialized only in hernia repair, I began to use more and more replacement mesh grafts. It made sense! Carefully suturing the mesh to cover the hernia opening without tension resulted in less post-op discomfort and far fewer recurrences. I cite two cases. One illustrates the need to persevere---never give up. The second carries with it an interesting interplay between myself and a concerned parent.

    1. First, it should be pointed out that groin hernias are of two types---the congenital, indirect type and a direct hernia, which is secondary to a weakening of the lower abdominal wall. It is the latter type which benefited most from the use of mesh grafts. Now, meet Earl. Earl had had 4-5 hernia repairs and recurrent hernia repairs in the right lower abdomen---all performed at the Mayo Clinic. It's easy to criticize the other surgeon when a hernia recurs, but when a surgeon performs hundreds of hernia repairs, there are bound to be some recurrences. The batter who goes up to the plate may hit a home run, but he also may strike out.

    Earl naturally was discouraged with the uncomfortable, unsightly, basketball-sized hernia he carried around. Although he wanted to talk about another attempt at surgical repair, he didn't have much confidence. Even with his history, I thought that mesh grafting might just be the answer. After freeing up the hernia contents and replacing them back where they belonged in the abdominal cavity, the edges of the hernia were identified and freshened. In this repair, we employed not one, but two layers of a strong synthetic mesh. Although the work was nit-picky and time consuming, it worked! With his newly discovered flat tummy, Earl not only could see his shoes---he could tie them.

    2. Especially when dealing with a minor, much of the attention must be directed to the parents or grandparents. One afternoon, a 5 year old boy was seen in the office with a good sized inguinal hernia. The surgical procedure, with emphasis on high safety and low risk, was explained to the anxious father, a young university teacher. As we discussed scheduling the surgery, the father abruptly asked, "Doctor, are you the very best surgeon in Eau Claire for this type of case?"

Perhaps I sensed the trap he was leading me into. I don't know what prompted my words, but without hesitation, I answered quite simply, "No, I'm not." With just the right timing, I then added ". . . but I'm as good as any. There are several surgeons in Eau Claire very capable of treating your son safely and with a good result." I give this account not to suggest that I was in some sort of a contest with the father, but to acknowledge that, for a moment, it might have been tempting to proclaim proudly, "Yes, I am." I'm not really sure what the father wanted to hear---or expected to hear. What I do know is that respect is gained with honesty and forthrightness---and may be stifled by bravado and showiness.

BEING IN THE RIGHT PLACE
AT THE RIGHT TIME.

More and more, I'm impressed that much of what happens to us is chancy---just related to the year in which we were born. In that vein, being in the right place at the right time may be sheer happenstance. In writing this book, I'm trying to recall words and events, but I have to admit to worries that incipient dementia and increasing forgetfulness are robbing me of acute recall of the past. Perhaps that's why I must finish my writing before I can't trust my recollection.

Maybe I should have listened more to Peggy, who often warned that, "You're going to get in trouble, the way you talk." I guess I was known for saying some outlandish things---let's just say that I was unconventional. My office staff won't let me forget my offhand remark to Pearl about her concern over excessive flatus. All I did for Pearl, even as we looked for the cause, was to suggest that there was a small redeeming feature to her problem---the production of pleasurable party-like bubbles in the bath.

Too frequently, former patients tell me of things that I supposedly said to them and I haven't the foggiest idea that I could have said anything remotely akin to what they think I said. In grocery store aisles, I'm having great difficulty in matching the past that I knew with what my former patients are telling me. Do you suppose that patients' memories are to be trusted more than mine?

Even so, I think it's human that patients subconsciously inflate their doctor's worth and reputation. It's only natural for people to want to believe that, "my doctor is the greatest." After all, who would want to admit seeing a fool? Thus, memories of things done, of words said, may be multiplied or influenced by the passing of years. It's not uncommon for a grateful person to insist, "You saved my life---or my mother's life, etc." Is it misplaced humility that I would tend to downplay my part in what they recall? Possibly, if stretched a little, the expert and timely treatment of colon malignancy, the neat management of ruptured appendicitis with peritonitis---might be considered life saving. Yet, in referring to being in the right place at the right time, I'm thinking of those relatively few times when one person, alone, was in a crucial position to help---when minutes counted and nobody else was around. With a measure of pride, subdued by humility, I remember a few instances when I, alone, was in the right place at the right time.

    1. Tobogganing used to be a popular wintertime activity and there's no doubt that there were thrills aplenty as long as the riders stayed on the toboggan and the toboggan didn't meet an impenetrable object. After an out-of-control toboggan crashed, Jeff was brought to the E.R. with acute respiratory distress. It was one of those blue, cold evenings when this 14 year old boy was seen---his skin blue and cold just like the evening.

    To TV addicts, transfixed by images of E.R. or other medical dramas, everything seems to happen right now! Friends, in real life, it's not that simple!!! In Winter, there are many layers of clothing to peel or cut away just to gain access to that blue, cold skin. Listening with the stethoscope to those labored shallow gasps, I heard no breath sounds. The immediate presumption? Probably bilateral pneumothorax (collapsed lungs). Hastily assembling chest tube trays, and with emergent confirmation of the diagnosis by x-ray, tubes were quickly inserted into the chest cavity, right and left, with prompt gushing of air and re-expansion of lungs as the tightly compressed free air in the chest cavity could escape through underwater seals. Those bubbles, indicating lung inflation, brought cheers, relaxation, and the relief of overcoming terror. Bathtubbian bubbles never could match the thrill of those pneumothorax-relieving bubbles.

With all of us breathing easier, Jeff pinked up---a tribute to the youthful dynamic. In treating emergency patients, there's no time for gender awareness. Babies have assigned gender colors, but Jeff was much more beautiful dressed in warm, pink skin than in cold, blue skin. Having survived the fearful trauma, Jeff later had to have a thoracotomy to permanently expand one lung. Happy days are here again! What an appropriate theme song as he left the hospital for home.

2. Anybody who worked in E.R.'s during the 1960's and 1970's had to be impressed and disgusted at the senseless, preventable carnage coming into the E.R. from the highway---too much blood and guts mixed with the unmistakable odor of beverage alcohol. Bonnie and her fiancee, students at UWEC, were returning to Eau Claire late one evening from a graduation party. Driving a small Volkswagen, they were broadsided by a young driver afflicted by AIDS (that's alcohol-impaired driver syndrome). Bonnie's fiancee was killed instantaneously. Only after difficult and skillful extraction from the wreckage, Bonnie was transported to the E.R., bearing little resemblance to a human being.

Rescue personnel wisely had transported her prone on the stretcher so that she wouldn't drown in her own blood and other secretions. As we carefully turned her face-up on the E R. table, I remember the haunting appearance and my gruesome thought that hamburger somehow had become attached to a human body. Every bone in her face had been shattered as she was thrown forward into the windshield---sinuses, nasal bones, malar bones, mandibles. By the time she was resuscitated and stabilized, 8-10 units of blood had been transfused. Helpers, who were aspirating blood from the nasal passages and throat, could hardly keep up with the flow. An emergency tracheostomy was necessary and probably life-saving.

Overnight, Bonnie remained unconscious. At that time, we simply didn't have ENT or maxillo-facial surgeons in Eau Claire who could handle such severe facial injuries---so she was transferred to the Mayo Clinic. With multiple operations, plastic surgery care gradually restored a pleasant face, but her features were thickened and couldn't match the pretty, petite face in her college photo, shown to me by her mother. With societal assent, an alcohol-impaired driver had wiped out one young life and destroyed the dreams of another young life. Why do I say, "with societal assent. . .?" The irresponsible driver, obviously under the influence of alcohol, never was deemed responsible for the crash in court even though he was considered totally at fault in the police report. Ho hum! Among many other cases, this was tantamount to a societal blessing on tragedy. Ho hum! It wasn't my son, my daughter.

Bonnie remained at the Mayo Clinic for several months, at least 4-5 weeks spent on a psychiatric unit because of depression, inconsolable grief, and loss of personal image. Eventually, she did try to get on with her life, re-enrolling at UWEC. However, she just couldn't do it. Unable to concentrate, blinded by the image of her fiancée as she walked across campus, she couldn't continue and had to leave Eau Claire. Subsequently, she did gain her elementary education degree and, never married, became a wonderful teacher. Blessed have been those young lives who have been influenced by a teacher who almost lost her own life.

Many years later, at the close of office hours (I think that Sandy, Janet, and Delores were still there), a young woman entered the office. Seeming shy and hesitant---and new to our office---she quietly announced, "Hi, I'm Bonnie." What an emotional downpour was released by her presence. Amid the hugs, I couldn't erase from my memory the picture of her mangled face in the E.R and I never have erased the bitterness as I recall the too-casual societal approach that never punished a killer.

3. I now am going to show you that a medical professional doesn't always treat with pills, sutures, or vaccines. Yes, in the rich lore of medical heritage, there is

ample room for the physician who just happens to be there---at the right time. Yes, just being there, even without scalpel or black bag, may be the only medication we can give---our presence.

The dead will be treated in some way by those who know how. What is too often forgotten is that treating the living in the presence of the dead is eminently important and especially difficult when grief and guilt are all consuming. The ground is laid for this vignette in a nasty divorce proceeding, an Eau Claire attorney being sued for divorce by his wife. Whether true or not, I have been told that, especially in smaller communities, attorneys don't like to get involved in court battles involving another attorney. They avoid it like the plague.

When the wife, suing for divorce, approached a local law firm for assistance, the most senior member of the firm side-stepped, suggesting that he might not be the best person to represent her. A brilliant and promising junior member of the firm stepped forward, agreeing to take the case with a blithe, "Hell, I don't have anything to lose." At that moment, he had no inkling that the "anything to lose" would include his life.

As the divorce drama played out, the attorney husband became more and more disconsolate, mean, and spiteful. Egged on by the seductress, Ethyl Alcohol, his profanities and threats were common knowledge---but, in peaceful Eau Claire, would anybody actually carry through on threats? Oh, no! On a Christmas eve, timing his action to interrupt a precious family time, the about-to-be-divorced attorney appeared at the door of the one he perceived as his nemesis---the young attorney. Armed with a shotgun, he shot and killed the young attorney when he came to the door---and then took his own life shortly thereafter.

At the same time this was going on, I had just completed suturing a laceration in the E.R. at Luther Hospital. On my mind were excited children, inspecting packages under the tree. There is possibly no lonelier place on

Christmas eve than a hospital---and I was the only doctor on the premises at that moment---the right place at the right time? As I reached the front door of the hospital, a distraught and almost hysterical attorney (the senior partner) came running after me. Powerfully gripping me by the arm, he pleaded, "Don't leave! My partner's been shot and they're bringing him to the E.R." As we waited together near the E.R., tension mounted. The ominous wail of the ambulance siren was penetrating, incessant (I still shudder at times when I hear it). Why the sirens? Both attorneys, the shooter and the shot, were dead on arrival. The dead need no further treatment, but there are the living---needing support, trying somehow to understand what never is understandable, groping for answers, engulfed in anger, grief, and guilt. It would have been cruel and unconscionable to leave the grieving attorney at that moment. He was so alone, spilling out his guts and his guilt, "I should have handled the case---maybe I could have talked to the guy---my partner might be alive."

Prior to that fateful Christmas eve, whenever we had been thrust together by chance, our relationship would have been considered strained and cool---at best. This man, now taken down, was among those who loved Ethyl Alcohol blindly and his defense of DWI cases usually was odious. When you're spilling your guts, either emotionally or into a barf bag, you lose arrogance and pride---you're so vulnerable. In this vulnerability, but with sincerity and genuine appreciation as we parted, this spirit-crushed attorney swore unending gratitude as he promised me, "I owe you one."

UNFAIR!
A FAMILY BROKEN!
A COMMUNITY AWAKENED

Little did I dream that a simple promise, "I owe you one," would be called in within a year. Indeed, initially interpreting the promise as perfunctory and emotion-driven, I had nearly forgotten it. What follows was life changing, a tragedy that should never have happened, but yet another societally enabled DWI death --regrettably.

To introduce the players in this tragi-drama, I had become active on the State Medical Society's Commission on Safe Transportation. Thus, in the 1960's and 1970's, I was seen as a highway safety expert. Increasingly, awakened by too many alcohol-related deaths and injuries in the E.R., I had become a thorn in the state legislature, known as an anti-DWI advocate there and through my newspaper Letters To The Editor.

Another player in the tragi-drama was John, the oldest son of a middle class family, the pride of his parents. John possessed those natural athletic talents and had that disarming, pleasing personality that made him a favorite with neighbors, teachers, and classmates. At about age 14, his athletic career was sabotaged by a freakish, horrendous, football injury---a fractured hip with subsequent overwhelming infection following the post-trauma hip surgery. Even now, I'm grateful that I wasn't a part of that surgery. Eventually, the hip had to be removed and John, in the eyes of the world, became gimpy. John's response? "I guess I'm not gonna be a jock---so I'll be the best photographer I can be." The other unwilling players in the tragi-drama were John's parents. John's father was a lieutenant in the fire department. John's mother was our office nurse and it was she who reported that John had repeatedly said, "I'd like to be a doctor---like Dr. Hudson."

Oh, I neglected to introduce the villain in the tragi-drama, a speeding driver, who eventually was apprehended and tested at BAC (blood or breath alcohol concentration) 0.20%, twice the legal limit. As the curtain rises, what a frightening night. It's only a one-act drama, cut short as young John, riding his bicycle homeward after visiting his girl friend, was struck by the villain, driving at a high rate of speed, alcohol-impaired. I don't want to see any more. Close the curtain.

At 11:00 p.m., I heard a mother's plaintive voice on the phone, "Dr. Hudson, can you tell me anything about John?" "Where are you, Janet?" "I'm at Sacred Heart Hospital. John's in the E.R. and I think they're doing C.P.R. on him." As I arrived at the hospital, I ran across the parking lot just as John's father arrived. In the E.R., there was an eerie, deadly silence. John lay dead on the table, a casualty---a victim of a crushing head injury. So senseless! Every resuscitation effort had failed and the E.R. crew was summoning up courage to talk to the parents. What an unsettling paradox---to see a vibrant young man with such potential lying on the E.R. table. His appearance was so normal---maybe he was just asleeep? No! He was dead!!!

Whoever preached that emotion must be removed from the practice of medicine in order to retain objectivity and competence---well, that person must be one cold fish. The telling of bad news to patients and families, not necessarily tuned to listening or believing---a physician's worst nightmare. I felt so helpless standing in that E.R. by John---not even having been involved in the resuscitation effort. Yet, something now had to be done---couldn't be put off forever. Around that E.R. table, in the eery hush, I volunteered, "I guess I'm the only one who can do this." Somebody had to talk to John's mother and father---and, at times, I've been somebody. As I walked toward John's mother, she was tearful and perceptive. I'll never forget her face and her words, "I don't like the way you're looking at me."

A numbing grief descended, at first unconsolable, bringing with it bitterness and anger. Weaving through the visitation, the sleepless nights, and the funeral---with hundreds of John's classmates attending---the grief was all consuming. Acute grief is just the preceder of a certain chronic grief which, with proper dosages of tincture of time, eventually assumes some degree of proportion. Lives go on, but are changed! The family goes on, but is different. The world? Why should society take much notice when, after all, John was just one of 800,000 killed in much the same manner in this nation during the last 4 decades?

Life changed also for the DWI driver who struck and killed John---the extent and quality of change known only to him. The wheels of justice, it is said, grind slowly---and, sometimes, the wheels of justice grind unevenly. A coincidence? The DWI driver's defense attorney was a member of the same law firm from which came the promise, "I owe you one." Properly, and with respect, I called in the promise by asking for an assurance that, in the event of a jury trial, no attempt would be made or even inferred that would, in any way, besmirch the dead youth's reputation. I knew defense attorneys and knew that sometimes, grasping at straws, they could become overbearing and insinuating, putting the victim on trial. My request was honored.

After many delays, the defendant finally pled "no contest," a maneuver which apparently helped him in the event of a civil trial. The sentencing phase of the deliberations was a laugh! The prosecution had honored my request for no plea bargain, but conceded, in return for not having to go to trial, that nothing would be said at the sentencing hearing. A mistake! The defense attorney, with a parade of unchallenged character witnesses, pictured the killer as a saintly church person, blah, blah, etc., etc. The judicial penalty for killing a person with a deadly weapon? A slap on the wrist for the defendant and a slap in the face for John's family. Probation! We heard the same lame reasoning from the bench, "This was regrettable, unfortunate---but nothing will bring John back---and the defendant has already suffered." Two decades later, a DWI death will command at least some jail time. In 1981, killing a young man was treated less harshly than illegally killing a deer.

An inscription on John's bedroom wall, "No goal is too high if we climb with care and confidence," now is etched on his grave marker. That quotation set me on an odyssey to change public policy toward DWI.

Society obviously doesn't like change. Rocking the boat causes discomfort and societal seasickness. It has been my experience that society cries for change only as a knee-jerk reaction to awful catastrophes, such as the Sept. 11, 2001, World Trade Center terrorist attacks. DWI deaths and injuries accumulate one by one, two by two---never attracting the same outcry for federal investigation as when a large airliner crashes. With the help of grass-roots organizations, the voice of victims, societal change has gradually occurred. With or without the help of the alcohol interests, society couldn't dodge the obvious when hit right between the eyes by the gruesome statistics. In the two decades prior to John's killing, this nation had nodded, asleep and in acquiescence, as 500,000 people had died and up to 15 million people had been injured as a result of alcohol-related crashes on the highway. Society couldn't face these grim reaper statistics and yet blindly carry on the love affair with Ethyl Alcohol. In the two decades since John's killing, such deaths have been reduced from 25,000 to 17,000 annually.

Progress can be a two-edged sword. Progress is to be lauded, to be sure, but it has a way of slyly blunting and pacifying public outrage. In response to further effort to reduce deaths, you'll hear, "Well, now, we must be on the right track so there's no need for so much hullabaloo." In this way, progress can be slowed by those who profit from alcohol sales. Who among you can be comfortable, knowing that 15,000-17,000 people still die each year due to the DWI driver? Does it lull you to sleep, listening to the alcohol advertising song, "15,000 is better than 25,000"?

In my odyssey, always thinking of John, I searched for an answer as to how or why society could so easily tolerate such carnage. It finally came to me! Ethyl alcohol, a drug never scrutinized by the F.D.A., had wormed its way into the culture as acceptable, a girl you could bring home to mother. Much of the acceptance and worship was a backlash from the prohibition era when we were told, "You shall not see Ethyl again." It became obvious to me. Society had fallen into a passionate love affair with Ethyl, she of the family ALCOHOL. Love affairs often are necessarily blind---resulting in, "She can do no wrong." Presently, our nation has been shaken by terrorist attacks from the sky. At the same time, isn't it strange and sad that this society has freely accepted another terrorist, stalking us on the highway---causing far more deaths and injuries than those incurred on Sept. 11, 2001?

Public health principles should prevail, of course. In public health circles, deadly illnesses have been combatted by vaccinations or elimination of the cause. Unfortunately, elimination of the cause in the dreaded DWI illness is well nigh impossible because Ethyl has become too seductive. In the alcohol/driving wars of the 1980's, we did win a few skirmishes and perhaps cleaned up the battlefield a little, but the war has always been won by the alcohol interests. A paradox! Those same alcohol interests officially decry abusive and underage drinking---but they laugh all the way to the bank as they profit from such activities.

Admittedly, John's death had created an obsession, an anger. I hope that I was more than a Don Quixote, flailing away against allowable BAC laws, which essentially allowed every driver to drive impaired---legally. My file cabinets are overflowing with letters and responses---to legislators, to the governor, to alcohol industry executives, to newspapers. In 1990, I received the "Citizen Activist Of

The Year" award from the National Commission Against Drunk Driving in Washington, D.C., receiving the honor in John's memory.

Nominated by Doris Aiken, founder of R.I.D. (Remove Intoxicated Drivers), a citizens' activist group in the state of New York---I was following in the tradition of Doris, a tenacious pitbull. R.I.D actually was formed before Candy Lightner's M.A.D.D. organization. A problem: In addition to R.I.D.'s anti-DWI and victims' support activities, Doris had the vision to see that ethyl alcohol, taken too much, too fast---CAN KILL YOU. Yes, alcohol poisoning is a leading cause of sudden death in our youth---and the F.D.A. has never studied this drug. Not a prohibitionist or teetotaler, Doris campaigned for S.N.A.P. (a Sane National Alcohol Policy). In so doing, she and her organization, R.I.D., drew the ire and wrath of the alcohol interests and she was blackballed by the national T.V. media outlets. Friends, a lesson of life: T.V. depends upon revenues for profits---and the alcohol interests and their advertising cohorts had spoken.

We like to proclaim ourselves as individual thinkers, but methinks that, as a society, a mob mentality takes over---whether in inappropriate action or inaction. We're conditioned to act because "everybody does it." Therefore, just as our society hoodwinks itself into thinking it's "saving" more daylight time at certain times of the year---we stifle a yawn of acceptance as the alcohol interests control the playing field. Oh, well. It must be o.k., as long as we're "under God."

Does a basic abbreviated description of this odyssey belong here? Obviously, I think the answer is affirmative because this book has to do with health care---and the odyssey was constantly involved with an illness and our attempts to control it and to eliminate the cause. You would read more? Seek out, "A Societal Love Affair With Ethyl," published by the Claymore College press. Finally, as you contemplate the terrorist in our midst, meting out death and injury year after year---yes, the alcohol-impaired driver, wouldn't you like to be on the other side?

WOULD YOU OPERATE ON THE POPE?

Ideally, each patient under anesthesia carries no banner---no labels of rich man, poor man, preacher, pauper, prostitute, banker, or judge. Hopefully, idealism is never swept away when identity of the patient is revealed to caregivers. At the Mayo Clinic, certain famous people receive special considerations in the areas of privacy and courtesies---the foreign princes, kings, and sheiks---a Billy Graham or a U.S. senator. Even in Eau Claire, I often commented to our O.R. crew, "What if this patient were the mother of one of you?" In the U.S. Navy, there was an old adage, "Rank has its privileges." That may be true, but rank, position, wealth, or importance can't increase a skill level among caregivers in health care. However, on at least one occasion, I was forced to confront the obvious---the importance of one patient can be capable of producing stress, with an added burden on caregivers.

Father Edmund J. Klimek, beloved priest and tireless hospital pastoral care person, has always been a common ordinary, gentle man. Although his priesthood began inconspicuously in a small town parish, someone had the vision to recognize greatness. When Sacred Heart Hospital initiated a pastoral care program, Father Klimek was tagged for the job, possibly even anointed. Years later, when I asked him where he received his hospital pastoral care training, he gave his usual smile and quiet comment, "It was all on the job training."

In the upper Midwest, many communities had two religiously affiliated hospitals---Lutheran and Catholic. These "Looderan " and "Cadillac" hospitals may have been competitive, but never as fiercely competitive as now exists within the "managed care" framework. Father Klimek was innovative. Surveying the hospital census, he found that nearly 50% of patients were other than Catholic. Although old time Protestants may have been wary of the fish eaters, worried that somehow their stay in a Catholic hospital would taint them or turn them, Father Klimek's mission was to serve, not to save. Not even worrying about permission from Rome, he established a hospital ministry in which Protestant pastors were included---and welcome.

Father Klimek and I became friends and we shared much as we made hospital rounds. We often were amused at some patients' wonderment as to, "Just who's the doctor and who's the priest?" Increasing this friendship, Peggy and I were privileged to fly with Father Klimek to Phoenix for an ethics conference. Hopefully, I didn't embarrass him in the presence of our Jesuit hosts when I wondered aloud, at a floor microphone, "I hear you using inflammator words such as 'killing' and 'murder' when you refer to end-of-life issues such as euthanasia and physician-assisted death. Haven't you ever considered that a compassionate physician might use a time honored and patient specific word---' treatment '---in helping a patient leave this world in terminal, futile situations?"

The friend can become a patient. Who knows? It may even be reassuring to the patient for the physician to be a friend---to be considerate and thoughtful. As a possible negative, a close relationship between doctor and patient might ever so subtly influence objectivity and decision making. This is the same principle seen in the unwritten rule that physicians not treat their own family members---especially as the level of seriousness increases.

I was convinced that Father Klimek was close to God---but he, nevertheless, had those human frailties of the flesh. For years, he had had repeated bouts of duodenal ulcer distress with pain and bleeding. He was no stranger to the O.R., having had gastric surgery in La-Crosse years before. We were told that, on that occasion, surgeons had to reoperate at midnight to control bleeding.

My first consultation with this beloved priest was before the assistance of endoscopy. By this time, I've blocked out details, but surgery obviously was necessary because of uncontrolled discomfort. Painstakingly, we sorted out the anatomical puzzle, re-routing the food pathway in an effort to alleviate his symptoms. In the process, we encountered extensive adhesions from previous surgery. We often jested at such times that "only a surgeon could mess up an abdomen like this."

Immediately post-op, we were feeling good, not smug, about what we had been able to accomplish. On the following morning, however, those good feelings went down the drain. There was disquiet in the intensive care unit---far too much bleeding. With all the fancy laboratory tests available, there still remains a need for listening, simple observation, and common sense. When the patient's face is whiter than the pillow, there's a problem. De ja vu! Controlling the bleeding by re-operation couldn't be avoided---much like his experience years before in La-Crosse.

All of a sudden I felt the weight on my shoulders and I faced the gravity of the situation. Would it mean any more if we were operating on the pope? In the Eau Claire community, Father Klimek WAS the pope. In surgery, there is an unholy alliance of skill, luck, divine guidance---whatever. It is so much easier to tell success stories. For decades since that battle, Father Klimek remains young and available to everyone, everywhere, anytime. The proof of the surgical success is seen in the way in which his body has withstood the abuse he heaps upon it by his continued insistence on answering calls at any hour.

It has been a privilege just to know him---to be his partner in the holistic healing mission. Is it now apparent why, when I've been on the other side, Father Klimek's simple prayer and holding of my hand has been so reassuring and meaningful? It occurs to me that, just perhaps, Father Klimek is the embodiment of Jesus.

YES, VIRGINIA, THERE ARE BUMS IN THIS WORLD

Raised in traditional small town Christianity, gradually impressed more by the social gospel than by the salvation gospel, I foresaw the healing arts as offering a unique blend of making a living while providing a service. With some naiveté, I still cling to the hope that physicians are baptized in the waters of idealism and that dollar signs won't destroy that idealism. For every person born, I'm convinced that there is a role to be played, a purpose, a mission. The real quest, as we struggle with "What's it all about?," "Why am I here?," and "Where am I going?," is the quest to find that purpose, that mission.

For some unspoken reason, "mission"---that is, real "mission"---is seen, in the religious world, as connoting service in some place far across the sea. As I pondered this, it came to me that, while religion is fulfilling the commandment to preach to and save the entire world, it's abundantly clear that we Americans extol such salvation for others as long as they stay where they are and don't want to work beside us or live next door. Yes, I suppose that I, too, once had a few stirrings for missionary service someplace, somewhere among the heathen---but that wasn't to be.

When my surgical partner decided to fulfill his lifelong promise to do missionary work in Africa, I was often asked, "Wouldn't you like to do that, too?" At that time (certainly not now), the answer was, "Yes, of course"---but the reality of feeding and clothing a family had a constraining influence on staying close to home. Not just as rationalization, a light turned on. Mission can be wherever you happen to be as long as you have the eyes and ears to see and listen to the needs of others.

Again, idealism! Even with idealism, a serious and compelling thought has come to me. Is it ever possible for the well intentioned to become overzealous---maybe too enamored of their role in helping others? With such idyllic phrases as, "I've never met a bad person," and "He's not heavy, Father, he's my brother," can we be blinded to the awful truth that there really are some bums in this world? You spell it B-U-M-S. The "bum" personality is well described in psychology and psychiatry---the charming person who always takes, never gives---the sociopath, incapable of treatment. Such a person came into our community.

Bill was an outwardly pleasant man, unfortunately down on his luck. Married and with a child, Bill arrived in Eau Claire and came to our church, in need of help. Our friend, Roger, had had the vision of social work as fulfilling Christian mission. Roger and I developed grand and glorious plans for assistance to and rehabilitation of Bill and his family, our work done within our definition of church mission. Furnishing clothing and financial assistance, we didn't have the smarts to recognize that we were dealing with a sociopathic personality---but, with subsequent lessons, we eventually saw the light and passed the exam.

A comeuppance, a disquieting revelation. In the E.R., I treated a St. Paul businessman for a fractured mandible and a badly swollen face, sustained in a beating. We were crushed to find that Bill was responsible for the injuries and had been apprehended by the police. Apparently, Bill's wife provided the entrapment, the come-on, luring the man to drive her to a remote place for some hanky-panky. Guess what? With the trap sprung, Bill ambushed the man, beating and robbing him. Even with the injuries, the businessman chose to avoid the shame and embarrassment of bringing charges. He just wanted to get out of Eau Claire.

Admittedly misguided, Roger and I still thought we could support Bill through these tough times---with church assistance. Predictably, his periods of charm were punctuated by outbursts of violence. On one such occasion, I was called by police to help handle a situation in which Bill had climbed onto his roof and was throwing furniture at the police. My role was to communicate, to understand, to talk him off the roof. Peggy recalls a scary occasion near Christmas when Bill called from the state of Washington, requesting help to the tune of $100. Distance is a great ally in refusing such requests. Scarier, still, was the time Bill appeared at our front door, asking for me. Peggy could envision the gun in his pocket. Feeling uneasy and threatened, she was glad to tell him I wasn't home.

Bill's life pattern matched perfectly the sociopathic personality---the model prisoner while incarcerated, but caring little for others' rights in the outside world. Our last encounter with Bill was more hurtful to another than to us. On a Saturday evening, fortified with alcohol and feeling sorry for himself, he filled a glass with the caustic alkali, Drano, and threatened that he would drink it and kill himself. Actually, that would have been better than what happened. With the parents sleeping it off on Sunday morning, their little toddler was ranging around the kitchen, looking for food and drink. Horror of horrors! The glass of Drano had been left on the kitchen table, where the little boy spied it and drank it, burning and destroying his esophagus. Treatment of this critically injured little one was touch and go---and eventually he had to be transferred to the university hospitals at Madison. Many months later, a segment of colon was utilized to substitute for the traumatized esophagus, providing a food pathway.

Yes, Virginia, there are BUMS! Mission can be rewarding and dream fulfilling---but mission involving a sociopath can give nothing but reddened eyes and nightmares.

LOOSEN UP A LITTLE

If only we could see ourselves as others see us. How fortunate that beauty exists in the eyes of the beholder. Most of us never quite measure up to our desires or others' expectations---from adolescence on, neverending. Even doctors might benefit by seeing themselves as they are perceived by others. The image of the physician, and this is changing, has been that of the somber, white-coated male. It doesn't always have to be thus! For my own reasons, I never wore the white coat, somehow thinking it conveyed slight haughtiness, even arrogance at times. Furthermore, when dealing with pediatric patients, I felt that the white coat, together with the smells of the hospital, was a little scary and unnerving. Loosening up, not taking yourself too seriously, can shorten the day and inject a little mirth into the humdrum. O.K. Maybe I wasn't totally aware of what I was doing, but in dress and conversation, these are instances of "loosening up."

1. This first remembrance illustrates that loosening up has more to do with attitudes than with dress. My uniform of the day featured a suit and tie. This seemed to be the expectation of most people, but let's face it! The world changes. During the latter years of my practice, younger physicians were much more casual, at least in dress, and felt no compulsion to "dress up." Quite to the contrary, some of them "dressed down" with jeans and sneakers.

An example of what was expected or hoped for by my age group was seen in the reaction of a gentleman from Fall Creek. I had been asked to see him in consultation in his hospital room. Before I left, he spontaneously shook my hand and declared, "I'm gonna thank Dr. Zboralske for sending me a real doctor." The inference was clear---I looked like a doctor to him. Hopefully for all of us, the Jesus principle still applies---that external appearances don't count as much as what's on the mind, the heart, and in the inner being. It is so clear---you can be casual in a suit and tie and you can be stuffy in jeans.

2. Summing up, loosening up has more to do with how we greet each other than it has to do with an appropriate dress code. There are times, indeed, in medicine/surgery when we must relax and just be friendly. An assistant chief of surgery at Hines V.A. Hospital gave this bit of wisdom while we were routinely closing an incision. "Sometimes we'll joke and laugh. You know why? Because---sometimes things are so serious that, if we didn't laugh, we might cry."

3. Have you noted, even in yourself, that we all tend toward a repetitive pattern of speech? Certain cerebral pathways have been used so much by our customary phrases that the weeds have been eliminated. This makes it easier for our predictable phrases to spill out of our mouths. Yes, we become known by our words. Every day in the O.R., I would remind the crew, "Don't worry about what you can't change. After all, this day, too, will end and tomorrow will come." Those words are printed on a T-shirt presented to me at a retirement party.

4. Again in the O.R., if something had been said in a complimentary vein, I'd sidestep and strongly suggest, "Chances are that, if I were gone even a week, you'd forget me." In unison, the chorus rang out, "Oh, no! We shall never forget you." Then, after several minutes of perfect timing, I'd abruptly say, "Knock! Knock!" Naturally, some unwitting straight man would chime in with the customary and necessary, "Who's there?," giving me an opening for, "You see, you forgot me already."

5. You can trick someone only once---so it was necessary to seek out the newcomer, the uninitiated in the ways of the sneaky surgeon. On very early morning rounds, I'd tend to see patients in their rooms by myself. If a patient with a naso-gastric tube in place had shown evidence of significant improvement, I'd remove the tube---

with profuse thanks from the patient. Then, approaching the nursing station, I'd offhandedly and deadpanly remark to the night nurse doing her charting, "Somebody removed the N-G tube from Mrs. Smith in 702. The nurse's shoulders would sag as she tried to envision how that N-G tube could have been removed when she had just been in that room 15 minutes ago. What could have happened? Not prolonging the torment unduly, I'd then deliver the punch line, "Yes, somebody removed the N-G tube---and I like to think that I'm somebody."

6. Motherhood---the blessed event---evokes warm feelings of tenderness, approaching veneration. The recognition we give to mothers on Mother's Day is not only appropriate, but rather minimal compensation. Sadly, though, national days of celebration too often cram human emotion into one day. Alas! Patriotism, thankfulness, thoughtfulness---well, they're too easily relegated to second fiddle in the days after July 4, Thanksgiving Day, Christmas.

Just so! At times, I've felt that Mother's Day is a national collective expression of love---and guilt---allowing mother to resume her servant role the rest of the year. Come to think of it, why should each mother share her day with every other woman in the world who happens to have given birth--for whatever reason? No doubt! A mother's most special Mother's Day is on the birthday of her children---a day for her children to say, "Thanks, Mom."

March 13, 1961, was just such a special Mother's Day for Peggy---the day on which wombmates Debbie and Diane were introduced to Luther Hospital and the world. Naturally, there was much talk and rejoicing around the hospital at the announcement that these wombmates had emerged from their watery playground. Flowers were abundant, free doughnuts were the rule in the cafeteria. Congratulations were flowing! In the medical records department, a transcriptionist innocently inquired, "And what did you name the girls?" Straightforward answers somehow have never found a place in my cerebral computer. Instead, and I can hardly believe it now, I replied, "We decided to name them Platysma and Placenta---but don't worry. We'll be shortening their names to Platty and Plassy." I then walked out without changing the deadpan face. As I retreated, I could hear the young lady fuming, "Did you hear what they named those twins?"

VASECTOMY CAN MAKE A VAS DEFERENS

In the convoluted thinking of the male human being, sexual activity often is assumed to be a God-given right and is taken for granted. By and large, men are hormonally opportunistic, leaving women to be responsible for reproductive control. This blatant comment, of course, is a generalization, but may be a small capsule of what fills volumes and volumes, dealing with sexual dynamics.

The original "mixed marriage" involved not a mixture of the races, but simply a man---and a woman. What a revelation as one tries to understand the other. The genders are so profoundly different both in anatomy and in feelings. Inherently, women are softer beings---with natural warmth, caring, and compassion. The womb, the nurturing place, always will be female. Down through the ages, it seems to me, society in general and the church have been womb-oriented. It has been the acceptable role of women to bear and care---caring for the home and the children. With the difficulty of housekeeping tasks, a physician should never, never ask a housewife if she works. Early on, I learned that a more appropriate question of any young woman was, "Do you work outside the home?"

In many cultures, even to this day, supported by religious dogma and tradition, the woman's role has been narrowly prescribed. Male dominance was the thing and even said to be supported by scripture. In this supposedly enlightened nation, male dominance was evident most tellingly in that women gained the right to vote only 80 years ago. Politics, ranted the preachers, was dirty and seamy---and genteel women shouldn't be sullied by it. 'Spin" obviously was alive in those days also. The hidden meaning, of course, was that women weren't strong enough or smart enough to be partners in the political decision making process. Their place clearly was in the home---having babies.

It's a new day! More men started coming forward, wishing to accept a role in family planning and contraception. Therefore, I began doing vasectomies (male sterilizing procedures) in the office, using infiltration local anesthesia. To help those who weren't so affluent, we tried to have availability and cost within reason.

Furthermore, it seemed only a slight reward to accommodate those men who were willing to do their part in birth control, even enduring discomfort---something many men find difficult to do. The procedure I devised was virtually foolproof, pinning the vas deferens (the sperm-carrying tube) with a needle so that I then could work casually and carefully with no worry of slippage. Without precise polling, the men who underwent vasectomy in our office were pleased---with minimal discomfort, virtually no complications, and minimal fee.

Perhaps later I'll discuss fee structures and medical costs in general. Hearsay suggested that complication rates in other offices were greater than we experienced. Against that backdrop, I share with you an interesting interchange between myself and our loyal office staff regarding fees. Occasionally, like every day, the office staff would gently chide me, "You don't charge enough." Trying to avoid or evade the subject, I'd just shrug my shoulders, acting unconcerned, and sigh, "Get off my back. The children have food and clothes---and we're getting by."

If the truth were known, I was incredibly naive. I did know that, in fees for major surgeries, our fees were in the lowest 10th percentile nationally. Well, without my knowledge, the office staff did their own clandestine investigating---calling the five offices in Eau Claire where vasectomies were performed. They used a simple query, "Hi, I'm Mrs. Smith and my husband is planning to have a vasectomy. Can you give me the cost of the operation?' Those offices, eager to have the business, gave the figures without hesitation. The staff then neatly compiled the figures and placed them prominently on my desk. O.K. So, I was naive! Even in retrospect, though, why should I worry about what some other office was charging as long as I felt I was doing the right thing? How did you guess it? My fee was the lowest on the totem pole with some fees twice as much. Most galling of all was that the Family Medicine resident training program had a fee higher than mine---and I was the expert. They were the neophytes. So be it! End of story.

With few exceptions, I insisted on a pre-vasectomy visit with husband and wife---and signatures of both parties. On a few occasions, I actually asked couples to delay the procedure, to re-think. A red flag was waving if either husband or wife had even the slightest reservation about permanency. Maybe they'd like to have another baby? Yes, reversal of vasectomy is possible, but it's more difficult to achieve and a lot of trouble.

The title of this section is taken from a wiseacre patient who joked, "Having a vasectomy really makes a vas deferens in how I look at the world."

DAY OF CARING

Although not dealing directly with the hands-on treatment of patients, this section has to do with all the employees of Sacred Heart Hospital and their feelings for each other. A gift was given---and I couldn't even begin to comprehend the reason. Perhaps the reason may come to you in a quiet moment. On a memorable afternoon in the surgical lounge, the surgical staff presented me with a colorfully wrapped package. It wasn't Christmas! It may have been someone's birthday, but not mine---and it wasn't April Fool's Day. With little formality, I tore away the wrapping paper and out of the box came a Care-Bear (pseudonym Friend Bear), glad to be freed from his imprisonment, confined to the box all the way from his birthplace in North Dakota to Eau Claire. Created by Garnet's mother, the soon to become infamous bear was mine.

Alter-ego, Dr. Friend Bear

Little did the O.R. staff suspect that an apparently inanimate bear would mysteriously become animate as we drove home to Claymore Lane. Most likely, the staff hadn't the foggiest idea of what they had initiated. On that strange day, a stranger relationship was born between the unpredictable surgeon and the rambunctious bear. You may think of such a match as not only strange but weird---and you will probably be right. Never could I elicit any rationale for the gift (you suppose they liked me?), but with the gift, a new era was born and Sacred Heart Hospital would never be the same again.

This stuffy and fluffy bear was overflowing with ideas. Together with Garnet, the O.R. head nurse, the three of us dreamed of a day on which the "care" in Care-Bear would become reality. When you think of caring, you simply assume that there will be caring between employees and patients, but what about the feeling that employees have for each other? The date was set, March 3, for the celebration of caring. Invitations were sent to President and Mrs. Reagan, but they had a prior commitment. Their tough luck! All the departments in the hospital were alive with anticipation and, fittingly, employees brought their bears.

The spirit of the day was magnificent---much more than we envisioned. Departments such as medical records and housekeeping all at once became proud and saw themselves as a part of the total hospital effort. Not unexpectedly, the administration had never given those departments much recognition and it was all too easy for them to crumble with the "we're not very important" image. You should have seen it! One whole wall in the medical records department was covered with bears. Most importantly, caring became a catchword. Employees began looking at each other with appreciation, meaning it as they said, "Hey, I care about you, too."

This embryonic event, "Day Of Caring," had become more than a dream. It blossomed into an annual event, complete with balloons, TV coverage, radio and newspaper interviews, and even a brief program with speeches written by ghost-writer Friend-Bear. The triumvirate had high hopes that this day would become ecumenical, involving health care workers in offices and clinics, even spreading to Luther Hospital. A roadblock! The hospital sisters weren't about to let this public relations baby be kidnapped, so the Day of Caring stayed provincial. Were physicians included? Most certainly, but participation was sporadic. Some physicians joined in the playfulness of the day while others, of sterner and gruffer stuff, were staid and stayed aloof. Their lament was a weak, "What's all this cavorting with bears?"

"Day of Caring" at Sacred Heart Hospital. L-R: Neil Miland, Dr. Hudson, Garnet Bast

Quite predictably, when Garnet left, the tradition waned, perhaps wisely so. Traditions can become hokey if the spirit isn't indwelling. "Day of Caring" is no more, but the very mission of hospitals demands that there be continuing expressions of caring between workers and patients---and among the employees. It has ever been thus and ever shall be. In reminiscence with those who received the spirit, it is rewarding to count the many who remember those days. This is confirmation that you never can destroy that which has been good---nor should you try.

FANTASY AND THE BEAR—
A DELVING INTO SCIENTIFIC RESEARCH

From the getgo, I realized that my relationship with that jealous bear was viewed as weird. Troubling, though, as the relationship flourished, were the inferences that I might be in the incipient stages of dementia. The furtive questions weren't even behind my back. "Gee, is the old guy slipping?" "You think he should retire?" In a court hearing, I'd have absolutely no defense if humanization and animation of care-bears or cars were to be introduced as sufficient reason for putting me away.

There were those who suggested that the little bear was my alter-ego. I leave it to you. All I ever did was convey to the world what was going through Friend-Bear's mind. Perhaps you would understand, more or less, if I would detail for you our symbiotic association amid wild confusion in the O.R. concerning the cause of pregnancy.

A coincidence, perhaps? The pseudo-scientific search for the causation of pregnancy was born when 6 young women, all of them working in the O.R., were noted to be in various stages of pregnancy. Overhearing their conversation, I found it mind-boggling. Although admitting their condition, and although expressing pleasure and anticipation of birth, not a one of them seemed to have the foggiest notion as to how the pregnancy could have come about. The offhand comments were slippery disclaimers, lacking the credibility of scientific verification. Have you ever heard such girl talk? "It must be in the air!" "Could it be the water?" "Get away from me---it might be catching." "Perhaps the toilet seats are contaminated." Those young women needed help and so, in a climate of confusion, I suggested to Friend-Bear that we embark on a collaborative scientific study to determine once and for all the causation of pregnancy in the Sacred Heart O.R. You should have seen the furry creature. Friend-Bear was bursting at his sewn seams, eager to be involved in the hunt. His great opportunity!

The details of the exhaustive study fill another volume, which is to be found in the Claymore College archives or in Garnet's files. Suffice it to say that this study has become recognized as a benchmark effort, one of a kind. Perhaps if you would refer to the original unedited text, you wouldn't have such raised eyebrows. To soften your skepticism, herewith a brief summary: Friend-Bear, through his nocturnal bedroom research, completely refuted as fallacious any inference that the germ theory was involved. He found no credible evidence that pregnancy was air-driven, water-borne, associated with toilet seats, or whatever. His brusque, emphatic conclusion? The cause of pregnancy was found to be parasitic---the ubiquitous, sperm-spitting trouser worm. With this revelation, the mood of the female O.R. employees approached hysteria until they were reassured by Friend-Bear that all the trouser worms in the O.R. appeared to be limp and lifeless.

There was no stopping him---his ego was out of bounds. With his new-found fame, Friend-Bear received a scholarship to college and, within 18 months, obtained his doctorate in meaningless clinical research. With a haughtiness, which we thought was too quick in coming, he insisted on being addressed as Dr. Friend-Bear---said something about his being as good as me. A rising star, he was installed as headmaster at Claymore College. Beware of being on the pedestal. It's a long way down.

Parents and students at Claymore College began to bristle at Dr. Friend Bear's abrasive, arrogant, and dictatorial headmastership. Why such a departure from the "Days of Caring?" Whatever the cause, parent and student disapproval resulted in canning him---coincidentally at the time I was entering retirement. Some of you bright ones will see the alter-ego. It's possible that there was an undue interdependency between the too clever bear and myself. Some pundits observed wryly that this unlikely pair deserved each other. Thus, when Dr. H., the old fogey now without scalpel, decided to retire---Dr. Friend Bear became a reclusive old fogey, too.

Dr. Friend Bear's rude ways and his peremptory dismissal led to the calling of the soft-spoken Gordon G. Groundhog as headmaster. Claymore College is now gaining stature under his furry leadership, thank you. You haven't heard of Claymore College? Well, we don't attract media attention or go out after publicity. It's the word of mouth thing that brings students to our door. The Claymore College motto is descriptive--"where fantasy is the norm and the pursuit of excellence is exceeded only by the retreat from relevance." In one era and out the other.

TO BE INVOLVED IN YOUR OWN FAMILY'S TREATMENT?

Should a physician ever treat his/her own family? Could not the answer be conditioned by the severity of the problem? Should it have to be an untouchable, a no-no, just to treat the common cold or other childhood illnesses, especially when the treatment consisted mostly of benign neglect? Yet, it's impossible to dismiss lightly the commonly held belief that emotion can bring the danger of impairing objectivity.

Accordingly, and undoubtedly for the best, if members of my family were having surgery, my place would have been in the family waiting room. Even unspoken tradition, however, may have to give way to common sense if circumstances should arise, demanding otherwise. Circumstances are unpredictable, can vary, aren't always envisioned or controllable. In short, occasions may arise when my talent perhaps was the only talent available---and the treatment of the family member couldn't be avoided or delayed. An obvious assumption is that the role of caregiver as well as parent or husband would impose extra care and caution.

Fortunately, or unfortunately, as seen in others' eyes---sickness was neither hoped for nor expected in our home. Indeed, sickness was viewed as with a jaundiced eye. As an inheritance from the dominant Esther figure, you were expected to go to school. Pre-school sniffles and runny noses were met with, "You're a little under the weather, but it won't last---you'll feel better, you'll survive, and you'll thank us for sending you to school." This, of course, was in an era unlike the present when school policy now treats a sniffle as something akin to the plague. Although Esther wasn't with us, her battle cry was commanding. Woe to him/her who pretended that he/she didn't hear it.

1. Laura was a shy, placid preschooler---hardly whimpering when she had the misfortune of catching a finger in a closing door. The finger was torn and looking a little grotesque what with the distal 1/3 of the finger not exactly lined up with the rest of the finger. No, there was no 911. Panic was at a minimum as Laura, holding her hand in a clean towel, rode with her father to the Luther Hospital E.R after the father first finished reading the newspaper. In those days, there was no physician on premises covering the E.R., so I began to think of who might be called to suture the finger. The more I thought of it, the answer came through loud and clear, "Who would Laura trust more than me?" Thus, with sterile preparation, some soothing words, and effective lidocaine, the finger was rearranged and sutured---again, without a whimper heard from her. A violation of the principle, "Don't treat your own family?" No doubt! But it seemed right. Today, Laura points out that she never was read her rights and she doesn't recall having given informed consent. She also mutters occasionally about bringing suit against the surgeon because the finger isn't completely straight.

2. As another example of treating a family member, I report some scary moments when there was nobody around but me to forestall possible tragedy. To set the stage, Peggy had been hospitalized for an abdominal laparotomy, exploring in search of a cause for vague abominal symptoms. A small ovarian cyst seen on ultra-sound exam, was sufficient to warrant the exploration. Surprise! My surgical partner immediately discovered the cause of the puzzling symptoms to be inflammatory disease of the small intestine, variably known as terminal ileitis or Crohn's disease---the very problem that afflicted President Eisenhower. A correct decision was made not to resect the involved small bowel for two reasons: 1) Surgical excision of Crohn's disease had a way of begetting further surgery and 2) There had been no chance to observe the ef-

fect of medical management of the problem.

Initially, Peggy did well post-operatively, but then developed a post-op ileus, in which the intestine becomes lazy or paralyzed, losing its peristalsis. Compounded by a previously known aerophagia (air swallowing), her abdomen became hugely distended, mimicking pregnancy---but without the happiness. She was miserable! While I was seeing patients in the office one afternoon, the phone rang and I heard a most plaintive voice, uncharacteristically pleading, "Will you come see me?" Arriving in her hospital room, I was alarmed at the degree of distention. Not being able to reach other physicians, and knowing that an abdominal x-ray was urgently necessary to assess the gas pattern, I simply took over. We took Peggy to the x-ray department in a wheelchair. With a patient in obvious distress in the hallway, I've always thought that the x-ray techs could have at least acknowledged our presence.

Finally! The x-ray confirmed what I feared---a massive acute dilatation of the stomach---the gastric air shadow almost filling the abdomen. Such massive distention can lead to disastrous electrolyte disturbances---so insertion of a naso-gastric suction tube was necessary---NOW! Retching and vomiting also assisted in the relief, a follow-up x-ray within an hour showing marked improvement. The lesson: There are times when you've just gotta do what you've gotta do---regardless of the dictates of tradition. I'm convinced that further delay on that occasion might have been catastrophic.

SUPPORT GROUPS

Perhaps we've had support groups in one form or another for eons, consisting of church groups, card clubs fraternal organizations, etc. What I have seen has been the emergence of formal support groups for every conceivable affliction or condition, imagined or real. Yes, support groups seem to be popping up everywhere, coming out of the woodwork. I confess that I have mixed feelings about support groups. On the very positive side, thumbs up are given to groups which are formed for the purpose of standing with, supporting, and helping others who are going down a path already trod by the members of the support group. These are my heroes!

An outstanding (the best) example of a positive support group is the ostomy support group, which encourages and educates others. In a spirit of sharing, this group offers living evidence that life, although changed, can go on triumphantly without the feeling of being hopelessly disadvantaged. Repeated testimony by patients gives lofty credit to pre-operative and post-operative visits by ostomy club members in helping them through a crisis time. This isn't just happenstance. Ostomy club visitors have to be qualified by training to give the type of reassurance and affirmation that worried patients need so badly.

On the negative side, be wary of groups in which members gather together only to share tales of woe. There may be a sympathetic reception, but missing are those members who have experienced the woes and yet survived---the ones who can cry out, "Yes, life is unfair at times, but I'm here to tell you and show you that you can be better than you are." Support groups are questionable when formed for trivial pursuits---as when broccoli haters gather to commiserate, to share their disdain with others of like mind. Negative support groups remind me of pigs in a mud puddle. There's such delight in sloshing around in the mud, rubbing up against one another, feeling good---but with nobody trying to climb out of the mud puddle.

The emphasis on "support" is exactly that---to support and encourage---not just to say, "Gee, you poor thing." When we're confronted by a tearful mess---let's say a marriage problem---it's probably a human reaction to seek out others with the same problems. The real trick is to find a listener who understands the problem, but who has gone through the valley and climbed to the mountaintop, becoming a person---not the one who has fallen by the wayside.

Kudos again to the ostomy support groups, composed of people who have gone through the valley, overcoming times of trial and testing. The camaraderie within such a group of survivors is inspiring.

One ostomy club member stands out for her faith, persistence, and courage. Her story was so bizarre that details are hazy. What I so keenly remember was the alarm in Dr. Leasum's voice when he described a young nurse with an emergent problem. Precipitously, out of the blue, Doris had suddenly started bleeding massively from the rectum. Later that day, before the time of much-needed endoscopic diagnostic assistance, we felt there was no other choice than to explore surgically. What we found was shocking and unexplainable---a horrible acute colitis with tissue-paper thin fragile colon mucosa, bleeding uncontrollably. The lining of the large bowel obviously had been attacked by an acute inflammatory reaction, cause unknown. The tissue literally crumbled at the slightest touch. With bleeding of that magnitude, the only life-saving thought was to resect what appeared to be an irreversibly damaged colon.

Doris somehow survived the day, but on the following morning, with a hemoglobin of 5 Grams %, we had to re-operate to control bleeding. We apparently were dealing with an acutely inflammatory Crohn's disease.

Having survived this initial onslaught, her condition was so precarious that she was transferred to the Mayo Clinic. Through the years, this petite nurse, educator, wife, mother, and Sunday School teacher suffered through fistulas and recurrent disease. At this time, she is functioning with an ileostomy and with a greatly reduced length of small intestine for absorption of nutrients. Yet, she is a smiling contributor---always ready to help others. She represents the heart of a positive support group--- bulwark of strength so that others, with similar problems, can see a person who has gone through the valley and emerged with a positive attitude.

TRANSPORTATION---IS A CAR JUST A CAR?

Those among you who are doubting Thomas's may think that I'm straying from the central theme of this book, which has been written to describe my travels along the healthcare highway. Well, how could I travel without a car? Furthermore, you will see, in this section, that my cars were embraced by the O.R. staff as more than ordinary vehicles. To the consternation of family and colleagues, the same weirdness that transformed Friend-Bear from the inanimate to the animate---well, this weirdness worked also with personal vehicles. Sam, Frank, and Bruno were much more than mechanized, motorized convenience. There was a bond, a trust that surpassed the understanding of non-sympathetic unbelievers. All three of these personal friends were treated with care and consideration---not to be sent to that great garage in the sky just because of some arbitrary mileage indicator. Admittedly, some of the treatment accorded these vehicles would stretch the definition of common sense. Ailments often were treated even though there was a promise of only a few more days, weeks, or months of service---even though, on the human level, the condition would be termed critical, the prognosis grim, and treatment tantamount to futile.

Although Bruno (Bruno Brougham)---he who accompanied me into retirement---endeared himself to everybody except possibly Peggy, Frank (Frank Fury) was the darling of the O.R. Staff. Descriptions of Frank's special day of honor are to found in the Claymore College archives. There you will find exhaustive documentation of an emotional and fateful day. On that day, the O.R. staff had decorated Frank with balloons, formed from inflated rubber gloves. Adorning the windshield and side windows were signs reading, "National Frank Day" and "Frank, We Love You." Frank's wheel covers even were festooned with O.R. caps. Rather obviously, all of this was done without my knowledge and, as I emerged from the E.R. door to go to the parking lot, photographers were capturing my facial disbelief. Frank, true to his stoic self, remained nonplused throughout the acclamation and celebration. I was the one who was shaken and overcome with emotion at this outpouring of love. Shaking as I was, Frank and I managed to make it home. As we crawled down Stein Boulevard, horns were honking and there were quizzical stares. The reaction of the family? In unison, "Wow! We're glad we weren't there!"

A GRATEFUL PATIENT---
WHAT IS ACCEPTABLE?

Let's face it! In any medical office, the members of the office staff are indispensable, partly because they are readily accessible. Patients quickly become comfortable with them and rapport develops. Nurses are treated by patients not only as understanding listeners, but almost as members of the family. With feelings of gratitude, it's not uncommon that patients will bring gifts to express that appreciation. Are there hard and fast rules about accepting such gifts? No, but common sense dictates that no gift should be accepted if there is any suggestion of a bribe to receive preferential treatment. Now, think with me. If there is a genuine outpouring of gratitude, wouldn't it border on the crude and insensitive to refuse the gift, perhaps demeaning the giver? Good intentions may and should be received graciously---with thanks. Admittedly, accepting a dozen cookies or a floral bouquet would be a far cry from a gift of a car or something else of great substance.

How would you have treated Werner? Werner presented a somewhat tangled problem. An elderly gentleman with an incurable sarcoma on the arm, he had been coming to the office for frequent dressing changes. Now, Werner had always been somewhat of a recluse and hadn't ever received such kind attention. He began bringing small gifts, giving him a good feeling. Then Janet, our office nurse, informed me that Werner wanted to give her some household furniture---sort of a pre-death gift. Understandably, this made her a trifle uncomfortable. As we discussed the pros and cons of accepting or rejecting his offer, it seemed best to give this terminally ill man the dignity of acceptance. Furthermore, we felt that Werner had little else to give him a sense of being worthy. If his gift, still treasured by Janet, made Werner happy, so be it! In a way, wasn't that a part of our mission?

A MOTHER GIVES BIRTH.
THE ROLE OF THE FATHER?

Where are the wise elders in our society who will teach us about gender responsibility? Where are the cultural role models to tell a girl what it means to be a woman---to tell a boy what it takes to be a man? Parents never can abdicate their important roles, but influenced by TV and movie exposure, learning about sexuality still is more by word of mouth on the street and playground. Rarely does such learning assume any structure---although there are applaudable strides toward correcting that. Much of gender wonder, in a heterosexual sense, seems to revolve around obvious anatomical differences. Development of appropriate feelings comes gradually, if ever, along the sexual highway, a trip often delayed or arrested by flat tires or battery failures.

Down through the ages, boys and girls have struggled through the maze of adolescence with the haunting and rarely spoken question, "How do I measure up?" Not only is there concern about how we measure up to individual, peer group, and societal expectations but, not often confessed, there is the measuring of body parts by furtive glances. Somewhere along the line, the mythical stork is placed on the shelf along with Santa Claus, the Easter Bunny, and the tooth fairy. With faltering steps, we eventually venture into the realm of the "sperm and egg" dance, understanding the concept more than the details. Marriages, long before "live-in" or "checking it out" situations, were initiated by dreams and starry eyes and sustained by cultural morality and the Golden Rule---surrounded by the blessing of the church.

We lived in a time when couples were considered suspect if, after a year of marriage, a baby wasn't on the way. Yes, a baby was born---and another---and another. The gender contributions to conception even were accepted by children who suddenly realized, "Gee, our parents did those things, too." The sperm and egg contributions to conception are timeless and changeless. It's the methodology that has changed and become innovative---sometimes artificial insemination rather than natural, in vitro development rather than in vivo.

Gender roles in the rearing and nurturing of children? The former sharp dividing line, which separated one side from the other side, has become somewhat blurred and indistinct A few generations ago, the role of the man? Breadwinner! The role of the woman? Homemaker, mother! But! Did these roles evolve as something etched on a tablet of stone and brought down from the mountaintop? No way! With change as one of our few constants, gender roles can, do, and will change with the passage of time. Placed on this sphere by the accident of the time we are born, we generally play out our parts in prescribed ways---ways that have been drilled into us by the culture into which we were born.

When my younger sister was about to be born, my father's role was to take the family for a ride in the car, circling and re-circling the house until a white towel appeared in the window, signifying the birth of a baby. I've searched and found precious little instruction re: gender roles there---except for male non-participation in the birth process. Gradually, fathers have been allowed out of their historical fretting and sweating role in the waiting room and have been given a precarious role in the birthing room---complete with cameras, of course.

A summation of gender roles: It's an accepted physiologic fact that men never will give birth, but there is hope that men can become more nurturing and supportive. Those of my generation can regret that our role was distant and work-oriented, but we can't change the past. We seemed to be possessed with a complacent indoctrination that said, "Well, babies are born and children grow, don't they?" To be sure, we can't change what has been, but yet-- we can wish. . .can't we?

WE ARE BORN AND WE DIE---
BUT WHEN?---AND HOW?

Look around you! You will find those with frailties of the flesh who, nonetheless, exhibit a spirit that soars like the eagle. I have seen abundant evidence, which has imprinted upon me the belief that tenacity toward life endures in all of us, undiminished, until the moment of our death. Indeed, examples of this tenacity have been chronicled in these writings. On a personal note, I have sensed this same tenacity in some of my own precariously dark days---that is, after I regained the wit and wisdom to know what had transpired. Life, I have always believed, is a spiritual journey---to be lived by faith, which is intangible and is the evidence of things hoped for, but not seen.

Even with this tenacity, I am convinced that there is a zone which we all can enter---when personal freedom should allow us the autonomy of discarding tenacity, leaving this world on our own terms---both when and how. Alas! These thoughts, though eminently logical and not radical to my way of thinking, are considered anathema by some. Surprisingly, and I think paradoxically, some of those whose voices are the loudest in resisting these ideas of personal freedom are the very religious leaders who speak with great authority of life beyond this sphere---that death cannot prevail---that there is a better life beckoning. More troubling to me are physicians who wash their hands, as Pilate did, when patients express a wish to leave this world NOW.

When patients are terminally ill and faced with the futility of no cure, when physicians themselves are the ones who have pronounced the certainty of no cure and looming death, wouldn't you hope that physicians wouldn't abandon the patient? Wouldn't you hope that physicians wouldn't abdicate their responsibility to listen and to hear what is said---and what is trying to be said? Is it too much to hope that physicians might embrace the precious word "treatment" in giving comfort to those who would like to choose the day on which they might bid farewell? Resistance to such requests seems strangely misguided, in my view, but surely I respect the feelings of colleagues who think differently and who are uncomfortable or who would find it unconscionable to assist a terminally ill person in ending his/her life.

Public opinion polls show that the status of dying in America is abysmal and painful in many cases, devoid of dignity. Redoubling efforts to improve pain control may be laudable, but this approach completely misses the point that not all pain comes from raw nerve endings. At the same time, wouldn't it be refreshing to redouble our efforts to embrace the word "treatment" and really listen to the patient as an individual? Ethical arguments seem pointless to me if the good of the patient isn't paramount, the central theme. Too often, I get an uneasy feeling that the good of the patient plays second fiddle to ideological religious beliefs, which somehow wiggle their way into physicians' thinking. Sad! I have attended many ethics conferences dealing with end of life issues. At those conferences, I have had some indecent exposure to some points of view, which represent the ultimate in physicians playing games, in my opinion.

1. Because pain control has been so poor in many suffering terminally ill patients, religious and medical bodies have finally acknowledged that heavy medication to control pain is justified---as long as the intent is the alleviation of discomfort and not the opening of the door to death, even though death might be hastened in the process. Doesn't anybody else see the semantic dance contained in that declaration? Isn't that just playing word games?

2. Later, I'll explain why I believe the term "physician-assisted suicide" (P.A.S.) is an inflammatory

misnomer. At an ethics conference just last year, I could hardly believe what I was hearing. An opponent of P.A.S. suggested that there really is no need for P.A.S. since, with present-day techniques of pain control, suffering patients can be lowered into oblivion---that is, unresponsive and in a near coma. This is asinine, ludicrous---and crosses the line of common sense. Trying to make a distinction between lowering a person into a state of oblivion and simply helping him/her to die by P.A.S. is the ultimate in playing games.

Now, think with me critically as I ask a few probing questions.

1. To physicians who oppose P.A.S., do you think that patients who are asking to leave this world will find much help in your playing of word games?

2. Shouldn't it be obvious that pain isn't measured just by raw nerve endings---but also by feelings of embarrassment and chagrin at loss of control, incontinence, dependence, and what is felt to be a selfish and needless waste of financial resources?

3. To physicians who are caring for gradually dwindling, frail cancer patients, why should helping to assist death not be seen as treatment? After all, treatment of patients on an individual basis has been the cornerstone of physicians' training. Nothing in medical training ever commanded physicians that life be maintained at all costs. Rather, the responsibility of physicians always has been to comfort and help.

Dying has been and forever will be a great mystery. That mystery will persist until some day when we may see as with a bright light, perhaps on that other side. Above all, death is not to be feared. Then, what's the big fuss? For some reason not clear to me, both medical and religious bodies occasionally slip into a fear mode. Totally inconsistent with their basic beliefs, they seem to resist death and insist that life must go on even in obviously futile situations. I now share with you my recollections of four patients, truly human and caring persons, who taught me so much. Would that you might also benefit by this brief glimpse.

1. What will we see as we're transformed? Perhaps we'll see with eyes which have somehow been sharpened. I think of Dave, a man with far advanced colon cancer, with extensive liver metastases. A colostomy provided some creature comfort by relieving awful cramping of bowel obstruction, but cure surely wasn't in the cards for Dave. This always smiling man wasn't one of those clamoring for release from his travail. He had an unusual patience and acceptance of what was to come.

One Sunday, I had a strange hunch that I should see Dave and stopped by the nursing home. It was an intuition-- both Dave and I knew that the end (or the beginning) was near. His pulse was thin and fleeting. The smile was still there. Dave's words seemed to be expressing something of what he was seeing. "The forest---the forest---can you help me out of the forest?" Dave's wife arrived at my summons to be with him at that precious moment of release. Certain words have been repeated over and over at visitations and memorial services when there has been a lingering and painful illness. How many times have you heard or said, "What a blessing"? In many cancer deaths, there indeed is a very thin line between grief and relief---and "What a blessing" brings a measure of comfort. Deep inside, I find myself thinking, "If such a blessing now---wouldn't it have also been a blessing, maybe a greater blessing, a week ago or two weeks ago?"

2. There is nothing quite as distressing and devastating as progressive neuro-muscular degeneration. Les was a happy-go-lucky outdoorsman. Bothered by progressive weakness, he finally was diagnosed as having amyotrophic lateral sclerosis (Lou Gehrig's disease). People may not be acquainted with the details of the disease, but most are aware of the creeping disability which this disease brings---progressive weakness and inability to use the arms and legs. Natural bowel and bladder function become difficult, impossible. Most terrifying of all is the inevitable weakness of respiratory muscles, with choking

and gasping for air. The awful decision---to use a mechanical ventilator to get more oxygen into the lungs---just for a little more time?

Les began to speak to me about having his life end on his own terms. He felt that he had achieved the impossible when, with the assistance of his sons, he actually had gone deer hunting with the guys, hunting from the back of his truck, strapped in his wheelchair. As an avid outdoorsman, Les felt that he had gone to the mountaintop in his last hunt. He told me, "I'm at peace and I want to be free." Sometimes, people will talk about doing themselves in to see what response they'll get. Les forewarned me, "I'm going home and roll my wheelchair off the deck, a drop of 20 feet". I simply told him that he was a good person and I'd support whatever he wanted to do. I cautioned him, however, "Les, if you do that, the human response of your family will be to call 911 and bring you to the hospital." His frustration with his weakness was relieved I think, when I promised him that, if he ever came into the hospital again, I'd just hook him up to an I.V. morphine drip for comfort.

Les never carried out his threat to push his wheelchair off the deck, but respiratory problems forced his admission to the hospital. It was long known that Les fiercely resisted the idea of a respirator. Nasal oxygen was given to make breathing easier and, as promised, the I.V. morphine drip was started. It was done! Do you suppose that the rate of that I. V. drip might have been increased a tad?

3. I couldn't have had a better neighbor than Bob. We were politically and philosophically on the same page---and we delighted in playing tennis with neither of us prevailing as winner. An indication of my liking for Bob was shown in that I often rode with him to tennis matches---on his motorcycle. From what I had seen in the E.R., I disliked the thought of riding motorcycles (in the E.R., they were called "donormobiles"). With Bob, it was different---I felt safe. One day, without warning, he com-

mented sort of casually about a hard lump which had appeared in his neck. One touch and I knew that this was a malignant lymph node. Outwardly, Bob seemed unconcerned. His words, "I did have colon cancer 4 years ago, but they got it all." That too commonly used phrase, unfortunately, isn't always borne out with the passage of time. Sure enough, Bob had extensive metastatic colon cancer.

In spite of chemotherapy, the disease began to take over. When Bob became so weak he couldn't even climb the stairs, he asked me in a backyard conversation, "How many sleeping pills would it take?" Just as with Les, I promised Bob that I'd support any deision he should make but advised him, "Bob, if you take sleeping pills, take them when nobody will discover you for some time. Otherwise, your family will take you to the hospital and they'll pump your stomach." He didn't take pills. Like Les, he just wanted to talk!

Are people with terminal disease depressed? That question must be high on the list of stupid questions. Why shouldn't they be? Of course they are, but not all the time. They're too frail to be turning cartwheels, literally or figuratively. Some dreamers in the "keep 'em alive as long as you can" crowd delude themselves, thinking that situational depression clouds valid judgment. When the terminally ill person says that he/she wishes the torment to end, these dreamers will say, "he/she doesn't really mean it." They preach that treating the depression will magically relieve the suffering patient of the thought that he/she would be happier only when the torment should stop. How naive! With Bob, any depression was surely understandable---as you will plainly see.

At his last hospice hospitalization, Bob woke up each morning, groaning and mumbling, "Am I still here?" He weighed only 1/2 his normal weight, he had tubes in every conceivable orifice, he was paralyzed below the waist, his pain was excruciating, and there were sores allover his body. That's living? Most important, recognizing the futility of his condition, he was at peace with his family. Yes, pain protocols are improving today, but only as a reaction to criticism. When Bob was going through the valley, we were in the throes of nurses' fears that their necessary injection of narcotic might be the last---might cause death. Perish the thought! They should have rejoiced, but yet they were alarmed and upset. Even with more enlightenment, I sense that some of that mentality still exists in that so many obviously have difficulty in helping a patient to die. You may have heard it said, "Doctors are so imbued by their training to pursue the saving and prolonging of life that they think of death as a failure---a personal defeat." This, at least in part, explains why end of life treatment is lateralled to hospice nurses, pastoral care, whatever. The escapist theme is loud and clear, "I've done my bit---now it's your turn."

Do you have a stark, gnawing picture of the man Bob had become---not to his delight? Can you dispute my plea, "If a blessing now (at the visitation), why couldn't it have been a blessing two weeks ago?" Society, sadly, has trouble burying those who are already dead in the eyes of those closest and dearest to them. The insistence on prolonging suffering to satisfy some weird and warped societal concept represents guilt and an amazing lack of compassion. Four-legged animals are treated with more kindness.

It was a Saturday morning and I was visiting Bob in the hospital---just as a friend. Suddenly, Bob's wife asked me a question for which I had no studied answer. Ever so quietly, but earnestly, she pleaded, "Can't you be the doctor? Can't this be the day?" Confident that the responsible physicians, who actually were just covering on the weekend, would take no affront, I had the courage to reply, "If you simply say I'm the doctor, then I am. It's your right." Now in charge, it's possible that I made the nurse a little tearful when I asked her how much morphine she was giving by hypodermic injection. When I found that only 15 mgm. of morphine was being given, I challenged, "Why not 30 mgm.?" With Bob incoherent, moaning, and having great difficulty in breathing, I did what I could to alleviate his misery. Wouldn't you? I was, at that moment, perhaps his one true friend, slowly giving him valium I.V. until his breathing eased, he was more at peace, and he died.

No questions asked! The hospital chaplain, the family, and I had a circle of prayer. Completely absent was any suggestion that I had done anything wrong, anything unethical. Let's just say that I was adhering to the Jesus principle, as quoted in the Beatitudes. In those passages of scripture, it is promised that there will be torment for him/her who refuses to give even a cup of water to the thirsty. From a philosophical, but also pragmatic point of view, I was just helping to quench Bob's thirst.

4. I didn't think I would be, but I'm buoyed by stories coming back to me in retirement, stories which reflect the way in which I worked with nurses in mutual respect. Dorothy was that top of the line nurse---the one you'd like to have caring for your mother. After my retirement, I heard through a third party that Dorothy had an advanced malignancy---and that she'd like to see me. I went! Wouldn't you? What transpired that afternoon at her farm home was a reunion, an exchange of reminiscences, a memory of how we worked together as physician and nurse. Strangely, little was said about her illness. She did something for me that day when, in parting, her words were, "Thanks for coming---and I hope that you now have a better understanding of who you always have been."

Dorothy had hoped to map out her journey so that she would die at home, but such was not to be. Terrible pain became the stumbling block that necessitated her moving reluctantly from her home to Luther Hospital. There, with the restraints of D.R.G.'s and the insult of managed care (which, from the start, has had more to do with money than with care), she was allowed to stay for 5 days and then was shipped, like merchandise, to a nursing home to endure her remaining days. Here is where I take great exception to those who insist that all pain can be controlled. Who are they kidding? Dorothy's pain was being treated by a reputable pain clinic. Heavy doses of morphine were being given by I.V infusion drip and, every other day, pain clinic personnel were injecting her painful ribs with steroids and anesthetics. Was she comfortable? Not really. No way! She had been turned into a zombie---and this lovely lady never was intended to be a zombie.

In retirement, without a license, I couldn't be the person for Dorothy that I had been for Bob. Yet, I could be there, I could listen, and I could use common sense, that missing commodity in Dorothy's management. One morning, I blundered into her room to find her husband doing his best to steady her on the commode. Retreating rapidly, I returned in a few minutes to find her back in bed, still in misery, unable to void. Since I wasn't the treating physician, I may have stepped over an ethical boundary, but nobody was helping her. If you had been there, you could have made the simple diagnosis. Clinically, I placed slight pressure on her lower abdomen and she grimaced, "That feels like I have to go." There was no doubt! She had a hugely distended bladder. I was never one to throw my weight around, but I confess that I used some of my remaining clout at the nurses' station, pleading that they just put in a catheter for relief. Following her death, her husband wrote me to thank me for giving her a peaceful day.

Family members often are hesitant, don't quite know what to say or how to say it. Dorothy's husband approached the oncologist with a thinly-veiled plea, "I don't want you to get in trouble---but isn't there something more that could be done to let her go now?" Let me remind you, as you search for an answer to that question, that Dorothy was only a shell of her former vibrant self. Her children were terrified at her appearance and couln't bear to visit her. Be ye not over-critical of them. The oncologist's answer, hardly comforting, "It shouldn't be long." Well, time sometimes stands still and sometimes seems to fly---but "not long" was another 2 weeks of Hell. At ethics conferences, I've cringed when hearing physicians hiding behind the Hippocratic oath, which directs physicians, "At least do no harm." To me, Hippocratic too often has been turned around as Hypocritic. There is a great danger in fundamentalism, whether religious or medical, when ancient writings aren't seen as historical and those writings are transposed to present day problems, which weren't even envisioned by the ancient writings.

"At least do no harm." For some reason, I've been a small voice as I have challenged all physicians to look in the mirror at night and ask themselves if Dorothy wasn't hurt badly by the end-of-life management afforded her. We do better for sick horses. Dorothy was asking to leave this world each day. Saying, "There, there---it shouldn't be long" was a strange commingling of cruelty and comedy. Cruel comedy isn't funny! It was sheer incompetence.

Think with me for a moment about words. Don't dismiss words as just semantics, as having little impact. Back in the 1980's, during the alcohol/driving wars, we in Wisconsin goaded safety-conscious organizations into discarding the word "accident," replacing the word with the more descriptive word "crash." "Accident" conveyed a feeling that it was an unfortunate occurrence, unintended, and just happened. Too bad! We countered with the obvious. When this society can predict, fairly accurately, how many people are going to die on the highways each holiday each year---in advance---then that's no accident. Societally, that's on purpose. We believe that replacing a word helped us to approach the horrible highway death statistics as violent events, anti-social.

In similar vein, I've actively resisted using the word "suicide" as in physician-assisted suicide. The problem? Suicide is an inflammatory word with a societal connotation of weakness. To be sure, we should do all we can to prevent suicide with treatment, encouragement, and education. The common denominator of suicidal thoughts, earlier in life, is that depression overcomes a person with feelings of "there's no hope---life's not worth living." This feeling of hopelessness comes from within. Now, think of the terminal cancer patient. The pronouncement of hopelessness comes not from within, but from without---from medical authorities. Patients faced with grim pronouncements will react variably, no doubt, but shouldn't there be autonomy and respect? Above all, wishing to leave this world at a prescribed time should never be seen as a weakness. Quite to the contrary! It takes strength to confront the inevitable and to say in acceptance, "I understand and I'm at peace. Can it be soon---on a day of my choosing? Do this for me---please." Dorothy, and others like her, was never suicidal a single day in her life. To treat her as a weak-minded person is heaping on indignity.

Darrel Aspenson

AND THEN THERE'S DARREL...

We're born and we die---but when and how? As you've read the previous life stories of real individuals, my patients, the "when" has been assigned a date and I've shared with you my sometimes painful and pleading account of the "how." Just as the writing of this book is a work in progress, I cannot, I should not escape the trials of my friend, Darrel, also a work in progress---an arduously slow progress toward leaving this world.

Darrel has been my golfing buddy---a constant companion as we have pursued the little white ball around the pastures together. There's nothing like the camaraderie of golf to assess a personality and strength of character.

A jolt! Nearly a year ago, Darrel had an excision biopsy of a nodule in the umbilicus---and was handed an unwanted diagnosis of out-of-bounds pancreatic malignancy. Ouch! Coincident with the almost obligatory and ineffective chemotherapy, we made a pact to play golf as long as we could.

We're now in precarious times, the tumor extensively infiltrating the intestinal mesentery (the attachment of the intestine to the back wall of the abdomen). To add to his woes, there is an omental cake of tumor---and Darrel has been hospitalized with a small bowel obstruction, necessitating naso-gastric suction and eventually a gastrostomy tube for palliative decompression. Shades of Peggy (her ordeal described in a later chapter)! Maybe it helps to write about it. Just five days ago, Darrel and I, together with his son, played our last round of golf together. We played as long as we could---just as we pledged.

There's an oppressive loneliness which comes with being on the periphery, unable to influence treatment (again, shades of Peggy)). Darrel is a stalwart individual, unique in speech and in his approach to life. He's just Darrel! Maybe he doesn't have the vision of Dave. His pancreatic malignancy has reduced him to dependency, but in a different manner than Les, who was crippled by A.L.S. Darrel is my friend and it's frustrating that I can't help him as I may have helped Bob and Dorothy. Never, never label Darrel as weak or suicidal when, on occasions, he has said to me, "Why can't we just get this over with?"

Darrel will surely die as he slowly becomes nutritionally bankrupt. I'm writing about a death in progress. One evening, as Darrel and I were alone in his hospital room, he asked his nurse a seemingly offhand question, "Will you give me 32 sleeping pills tonight?" Taken a little aback, her response was, "Well, I can give you one sleeping pill." I sat there contemplating and suddenly blurted aloud, "Tell me, why NOT give him 32 sleeping pills? It might be excellent treatment."

As so often the case, my rumination was a combination of jest and seriousness. A revelation! I suddenly realized---it's so obvious---that health care personnel, in discussions over the extent of assistance in dying, remain hopelessly handcuffed by the words of Hippocrates, "In whatsoever you do in treating the patient, at least do no harm."

The dilemma, it seems to me, arises when professionals read either sacred or medical writings as non-historical, attempting to apply ancient writings to present-day problems, problems which weren't even envisioned by the ancient writers. Helping a patient to die peacefully NOW---a patient in whom the medical profession has adjudged treatment to be futile and death to be imminent---helping is now interpreted to be harming. Bizarre, to say the least! The harm has already been inflicted by the invading malignancy. Good Lord! How, then, could we do any more harm?

Fortunately, in stark contrast to the treatment of Bob and Dorothy, described in the previous chapter, there have been great strides in improving end-of-life management. I have nothing but praise and appreciation for the compassion, care, and competency in the treatment of Darrel by pain clinics, hospice, and palliative care specialists. Furthermore, Darrel's family has been immeasurably supported by those truly caring individuals.

It seems to me that the mark of staying young is to be open to change, to acknowledge that another person has a better idea. In a sense, the world would be a better place if we'd work together with nobody caring who gets the credit for accomplishments. In going down the path with Darrel, I've experienced a change in my feelings. I've watched as the hospice workers have literally removed frustrations and have allowed a most wonderful and loving interaction between Darrel and his family.

I still think we shouldn't get panicky about whether or not pain suppression suppresses respiration. Who cares if respirations cease? I still would uphold the autonomy of a patient who expresses outrage at being held captive by disease---and requests to leave this world NOW. Even so, being with Darrel every day, I'm not so sure that I, myself, would pursue a path any different than the path Darrel is treading. Indeed, insisting that I leave this world NOW might even be a tad selfish, taking away some precious moments so valuable to family.

Now, as Darrel becomes weaker each day and his speech is hardly a whisper---he's still my friend, a work in progress.

WHEN AND WHERE
IS A PHYSICIAN A PHYSICIAN?

    Such a simple question---but with answers and implications that may surprise you. Stereotypes are simplistic, but we can't get rid of them. The doctor is frequently portrayed in white coat with head mirror and stethoscope---in an office or hospital setting. Why not expand that image, venturing into settings which you may never have imagined? The truth is that a physician is a physician whenever, wherever---with or without the external trappings of stethoscope and black bag. Wherever she/he happens to be, the aura of physician isn't turned on and off like a light switch. It's simply a matter of presence. Some of these following glimpses into a world unfamiliar to you hopefully will be believable. Others may serve to intensify my reputation of being maverick or different.

    1. There wasn't anything especially noble or unique about house calls. Wasn't this a common practice with Henry Stengel? It didn't seem unusual to visit pa-

Henry J. Stengel, M.D. (right) with colleague, Ralph Hudson, M.D.

tients in their home so it seemed only right to see a sick child at home so that worried parents wouldn't have to wrap the feverish and chilling little one to go to the office or E.R. It just seemed right to see a post-op patient on occasions when there was an urgent problem---when transportation was non-existent for that patient. This philosophy extended to the frail and elderly in nursing homes---

the only home for them now. Furthermore, transport to office or E.R. by any commercial means was, and is, prohibitively expensive. Dr. Kincaid, a cardiologist, and I played a doctors' lounge game in which we tallied the numbers of our house calls. Finally, I had him! He couldn't top this story.

Mr. S. called our office, reporting that he had fainted and fallen, gashing his scalp with lots of bleeding. This seemed to be valid reason to suggest that he go to the E.R., where I would meet him. Having experienced Mr. S.'s reluctant nature, we weren't surprised to hear him say, "No E.R. You come here or I'll just keep bleeding until it stops." Was there any choice? The office nurses made up a clean package of towels, instruments, and dressings---and I headed out. He wasn't kidding! The gash in the scalp was wide and deep---you could feel the skull. With Mr. S. sitting upright---as in a barber chair---I proceeded to suture that laceration without anesthesia. Meanwhile, his wife (an Alzheimer patient) was walking aimlessly around the house, humming and oblivious of what we were doing.

You can be sure that Dr. Kincaid heard about this house call---and he was duly impressed. Later, he got into the act. When the full story was known, Mr. S. had fallen because of Adams-Stokes syndrome, a momentary heart stoppage---and Dr. Kincaid was able to help by inserting a cardiac pacemaker.

Real life stories don't have beginnings and endings---they just wander. In other calls at this couple's home, I could see the anguish of Mrs. S.'s dementia and the torment it caused her husband. We know that patients have an absolute right to refuse any recommended treatment. When this happens, however, it gnaws at our sense of responsibility when a recommended surgical procedure would be life saving.

The story wanders and here's Mr. S. again, this time in the hospital with an obvious perforated duodenal ulcer and peritonitis. The problem would have been easily corrected by surgery, but I told you that this man was reluctant. He was firmly adamant---"no surgery." We did our best to support him with I.V. fluids and naso-gastric suction---to no avail. He died! As his daughter and I tried to sort out what his thinking might have been, we were agreed that he was exhausted by the ordeal of caring for his Alzheimer wife---and he wanted out. With more awareness and knowledge these days, respite help is available for Alzheimer families. Knowing Mr. S., would he have accepted the help?

    2. Can a physician still be a physician in a bank vault? Conduct your own survey. Ask around to see if anybody can match this tale. Lillian B. was an 88 year old ex-teacher, prim and proud spinster. She already had attained some importance in my eyes as the oldest woman on whom I had performed a hysterectomy. At that age, the indication surely had to be solid. Although not a malignancy, she was bleeding persistently, vexingly---staining her socks, shoes, and carpeting.

    It was 3-4 months post-op when Lillian and I met by chance in the bank vault. I was clipping a few coupons to buy shoes for the kids and Lillian was pursuing the pastime of the elderly---inspecting the contents of her safety deposit box---and visiting. She was chirpy, "Why, Dr. Hudson, I'll be seeing you in your office this afternoon." I didn't want to slam the door in her face, but I happened to know that her appointment actually had been three days prior to that day.

    I interject that the office visit wasn't about the surgery. It was just to be a casual exam, not needing much hoopla or equipment. So, rather than cause her grief, I suggested that we might as well save her a trip by doing the exam right there. We correctly obtained the permission of the vault supervisor. "Say ah," "Breathe in and out." With some tapping on the chest, feeling the tummy, listening with the stethoscope, Lillian had her medical visit---in the bank vault. A sense of obligation caused me to write the bank president an appropriate note of thanks for allowing the physician to be a physician---even there.

3. Weirdest of all, a physician may be a physician in spirit---that is, whenever the patient even thinks the physician is there. There were parts of John B.'s life style which you would have found to be unhealthy. John had an engaging habit of asking me questions, questions for which John already knew the answers. Why not eavesdrop?

John was one of those dedicated 2-3 pack a day cigarette smokers. For undisclosed reason, he asked me, "Doc, you think I should quit smoking?" I replied, "John, you know the answer to that---of course! ---but it won't be easy kicking a heavy habit." "No problem, Doc, I'll do it." To my surprise, he did it! He did it cold turkey and never smoked again. With that as background to show his sincerity, I was better prepared when John was back within a year with, "Hey, Doc, do you think I should stop drinking?" Now, there are heavy drinkers and there are heavy drinkers. John belonged in either category, but he was sneaky and evasive. He didn't consider himself an alcoholic because he never drank until noontime. Having arrived at the normal, more acceptable time for drinking, he proceeded to prepare a quart of brandy mahattans, which he sipped for the rest of the day. I admired his resolve although I didn't understand what had pushed or persuaded him to take the non-alcohol path. "John," I said, "you'd be a lot healthier if you stop drinking, but it's even more iffy than quitting cigarettes. You'll have to go into the hospital for 5-7 days."

After John was admitted to the hospital and the treatment plan was underway, we now have the physician "in spirit." Oh, woe! Oh, mortification and embarrassment! It should never happen and I can't explain the blunder---but it happened. I missed seeing John for several days and the nurses, strangely, didn't send up any red flags. When I came to my senses and visited John on rounds, he was sweating, a little shaky and trembling, but apparently thought my absence was just part of the plan. He came out of that hospitalization alcohol-free and remained such for the rest of his life, partly because he had trust and sensed that the physician was still a physician---though in spirit.

4. I've always felt better---never felt threatened---if only I could have personal contact with a patient---up close, not at a distance. At times, situations could be precarious and confidence could be shaken by the seriousness of problems, but I could feel warm inside if I'd seen the patient and really knew what was going on. Phone calls don't fit my definition of "up close." Phone calls, of course, are the start of communication, but I'm fearful when courses of action are determined by nothing more than a phone call.

A physician is a physician---even over the phone. It matters not whether it's the physician or a physician designee who lifts up the receiver. I may be a minority, but I worry about the risk inherent in phone consultation---giving advice without seeing and examining the patient. The risk escalates, it seems to me, with the increasing business practice of charging a fee for phone calls. Communication is a tricky thing even under the best of circumstances. If there is too much emphasis on phone calls because of crowded schedules, the convenience may rise up and bite the unsuspecting physician. In a medical-legal sense, there could be value in recording phone consultation. There often is a world of difference in what was said, what was heard. Down the road, if medical outcome is not so good, it might just be relieving to know exactly what was said, what was heard.

5. A physician is a physician whether his/her impact on patients is specifically personal or as part of a broad social picture. Maybe this is my plea for physicians to be involved in community activities where their medical knowledge and experience may make a difference, may help make a better community. Sadly, the medical profession hasn't always been recognized widely for such involvement. There has too often been an air of "I gave at the office."

Locally, I found great satisfaction in membership

on the City-County Board of Health. One of our times of testing was when there was an outbreak of Legionnaire's disease, causing 5-6 deaths and with the source of the disease a public health nightmare. A physician is a physician---even in communicating with the media and calming the public. Also, serving on the Visiting Nurses Association board brought me into association with like-minded people, those interested in health care and home care for the needy and less fortunate.

Physicians vary widely in their willingness to be involved in their professional organizations. When the stated and actual mission of the organization is to improve the climate for better patient care, a physician may become even a more effective physician in working for goals that encompass all of society. The image of the A.M.A. (American Medical Association) is seen with differing degrees of enchantment. Alas, there is a lingering, widespread feeling that the A.M.A. is a highly political organization, more interested in M.D. turf and income protection than the welfare of patients, the overall health of the nation.

The State Medical Society of Wisconsin (now the Wisconsin Medical Society) always seemed different, perhaps because I was closely involved. The spirit pervading the organization was one of concern for the best climate in which to give high quality patient care. Who knows? Maybe I could have been president of the organization---I knew how to achieve the office---but I feared that it would take too much time away from patients.

A physician is a physician when, in the Commission on Safe Transportation, we worked tirelessly to impact legislation which would make for safer highways. We treasured the compliment of Earl Thayer, executive secretary of the society at the time, when he used our commission as an example---saying, "We'd have no public relations problems if every commission would work for the common good as your commission does."

NEPOTISM---NATURAL AND NEAT

Should family members be a part of the medical office staff? Why not? In the early days of our Eau Claire adventure, our daughter, Janet, then a high school student, worked in our medical office. Meeting a sometimes anxious and demanding public was good experience---and an awakening. An accompanying side benefit was the opportunity to work with older women who mothered her, praised her work ethic, and increased her confidence.

Have you ever noticed that, for some unexplained reason, people who have complaints, legitimate or otherwise, will sound off at people who can't even come close to correcting the problem? From her vantage point in the medical office, Janet quickly found out that gripers often complain to the wrong people---to those who can do little about the supposed problem. Schedules in medical offices are subject to the vagaries of emergencies, very sick patients who require added time, and the popularity of the physician. It, therefore, was only natural that, if the schedule was tight and hectic, a backlog of patients might develop in the waiting room---with rumbles of unrest. Needless to say, these impatient ones, were they the ones in the examining rooms, would have liked sufficient time given to their problems.

Occasionally, Janet would hear murmurs of discontent such as, "Well, I suppose he's back there drinking coffee." She would bristle at such untrue speculation, loyally assuming the role of father protector. You guessed it! By the time the complaining person met me back in the consulting area, there was a far different picture. After I gave the sincere greeting, "I'm sorry you had to wait so long," the universal response was, "Oh, that's all right, doctor. I know how busy you are. Thank you for seeing me."

I had never thought of Peggy's involvement in the medical practice as nepotism---it just seemed to come with the territory. Would you believe that, in our marriage vows, Peggy promised to "love and obey?" (She later recanted and admitted, "I lied.") She recalls no mention in the marriage vows about answering the phone at all hours, trying to track me down whenever and wherever, keeping the family together, placating patients and office nurses, and then putting up with my unpredictable moods, which shifted from glee to gloom, depending on the condition of my patients. She did all this with a mellow telephone voice---and only once, by her own admission, did she lose her cool completely with an obstreperous, intoxicated woman from Chippewa Falls. This unreasonable, demanding woman couldn't understand why I couldn't drop everything and call her immediately. Slamming the phone down with an uncharacteristic outburst of anger---the human Peggy was revealed.

Years later, our business management consultants advised us that it would be appropriate to include our wives on the payroll, helping to fund their personal I.R.A.'s. With parental small town integrity drummed into me, I'd never have done anything not strictly kosher in the eyes of the Internal Revenue Service. No problem! The compensation Peggy received was minimal for the many things she did to facilitate my comings and goings. Jubilant she was, doing cartwheels, when she received her first paycheck. Then we entered the realm of contentious labor relations. Just six months on the payroll, she began pouting and wondering, "Isn't it about time for me to get a raise?"

POTPOURRI:

Where you sense repetition in these musings, you must realize that the repetition may be purposeful---for better learning and retention. To repeat, it behooves us to remember that patients (and the people you meet every day, including family members) come in all sizes, shapes, ages, and temperaments. Again, the magic touch in our office was that patients sensed an acceptance of their individual idiosyncrasies, humorous or kinky. You would never forget Shirley---a fashion plate with hair swept up so high that birds might nest in it. Shirley was the personification of all who would protect body image at all costs, never wishing to be seen in disarray.

Shirley was a young woman, but had false teeth. Just why her teeth had been extracted at a young age is still a mystery. Whatever the reason, the secret of her false teeth was zealously guarded---never to be revealed. Patients facing surgery are required to remove rings, makeup, and dentures. Shirley was adamant. Digging in her heels, she must have bribed the anesthesiologist or entered into some private dispensation. At any rate, those dentures were in her mouth when Shirley went to the O.R. You've heard of the phrase, "As difficult as pulling teeth?" Well, 40-50 years ago, pulling teeth apparently wasn't that difficult. It may not have been commonplace, but many people sported false dentures, perhaps a mark of fashion. I was more than skeptical and felt that dental recommendations to remove teeth were too often imprecise, haphazard, and willy-nilly. "Got an infection somewhere in your body and the cause can't be found?" "Got a bad taste in your mouth?" I had the feeling that dental extractions were treated almost as part of the work-up just to see if it would help.

In the gentle art of communication and history taking, it's unsettling to find that there's a marked difference in how a phrase is intended and how it's received. In the process of interviewing an elderly gentleman, I simply asked in the vernacular, "Are these your own teeth?" His prompt reply, with a smirk, "You bet they are. I bought and paid for them."

Entering the urological system review, I asked the same witty gentleman, "Do you have to get up at night to pass your urine?"

"Nope," was the answer. "I keep a coffee can by my bed."

A case of one-upmanship: Offhandedly, as a part of my banter while examining an abdomen, I'd ask if the patient was aware of the purpose of the navel, the umbilicus, the belly-button. Routinely, they would profess total lack of knowledge on the subject. I would then illuminate them with this senseless drivel, "The purpose of the umbilicus is widely known as the repository for storing salt when you're eating celery in bed." That bit of doggerel had been repeated over and over, finally being accepted as gospel truth, at least the gospel according to Dr. H. From the most unlikely source can come the comeuppance. A petite, middle-aged woman was being seen in the office following abdominal surgery. I should have been suspicious of her intent because she was grinning from ear to ear as I pulled back the sheet covering her abdomen. There, glued carefully in the umbilicus, was a decorative mink fur piece. She was ebullient, "There are other purposes for the umbilicus." She won that day!

Who could forget or completely understand Ruby? Known as the "bird lady" because her back yard, filled with bird feeders, was home to thousands of birds, she was just as colorful as her birds---with bright-colored ribbons in her hair and non matching orange or yellow skirts. No question---Ruby had had a tough life. At age 83, that toughness may become your own worst enemy, because you may not be willing or able to recognize an illness when it comes knocking at your door. Ruby was always a smiling person and as chirpy as her birds, making it well nigh impossible to tell if she was in distress. Good Lord! On one occasion, we almost had to hogtie her to get her to the O.R., where we found a grossly distended gall bladder, ready to burst. Would you believe that that gall bladder was the size of a small watermelon? You say I'm exaggerating? Well, I did say "small." The imponderable question is why Ruby, with this inflammatory, surely painful mass would still be wanting to finish her housework?

Dear old Henry used to come to the waiting room door and call out, "Next." We were a step advanced, sending the nurse to the waiting room door to call for patients. Why the prolonged silence in the waiting room? The schedule was in longhand and not clear. In parentheses next to one smudged name was the reason for the visit---"mass in axilla." Now you can appreciate the silence which descended upon the waiting room---nobody responding---as the nurse called out in stentorian tone, "Moss Axilla --next."

After retirement, I wrote a monograph one morning at the kitchen table, dealing with the oh, so important communication between physician and patient. "How Do I Talk To My Doctor" was intended as a springboard for discussion in presentations to service clubs, church groups, and anybody who would listen. One evening, as people were making ready to leave, a very kind lady approached me with complimentary tone, "Oh, Dr. Hudson, you missed your calling." To this day, I regret my response, which was given before I got my brain into gear, "Do you say that I missed my calling because you just heard me speak or because you've seen my surgery?" She was, of course, flustered---and I had to do some backflips and mental gymnastics to retrieve the situation for her and myself.

In dealing with physicians' families, it was forcefully driven home to me always to treat the patient as a person, apart from the physician in the family. Donna, the wife of a physician, had had numerous visits with specialists in her unsuccessful search for any way to survive a breast malignancy with metastases. How well I remember her soft, plaintive, almost tearful voice as she confided in me one day, "Why is it that, when I see those doctors, they all talk to my husband---and not to me?" What a lesson!

Recipients of Meals on Wheels appreciate not just food---but the accompanying conversation

THOSE CANKER SORE BLUES

To bring sense to much of what occurs in our lives, I've subscribed to the consequences of natural law---whether that be divinely instituted or just "that's the way it is" If there should be a purpose for every event in our lives, then the purpose of canker sores surely would be the bestowing of humility and the teaching of patience. Had Ripley established a category for the most canker sores in one mouth at one time, I would have been the world's record holder.

Everybody yearns for a cure for the common cold. All the attention goes to the common cold---probably because of sheer numbers of those afflicted. Oh, how those common cold sufferers put on---with their whininess, sniffiness, stuffiness, and sneeziness. They look and act miserable, the wimps often staying home from work---bemoaning their fate whilst sipping soothing syrups such as Nyquil. In stark contrast, the ones with canker sores are the silent sufferers---stalwart, noble, stoic, always at work---but not smiling. Not smiling? Can't smile! Can't eat, talk, rinse, or romance.

It is said that the common cold, untreated, will wane in a week; with treatment, it will go away in 7 days. Just double those figures for the virulent canker sore. The cause---viral? Possibly, but most certainly egged on by the slightest insult to the oral mucosa---in a type-A personality. How else would canker sores know when it's final exam time?

The breast cancer genetic linkage is a mother/daughter thing. To my shame, the canker sore genetic linkage is a father/daughter thing. As I pity each daughter for her misfortuune at entering this gene pool, I sing the Canker Sore Blues---"Boo-hoo, it got you, too?"

Though interfering with sleep, study, dating, and drooling---canker sores are a source of delight for dentists and orthodontists, who prod, probe, and push cotton against the canker sores---then ask, "Does that hurt?" To my daughters, I've tried to put on the false front of encouragement and rationalization. Hang in there, girls. Remember, canker sores single out the intellectually brilliant--- and they won't be with you forever. Canker sores get tired too and seek out younger targets. Put on the armor of patience! If you last until age 70, you'll outlive the little beasties.

Tell me, why is it? Why is it that each daughter, especially when afflicted by those sadistic canker sores, hasn't bought into my weak and flimsy subterfuge?

A LETTER FROM THE OTHER SIDE

Have you ever gotten off on the wrong foot on first meeting a person? Welcome to the "foot in mouth" club. I'm here as living proof that when things start badly, it's yet possible that something can be retrieved---with life-long gratitude. As preface, I fear that I had become self-congratulatory in my self-assessment of my ability to communicate with patients. Thinking that I excelled, that I was right up there at the top, I was ripe for a fall. I felt so small and thoroughly taken aback when my best efforts were completely misinterpreted and rejected by a young woman with metastatic breast cancer.

I first met Betty in her hospital room on a Sunday morning---she having moved from Milwaukee, where she had been a concert violinist in the symphony. Her breast malignancy had been surgically treated by the outmoded, disfiguring radical mastectomy. With metastases demonstrated, she had been seeking many alternative treatments, including laetrile, an off-beat anti-cancer substance popularized in Mexico, but declared to be illegal by the Wisconsin Supreme Court. Few of us have a thermometer to determine the boiling point in another person. An innocent movement of my hands---it's well known that I can't talk without using my hands---caused an abrupt eruption. No, it was more like an explosion. Something snapped in this distraught young woman as she lashed out at me, "Don't wave your finger in my face. You're no different than all the other men. My father beat me. A male surgeon mutilated me. A male Supreme Court denied me my medication." Tears cascaded down her face.

Rapidly retreating, trying to re-group, and without hand motions, I started down the only path that seemed reasonable, given her obvious mistrust. Trying not to be too male, I sort of placed myself on her mercy with, "Betty, I guess we haven't had a very good start---and I'm sorry that I haven't come across very well. Maybe, if we start again, and if we promise to work together, we can find a way out of the woods." Thus was born a professional, but warm friendship which extended beyond her death. On several occasions, sometimes with Peggy along, I visited Betty in her home. It wasn't a matter of dementia or being drowned in medications when she described to me the angels around her bed. "Why, oh why," she wondered, "can't my Lutheran pastor see the angels?" It wasn't a matter of visual acuity. I had no trouble seeing the angels because it was just a simple extension of believing the patient. The patient has pain? Believe him/her. The patient sees angels? Try seeing through her eyes, with her understanding, with her hope. Then you, too, will be able to see what others can't see---if for no other reason than that Betty was seeing angels.

Although, in our initial meeting, Betty seemed so derisive of males in general, she wasn't without the strong support of her husband. After her death, he brought me an envelope unopened, addressed to me. To read words from beyond the grave carries haunting overtones, to be sure, but the words were Betty's. A reward far greater than money was bestowed by these words, "Thank you for coming to see me, for treating me like a person---and for seeing the angels."

DO I REALLY WANT
TO GET TO THAT OTHER SIDE?

In trying to explain why life, though boring it might have been, wasn't that bad---my mother relied on the old saying, "The pastures are always greener on the other side of the fence." From this distance, my mother truly was blessed with wisdom. Yes , pastures as seen from a distance are brilliantly verdant, but when we climb the fence, we so often encounter prickly weeds. What was verdant can become vile. Now, motherly wisdom was never intended to keep young ones close to the apron strings. Perhaps those words were just cautionary, envisioning times when the inevitable would come---we'd be on our own.

Perhaps, by now, you have realized that the determinant of what side you happen to be on depends largely on where the dividing line is placed---and on those who have established that dividing line. Sometimes artificial and arbitrary, dividing lines can serve to set one side against another. We may proclaim that we yearn to understand those on the other side---even as we grit our teeth and do everything possible to remain on our own side. We play games when we see others as on the other side. Unfortunately, playing games leads to feelings of superiority over the other side. Feelings of superiority naturally blend into efforts to persuade those on the other side to join us, to be more like us (the missionary principle).

In health care, ideally there would be no dividing lines---no sides. There would be only one abiding principle---the welfare and comfort of those who are hurting. Realistically, no health care worker can use the word "empathy" correctly unless pervaded by the same problems and torments of those on the other side. Health care workers, after all, are perfectly human, responding to injury just as everybody else in this vale of tears. When assaulted by injury to their own being, they experience an awakening, a dawning of what it means to walk in another's moccasins, to be on the other side.

In retirement, I have gained in visual acuity across that great divide. Frailties of the flesh have become rampant and have brought a stark realization of the view from the hospital bed. Prior to that time, singing the stalwart Esther theme song, "Perfect attendance forever---down with illness," I hadn't missed a day of work due to illness or injury in 32 years. To those who expressed amazement at such a record, I could offer only this weak reasoning, "First, I belonged to a fairly resilient gene pool. Second, I occasionally pursued good health practices, which others disputed. Third, I was a product of the snotty-nose generation, in which school children shared their germs and gained a lifelong fortress-like immunity. Lastly, and most importantly, I imbibed with generous doses of stupidity." Everyone indoctrinated in this stern work ethic, and falling victim to being over-impressed with their personal importance to the success of any given project, has shared in this stupidity---refusing to acknowledge not feeling well, working when wounded, etc.

In 1995, some of my golfing buddies and all of my family described, in snickering tones, that my walking was a copy of a duck waddle. Blissfully unaware was I, but children will tell it just as it is. One day, in the parking lot of Hillcrest Golf & Country Club, I became aware of three little granddaughters following Grandpa across the parking lot, walking just like ducks. Children are honest. Children are forthright. Children have no qualms about asking, "Grandpa, what is that bump on your forehead?" or "Why do you walk like a duck?" X-rays revealed the worst set of arthritic degenerated hips that I or my orthopedic surgeon friend had ever seen. Fortunately for the lame, we now have almost an inexhaustible supply of spare body parts. Without too much flourish, a right total hip replacement was accomplished. Still in the Esther mode, I strove to be the gold star on the forehead, pain tolerant patient. Hallelujah! I received A+ in physiotherapy and was playing golf in 6 weeks.

Although my gait now was said to resemble remotely the walk of a human being, you can't take the waddle out of the duck by giving it just one artificial hip. After a brief hiatus, the discomfort ("pain" wasn't to be found in my vocabulary) and the waddle gradually re-surfaced and led to the decision for left total hip replacement---just after our 50th wedding anniversary.

Somewhere along the line, whether it was at home, in school, or in church---we were warned that "into each life some rain must fall." O.K. That's life---but does it have to be torrential downpours? Encountering post-operative hip dislocation, five subsequent surgeries, intensive care, renal shutdown, and septic shock due to infection---it finally was thrust through my brain barrier that the Philistines were winning the battle and that small opening leading to the other side was looming larger. Ah, survival reigned---gained by months of I.V. antibiotics, in spite of having no hip for 4 months. Try picturing the hospital bed in our living room and Peggy forced into getting her nursing degree on the job.

That tenacity for life, that remains undiminished even unto death, brought me back to the golf course, where camaraderie hath no equal. Buoyed by pars, occasional birdies, and the 19th hole, life regained composure. Yes, life was indeed good on this side! In theological jargon, Heaven may be my home, but I just wasn't homesick. There's more---the torrential rainy season wasn't over. In the summer of 2001, there probably were warning signs of weakness and discomfort on walking. My golfing buddy, Darrel, and Peggy apparently had better vision, both of them saying, in retrospect, that they had seen the warning signs clearly. However, once again the stupid stoic, determined and resolute (more acceptable words than "stubborn"), was totally unaware of such things until Dec.

5, 2001--when golfing was curtailed and crutches became not just fashionable, but necessary again. With some urgency, an MRI revealed a profound spinal stenosis---a bony encroachment on the spinal cord, which leads to paralysis unless surgically relieved. Here I was again, caught out in that torrential downpour without protective rain gear. The only refuge nearby was the O.R., where a decompression lumbar laminectomy immediately relieved the pain.

Well into recovery, naturally insisting, "No big deal," I awaited the coming golf season, mistakenly firm in the belief that my golf game would improve because my golf swing now would be slower and more deliberate. Wow! This journey from one side to the other takes a person over some rocky, bumpy roads. I've now decided that I'll just straddle the dividing line for a while, in awe and appreciation of everything and everybody around me. I've always been aware that I can be comfortably alone in a crowd. Yet it's lonely in this straddling position, everybody else appearing to be on some other side.

THE LONELINESS OF
BEING A FAMILY MEMBER

A revelation descendeth! A startling eye-opener! It's one thing to be the model patient on the other side---it's a whole new world to be on yet another side as a family member of someone having a battle with the Philistines.

Harken back to the Peggy woes when Crohn's disease was a surprise finding at exploratory surgery. Imagine, if you can, how she co-existed with this inflammatory bowel disease for 13 years---sometimes helped, sometimes hurt by medications. Prednisone (cortisone), in long term dosage, can be a crippler. Trying so hard to be the "good" patient, Peggy deplored the "cortisone dance" and the profound weakness. Something surely must be wrong when weakness makes climbing stairs laborious and falling or nearly falling becomes commonplace. During that travail, Henry Stengel was so solicitous, never failing to inquire about Peggy's health. In Henry's declining years, I believe that our clinical conversations would bring Henry back to his own clinical years, giving him a sense of purpose, perking him up. In characteristic Henry fashion, he would hold forth with wisdom, "Ya know, Peggy shouldn't be taking that much prednisone." Now, with a bit of Henry in me, I say unto you, "Ya know, the great one was right."

A promising new I.V. infusion medication, Remicade, initially was effective in alleviating abdominal symptoms. What was promising and hopeful, however, turned out to be highly allergic---dangerously allergic. With medical management now limited to measures for symptomatic relief, surgical resection of the localized Crohn's disease was recommended and Peggy, with combined trepidation and hope, put on the armor for her battle with the Philistines. When I was an orthopedic patient, I easily could be relaxed and accepting, non-critical of orthopedic management. After all, as said before, I didn't know that much about orthopedic surgery, which I thought was anatomical carpentry. It was easy, then, just to trust those surgeons who spent their time in joints. My problem as a family member? The intestinal surgery which Peggy faced was squarely in my field of expertise---and there I was on the periphery, looking in.

From this peripheral vantage point, I became restive as the surgery approached 3 hours. My surgical clock was telling me that, were I the surgeon, the operation would have been brought to closure in 1-1/2 hours. Peggy now has great hope for a future free of obstructing Crohn's disease---but the getting there has encountered a few obstacles. Who among you has ever had a naso-gastric tube in place? Only those answering in the affirmative could empathize with 14 days of naso-gastric suction. Bless that nurse who finally offered some throat lozenges. Bless the person who instituted total parenteral nutrition by vein so that Peggy could weather the storm of negative nitrogen balance. After so many days in the doldrums of ingesting no food or fluids orally, Peggy now is learning to eat again---just as a person, bed-ridden for months, may have to learn to walk again.

We are never too old to learn. I offer you some insights into things that I learned, from another side, during Peggy's ordeal:

1. A lesson, learned from Henry decades ago was brought home to me. When I was age 18, during our trip to Freeport Deaconess Hospital to observe an abdominal operation, Henry impressed me that both he and the surgeon would be much more at ease when they had a chance to get closer to the problem. There seemed to be a sense of urgency. With that same sense of urgency, I recall awakening and worrying about patients in Eau Claire. I couldn't wait to get to the hosital to see for myself what the prob-

lem might be. It's just that I felt better when I personally could see the patient, feel the pulse. Now, during those dragging days of naso-gastric suction, I found myself reliving the lesson, arising at 5:00 a.m., driving over to the hospital so I could see Peggy myself---and feel the pulse.

2. When physicians and nurses suggest, in the face of adversity, "We'll just have to be patient," it strikes me that the "we'll" in that phrase is nebulous and well nigh meaningless. After all, physicians and nurses go about their duties, seeing other patients, spending time with family, getting rest. Patience isn't even operative with them. Guess who that leaves to be patient? Appropriately named "patient," the patient is the only one who has to endure the annoyances and torment 24 hours a day, hoping to see light at the end of the tunnel.

3. Surgeons, being human, are capable of having ruffled feathers on occasions. Medical clinics and hospitals proclaim by pamphlets and wall plaques that they would be as nothing without the patient. Patients and families are urged to be a part of decision making. In spite of all those high-sounding and selfless declarations, we found that simple comments, questions, or suggestions were sometimes met with reluctance and defensiveness.

4. It's no secret that health care costs are skyrocketing, threatening the national economy. More discussion of escalating costs will be found elsewhere. Hospitals may be cost-conscious in certain areas, but we were exposed to the ridiculous. With a $32,000 hospital bill, how much was saved by providing the lowest cost, raspiest facial tissues? Tender nostrils needing soft tissues, we did the common sense thing, bringing in our own supply.

5. A lesson of monumental proportions! We treat others so casually, perhaps taking them for granted until a catastrophe forces us once again to appreciate their real worth.

THE MALE CURSE

When standing in awe of creation, I instinctively think more of blessings than of curses. This house we live in temporarily is a blessing and is marvelously constructed. Indeed, it is miraculous that combinations of cells and systems produce a living, breathing, vibrant, thinking organism---mobile, feeling, and rhythmic---with built in waste management and reproduction potential.

Assaults on this wonderful body are seen variably by people with different vision. To some, an assault is a hurt---to others, an opportunity; to some, disability---while others claim the time for service; to some, a hindrance---to others, only a time of testing; to some, a curse---to others, a blessing. Is it just semantics? Actually, terms and phrases are often descriptive and find their place in folklore by common acceptance. It wasn't uncommon for me to hear about the "female curse"---encompassing the woes, both physical and emotional, of the menopause. Physiological hormonal decline brings a mixture of joy and sadness at the cessation of those cyclical bloody tears of a disappointed uterus. The evidence of non-fertility is greeted by many with a sense of relief; by those who haven't borne children, there may be a sense of finalization and frustration. No individual can withstand the passage of time!

Whether or not "the curse" is proper terminology, menopausal changes occur at an age when, physiologically, women can handle almost any onslaught without blinking. Difficult for men to accept is the documented truth that females are physically and emotionally more resilient than males---from birth until death. Have you recently checked out the female:male ratio in the above-90 group?

Now, let us give heed to the "male curse," the prostate out of control. All right, class, it's p-r-o-s-t-a-t-e, not p-r-o-s-t-r-a-t-e, a pronunciation too often heard. "Prostrate" may be prophetic, but grossly inaccurate. In sharp contrast to the "female curse," the "male curse" arises at a time of physical decline and weakness---when a strong wind might blow over the vulnerable male who isn't well planted. In the urinary waste management department, women have long felt that they were short-changed because they were provided only one muscular sphincter to clamp down on the flow of urine. On the other side, men have been endowed with two such muscular sphincters. At first glance, this insurance against incontinence would seem to be a boon---but, for the male, the curse isn't so much the lack of control as it is that the water faucet won't even turn on.

The creator surely bestowed a blessing on urologists by tunneling the urethral tube, draining the bladder, through the prostate gland. With prostatic enlargement of aging, the urethral tube is squeezed upon and choked off. There's no avoiding it. It's an awful reality! Sleep is often interrupted by getting up to void. Sleeplessness may be a bother, but worse than the bother is the worry, "Will I ever get back to bed?"

I anticipate, not with glee, moving to the other side of the prostatic enlargement and urinary slowing dilemma. The dividing line, prostatically speaking, is a narrow yellow stream. In urinary problems, if you wish to stay on one side, you become adept at moving the dividing line and thus resisting the inevitable. Actually, I've taken one hesitant step toward the other side with a biopsy discovered focus of low grade malignancy.

In medical school and residency training, the subject of prostate malignancy was far too casual. It was generally felt that all men would develop prostatic malignancy if they lived long enough, but no big deal! They simply would die of other causes. What a great awakening, a rude awakening, to find that cancer is an animal with different coats and colors. A dormant mild prostate cancer may be a dream, never really changing your life. But! There's a wild, virulent prostate cancer, which produces nightmares. My brother, 10 years older than I, was tangled up with the wild type and died with a slow, miserably uncomfortable last year of life. How's that for family history? It's grabbed my attention.

At the present, I bask in the belief that prostate malignancy and I will coexist amiably---with mutual respect. The reality? Who knows? To be on the safe side, I plan to stay on good terms with my urologist friend---the physician who is justifying benign neglect toward my malignancy with the condescending introducer, "At your age. . ."

HOW BLESSED TO HAVE QUALITY CONSULTANTS

Although family practitioners have the awesome obligation to have an acquaintance with every aspect of medicine, they don't have to have the expertise to handle the more complicated problems. With the broadening scope of medical needs, one person simply can't handle everything. Gone are the days when old Doc Smith knew everything, could do everything. Likewise, surgeons don't have to be everything to everybody, possessing knowledge about every complication imaginable. As an aside, it was unnerving, on surgical board exams, to be presented with question after question about cardio-vascular, pulmonary, and renal complications---in detail---and almost as if we wouldn't have consultation available. The paradox arose, realizing that the questioners would be highly critical of us if we didn't use the expertise of consultants.

Two consultants, arriving in Eau Claire long after I started practice, were God-sends, easing the burden on my shoulders. One was a gastro-enterologist who, with endoscopic expertise, could manage gastro-intestinal bleeding---more precisely determining the need and the timing of surgery. The other God-send was an internal medicine intensivist, an uncanny diagnostician, who was available at all hours. More important to me than the light he brought to vexing problems was his graciousness. An example: A carpenter had been seen earlier in the evening in the E.R. complaining of chest pain. The history was confusing, but there was a possibility that, in pounding a nail, a metal fragment had struck his chest wall. However, there appeared nothing visible except for a small bloody indent on the skin. He was sent home by his family physician only to return a couple of hours later, still quite uncomfortable.

I was called to examine him and felt he should be hospitalized for observation, still confused about the diagnosis.
Oh, yes. A chest x-ray showed a small metallic fragment within the chest cavity.

It wasn't that we weren't aware of that metallic fragment. It's just that there wasn't any pressing need to go after it. After all, it could have been the needle in the haystack. About midnight, the night nurse called with concerns about a falling blood pressure. I asked the internal medicine specialist to consult and he was soon there---johnny on the spot. On careful examination, he found the clues that led him to a correct diagnosis of pericardial tamponade. Yes, in this freak injury, the metallic fragment had nicked the heart, with resultant collection of blood under pressure in the pericardium, the membranous sac around the heart. The O.R. crew was called and surgical correction of the tamponade was achieved before sunrise. When I expressed chagrin that I hadn't tumbled to the possibility of tamponade, the consultant was so gracious, pointing out the obvious---that this wasn't a set of circumstances which we saw every day.

ON THE JOYS OF VISITING THE SICK

It matters not whether the patient's bed is in the hospital, the nursing home, or his/her own home. It matters not whether the care is acute, chronic, or somewhere in between. The common bond is that patients are temporarily or permanently not the same person they once were.

Every health care facility I have visited, be it clinic, hospital, or nursing home has declared that its mission is totally for the good of the patient. If mission statements are to be believed and, knowing that patients are exposed and vulnerable, wouldn't it behoove us to help, not hurt the patient in our visits, our attempts to support?

Whether physician, nurse, clergy, family, or friend---I've seen the good and the bad when each of these has entered the patient's room. Some groups do it just right. For instance, the ostomy support groups send visitors into patients' rooms only after specific, intensively appropriate training and with the permission of the patients. Enlightened clergy, definitely not all clergy, also have had lessons in how to modify messages and approaches to and for the sick. Yes, visitation can be so encouraging and strengthening to the spirit, but it can backfire when motivation is centered more on the visitor than on the visited.

As with almost every other subject in these writings, you are referred to the Claymore College archives for more complete disclosure of my feelings on this sensitive topic. Whether visitors are motivated by biblical obligation or simply by feelings of concern, there are some guideposts which will help to protect patients' rights and privacy. You might consider the following comments or suggestions:

1. If you are uneasy and find certain odors and

sights to be unsettling in a health care facility, isn't it likely that those conditions aren't easy for the patient either?

2. Always check with nursing staff before visiting. It might not be the best time to visit because of change in condition or need for rest.

3. Always read signs as if they were intended for you. If the sign indicates, "Family only, please," don't assume that the restriction couldn't apply to you, that special friend.

4. In general, don't stay long in acute care situations. Patients instinctively will try to be host or hostess and they may tire easily.

5. If the door is closed, it may be for a purpose. Knock first! There may be a commodial occasion. Testing or treatment procedures may be in process. Maybe the patient is sleeping.

6. You don't know what to say? Send cards or flowers. Flowers are a wonderful expression of caring, which the patient can see all day long and not once wish they would leave.

7. Don't submit the patient to an inquisition. "My dear, what do the doctors say is wrong with you?" Most patients are too reticent to tell the truth, "That's none of your business."

8. If you enter a two-bed room, be ever so considerate of the other patient. A drawn curtain doesn't shut out conversation.

9. Be considerate of full bladders.

10. Be not the visitor who delights in giving unsolicited advice---"Don't you know you should. . .?"

11. Finally, grandpas and grandmas all will tell you that their most special treasures are those crayon cards that Hallmark can never match.

After many years of hearing patients' deepest secrets, I've seen and heard the gamut of hospital visitation stories---some humorous, some horror laden. Much of the problem, I believe, lies in the uneasiness with which most people approach those who are different---and illness is different. Whatever! The worst example of visitor invasion---a true story---was the visitor who found out that the patient's diagnosis was "carrot disease." What followed was unforgivable. "Carrot disease? Wow! My Aunt Hepzibah had carrot disease and she died."

Do you suppose that the Golden Rule was written for visitors of the sick?

An afterthought: Take special care to embrace the Golden Rule when visiting the one, old in body and spirit, who wishes to die. You're uncomfortable? Possibly, by listening to the story of Ken, you'll find the strength to understand and to help the lonely and discouraged.

Ken was no different from all of those before him and after him---he really once had a life. As a young man, he had natural baseball talent, pitching himself into a professional contract. Polio took away his fastball and curveball, but not his wit and change of pace. When he retired from the Uniroyal tire plant, he became a friend of squirrels---humoring them, talking to them, feeding them peanuts. Is it possible that, in Ken, I saw a vision of my own old age---alone, talking to squirrels?

Years passed in which Ken didn't call---he was a considerate man, didn't want to be a bother. Then, after my retirement, Ken's daughter called, asking me if I'd visit her father in the nursing home. Her words were compelling, "Dad is so discouraged and he thinks that you're the only doctor who knows anything." Doing a quick, quasi-professional assessment of Ken's condition, it was obvious why he was so unhappy. His mobility was gone, he was age 94, he was incontinent, he couldn't eat, he wanted to leave this world.

Yes, the first line of attack, of course, would be to try to improve his physical well-being, but all efforts to put the brakes on his physical decline had been unrewarding. What, then, about his spirit? A solid rule: If a person expresses the wish to die, don't take him/her down by lecturing, "Don't talk like that!" In such tones, you become chiding and critical, not understanding---even though you may intend to be encouraging. Gradually, I eased the conversation with, "Ken, I understand why you want to die. What do your kids say?" "They say I'm going to live a long time---and I should eat." Obviously, this is exactly what he didn't want to hear---plus the fact that he simply didn't want to eat.

As I held his hand that day, I left him with this thought, "Tell you what, Ken. I'll rejoice with you when you're feeling better---even if that means death. But for now, I want you to know how good it is just to see you, to talk to you." Ken's family listened to my advice, appropriating my words as their own, and were able to give their father permission to leave. The bottom line of visitation is seen in Ken's story---that the motivation be to help the visited, not the visitor.

LEARNING---A YEARNING
NOT CONFINED TO THE CLASSROOM

Call it insatiable curiosity. Call it nosiness about others' lives. Whatever you call it, learning is a part of our very being from the time we're born until the time we die---and even then we may continue to learn on the other side. The teaching profession's greatest reward, it seems to me, is that many of us have remembered our favorite teachers---teachers who have influenced us through the years. Never having met him, of course, I still harken to the words of the wise Dr. William Osler, who counselled his medical students, "If you're alert and listening, you'll learn from even the most unlikely sources."

Indeed, learning has to be a way of life. You must be programmed early to enjoy new opportunities, new vistas. I treasure a compliment from nurses and technicians in our O.R., telling me that every surgery was a teaching and learning experience. Among obstacles to learning, perhaps the greatest obstacle is a know-it-all attitude, a stubborn resistance to change. It shouldn't be, but there can emerge a subtle danger in formal professional training. In certain students, with graduate level education, there may develop insidiously a feeling of superiority and invincibility. Again, it shouldn't be, but therein is the birth of the physician who begins to project the image, "I'm the doctor and I know best." Too bad. So sad!

Let us sit at the feet of Dr. Osler again. His unusual wisdom is seen in his insistence that the patient is the physician's ultimate teacher. I have found it to be thus---and much of what I have written surely reflects this.

THE COST! THE COST!

First, a true story: It was our first year in Eau Claire and the medical/surgical practice was growing slowly---at what seemed to be a snail's pace. When I was asked to visit an elderly lady in Eleva, about 15 miles south of Eau Claire, I jumped at the chance. It was a fact---during those days, there was ample time to do such simple things. Mrs. F. was obviously very sick, suffering from an advanced stomach cancer---and her outlook seemed hopeless. However, her daughter hoped that I might be able to help her in some way, perhaps bringing something new to the table.

On cursory examination, it was apparent that Mrs. F. wouldn't live long. Yet, she was happy to see me and I did my best to give her a sense of importance, perhaps making her day little happier. Before leaving, I gave her a narcotic injection and wrote a prescription. I thought little about that house call until near the time of my retirement when Sylvia, Mrs. F.'s daughter. came to my office and said, "Here, I think you should have this." Bless her! All those years, she had saved the receipted bill for services, which read:

House call---Eleva, Wisconsin

Examination, prescription, injection $6.00

Together, we smiled and shared the memory, mindful of how that bill compares with the present runaway escalating health care costs.

Now, an imaginary tale: Zeke was a grizzled and skeptical old farmer. One day, he decided he'd visit the new young physician in town---sort of to check him out. The neophyte gave Zeke a most thorough exam, complete with some lab tests and an electrocardiogram. When Zeke received the bill for services, he was outraged and stomped into the doctor's office. "Your bill be a might high, doctor." The doctor's reply as he pointed to his diploma and all the equipment in the office, "Well, Zeke, you see that diploma on the wall, documenting my training, and all this high priced equipment? Somebody has to pay for these things." Pondering slowly, with his hands in his pockets, Zeke muttered, "But---all by myself?"

Whether true or imaginary, increasing concerns about health care costs created the atmosphere which gave birth to the "managed care" concept. I think I was a prophet. It's certainly been borne out that "managed care" has had more to do with money than with care. Although embraced enthusiastically by the business community as a cost-saving competition model, it completely missed the point. Health care just isn't a product like a refrigerator or a loaf of bread. When this marvelous, but vulnerable human body falls into disrepair, there are unleashed emotions, feelings, and vagaries---which just aren't a part of buying a loaf of bread. When emotions and feelings weigh in upon us, the urge for bargain hunting is invariably set aside.

As a generalization, merger mania in health care has created large corporate providers of care. In true corporate fashion, personal attention to patients' needs has too often been downsized to protect the bottom line---the almighty dollar. It was predictable! The business model has prevailed, especially in metropolitan areas---with exorbitant CEO salaries and bonuses. Meanwhile, an insidious and odious business reality has crept in. The word filters down to the treating physicians, employees of the corporation, "Your income, you know, is increased with a lessening of services and consultations available to patients." I see this as scary. As part of the business model, we now hear of providers, consumers, and a product---rather than physicians, patients, and health care. You say it's just semantics? To me, it's detestable and onerous.

Several decades ago, stimulated by the rising costs even then, I wrote a newspaper opinion piece, listing many of the reasons for increased costs. My central thrust was, "It's going to get worse before it gets better." Again, I was a prophet. With almost unbelievable annual increases in health care insurance premiums---35% to 50% this year in Eau Claire---it's obvious to everybody but the gullible that it's not getting better yet.

I hope that I'm not seen as an incurable alarmist nor to be found wandering around aimlessly and clucking, "The sky is falling." It seems to me, however, that any rational person would have real concerns. If increases in health care costs go unchecked or unchallenged, there certainly will be a negative effect on our economy as labor negotiations will be bogged down, leading to higher costs of products. Mind-boggling, to me, is that I'm not hearing the pertinent questions on the national level:

1. Why ARE health care costs so high?

2. Are we perhaps receiving more health care than we need?

Who bears the responsibility for these high costs? Obviously, both the health care system and the general public have to share responsibility or blame. How often have you heard, when health is critical, "To Hell with the cost---we want the best." There must come the time when we'll all have to take a hard look at the reasons for high health care costs---and make difficult decisions as to what we need and what we might discard. At least, we could try. Think with me about the following topics, all of which should come to the table for discussion.

1. A burgeoning technology certainly has been the principal factor in driving health care costs, but technology can be a two-edged sword. You will find no one who doesn't appreciate and value technology which has brought us more comfort and mobility. In an entrepreneurial nation, however, the clamor for newer, more intricate technology may be more profit-motivated than patient-motivated. I hear you saying, "Well, this is a free enterprise capitalistic system, which has given us many life-saving advances." You are right, of course, but new tech-

nology is ballyhooed with lobbying and advertising because of the profit motive. Furthermore, there should be continuing ethical discussions looming when technology, with its potential for keeping people alive, does little more than prolong the dying process---at great cost.

2. If you've been a patient, you should be able to identify much duplication and waste. Have you ever known a hospital administration that didn't bemoan the lack of profit? Yet in spite of claims that money is scarce, we see continuing expensive building and program expansion---whether or not new programs may duplicate what already is provided by other hospitals. Hospitals have "spin doctors," usually known as public information specialists, who explain that each and every expansion is done only for the benefit of patients and the community. Who do you think pays for all these building expansions? You're right if you say, "The patient." Yet, in spite of annual increases in room rates and allied costs, there will be the predictable public fund appeals.

3. Health care always has been acutely labor intensive, but it seems more so with technology spreading into more specialized areas. Health care is one of the few disciplines which requires 7 day/week and 24 hours/day coverage. This coverage isn't limited to nurses and aides, but extends to other treatment areas such as pharmacy, rehabilitation, intensive care, physiotherapy, dialysis, etc., etc. It's difficult to foresee anything that can or should be done to change the necessary level of personnel charged with direct care of patients.

4. Many years ago, it seems eons, the physician and nurse were the sole providers of care. Remember Henry, my venerable mentor? Henry had an office practice with no nurse, receptionist, X-ray or lab tech, or billing clerk. For all I know, maybe Henry swept out the place, too. With increasing complexity of treatment and greater possibilities of helping patients, the physician is surrounded by X-ray and lab techs, physiotherapists, occupational therapists, speech therapists, psychologists, nurse

practitioners, geneticists, programmers, transcriptionists, etc.--- and of course, the hundreds of workers employed in the business management. As an aside, and this just won't go away, some of this delegation of responsibility has been due to or resulted in physician abdication of some meaningful dialogue with patients. Without documentation, it appears to me that each physician now is surrounded by 10-15 employees. Many ancillary services bill separately for what they do---but there are many other services which are part of what the physician charges. This accounts for what, on the surface, appear to be exorbitant physician charges---charges, incidentally, which are reduced markedly by government contracts of Medicare and Medicaid. That's another ball game in which the rules are laid down by those same governmental organizations---capriciously.

5. Although designed admirably to reduce the risk of infection, disposable products are terribly expensive and often wasteful. I'll even acknowledge that the numbers-crunchers on the hospital staff will somehow justify the avalanche of disposable equipment as cost-effective, but it just doesn't equate with common sense. It seems that, for every procedure, there's a disposable tray---much of the contents of said tray not even used in the procedure---but adding to the earth's waste heap.

6. You've probably heard the recurring discussions about the role of litigation in increasing health care cost. This discussion often spills over into the political arena, with trial lawyers and insurance companies going at it. Partly because of the public's love affair with technology and unrealistic expectations, we live in a time when "nothing should go wrong." Part of this unreal expectation, strangely, is because of the excellence of care, which has increased life expectancy and given greater mobility and comfort to patients. Because of the recognized excellence and promise of life, the public has difficulty understanding results which seem to fall short. For whatever reason, whether it be ambulance-chasing trial lawyers or

an unrealistic utopia-seeking public, we are suffering some of the consequences of "nothing should go wrong."

Obviously, worry about making a mistake can lead to exhaustive diagnostic workups, with imaging CT scans and MRI's adding greatly to costs. Alas, the feeling that "I can't make any mistake" tends to throw common sense out the window. My brother, a brilliant law school professor, used to delight in goading me with questions about "defensive medicine." My brother tended to win every argument---at least, in his opinion. Yet, he gained points when he would insist, "Forget defensive medicine. The question is whether or not it's the right medicine---and, if it's not right, then the physician isn't true to his profession."

Does every headache need a CT scan? Of course not! Yet---one headache subsequently found to be due to a brain tumor or vascular malformation and a CT scan wasn't done? There has just been created fertile ground for a lawsuit.

7. Pharmaceutical costs have experienced a staggering climb. It's a mystery to me that legislators and other supposedly intelligent parties debate whether, how, or why to give prescription drug coverage---but nobody bothers to ask the most vital question, "Why are drug costs so high?" That's a discussion that would take several more chapters, but someone, somewhere should at least be stirring the waters of discussion. It has become a political football! As such, when it becomes political, the public is held captive to extensive lobbying by for-profit corporations; clever, but misleading advertising with the likes of Harry and Louise. Again, this is a free enterprise nation and pharmaceutical companies are prime players. Yes, we are told over and over, we are a people blessed by pharmaceutical companies and their research and development of new drugs. We're told very little about the availability of less expensive generic medication, about excessive marketing techniques, which provide perks (bribes?) to physicians.

The magic words, intended to obligate a willing public, are "research and development." We are the leaders of the world, beating the bushes for remedies which will benefit the diseased, the infirm, the downtrodden. Sounds downright humanitarian, doesn't it? Why, there's hardly any consideration of corporate profit or stockholder welfare. Let us, at the outset, be grateful for those medications which have come on the scene, especially in the area of oncology medications. However, be ye not fooled entirely by "research and development." The great preponderance of new drugs coming to the marketplace are "me-too" drugs---drugs which merely do the same thing as other drugs already available---drugs which generally are less expensive. You've seen the direct advertising campaign, "Ask your doctor if this is the right drug for you?" What's common to most of those heavily advertised drugs is that they're expensive, but if people can get hooked on them, it's worth the advertising cost. Even while we're grateful for promising new medications, let's not lose sight of the fact that the research and development budget is far outstripped by the marketing budget, which still includes amazing perks for physicians---and nurses.

8. Our increasing life span obviously is a humongous factor in increasing demands on the health care system. Weighing costs against what may not be meaningful life is touchy, to say the least. "Meaningful" is highly subjective and not easily defined. Should costs be saved by not giving as much care in futile situations? That, again, is a very personal question. Peggy and I have attempted to answer the imponderable question by including in our directions to power of attorney for health care matters, "When there is no hope of recovery, no tubes and no resuscitation---and, in addition, we would ask that money be a definite factor." In other words, we believe that $50,000 spent on our care in the last 2-3 weeks could be better applied to grandchildren's education. At last, a solution. A clever wag has opined, "Since 50% of health care costs are incurred in the last year of life, we could save 50% by

just eliminating the last year of life."

9. It bears saying again! In health care, we have become more and more procedurally oriented. Think on these procedures: joint replacement, organ transplantation, ocular lens implants, coronary artery bypass and angioplasty, cardiac pacemakers, respirator management, intensive care and E.R. resuscitation, neonatal support, computerized guidance in imaging and in surgery, bone marrow transplants---and this is a partial list. What is common to all these procedures? Not one was available when I started surgical practice in 1958---and all are very high tech, high-cost. I think you'll agree, with the benefit coming from these procedures, that we won't retreat from these advances, regardless of the cost.

10. It's well nigh inescapable that, at some time, high costs of health care will force this nation to revisit the discussion of how we should finance health care. Unfortunately, whenever a national health plan of any description is envisioned, there is always the boogey-man connotation of "socialized medicine" lurking in the shadows. Consider history! In my medical school days, "socialized medicine" was akin to communism---or so said the A.M.A. Think with me. Would it not have been better all along to think not of "socialized medicine" but of social medicine, that which wouldn't leave anybody out, that which would envision what might be best for everybody?

Sometimes I'm confused by religious zealots and politicians who pontificate that this nation is blessed to be a Christian nation---under God. The last time I talked with God and discussed the Jesus principle, there was great concern over millions of people without adequate health insurance---or access to care. Possibly, the ho-hum attitude toward the poor and unfortunate may be the same as my mother's philosophy toward squirrels. She essentially said, "Good squirrels get their nuts in for the winter. If others don't succeed in nut gathering, are too lazy, or even too sick---tough luck." It suddenly occurs to me that the definition of Christian may even be subjective.

You'd think that business-savvy folks, aghast at escalating health care costs, would be even more aghast at the middle man insurance companies, which carve 20-25% up front out of the health care premiums. You'd think that physicians would be up in arms at interference in the physician-patient relationship---and there is evidence that this is coming about. Yes, you'd think that all parties would realize that a national health plan would help to control costs, increase access to care, and protect the physician and patient. Will there be opposition? Yes! There are devout ideologues, who hate government---who fail to appreciate government as the way in which we do things together. Then there will be the vested interests that would lose huge sums of money, namely the insurance companies. Threatened with losses, they will, as in the past, mount huge advertising campaigns to confuse the issue, to distort, to scare, all to protect their turf. Idealism, with which I entered the medical field, is still alive. Ideally, a national health plan would allow, perhaps force, all parties to sit around a table, with give and take to determine just what, realistically and socially responsibly, their share of the pie should be.

Those who had the rare privilege of knowing Henry J. Stengel, M.D., will surely recognize that many of the thoughts I have presented herein were previously propounded in one way or another by Henry. He was, indeed, a pioneer and a visionary in his own way in a small town.

Henry J. Stengel, M.D.

THE NATURE OF HEALING---???

Really, the precise nature of healing, what facilitates it or how it occurs, is a mystery even in the here and now. Throughout history, in awe and wonderment, the human species has looked to every conceivable means to drive the demons out. Sometimes herbs, the forerunner of modern medications, have been used to alleviate suffering and to promote well being. Not necessarily as a last resort, the deities have even been invoked, by prayer or incantations, to intervene for the good of the faithful.

In low-tech days, practitioners such as old Henry recognized their limitations. Furthermore, they recognized that healing is a natural phenomenon and that the art of healing is to be found in the one who somehow can instill in the patient a calm and the anticipation that healing can actually occur if we will allow it. Henry's black medical bag contained many vials of variably colored pills (I always suspected that they were just different colors of aspirin). Most importantly! Henry's black bag contained ample doses of that precious fluid---tincture of TIME---patience.

In high tech days, nothing much has changed. The nature of healing remains the same and its vagaries are still imponderable. A notable difference is that Henry's black bag now contains precision tools and computerized imaging devices. Is there a problem in such advances? Amen! Whenever mankind makes great advances in understanding, there is a sense of smugness---the feeling that we've finally arrived at the zenith---that there's nothing beyond. When this occurs, technology can become the focus of worship and wonderment, not the awe-inspiring healing process. When this occurs, we lose sight of where we've been and where we can yet go. Now, this is sadness.

In every generation, there are external influences

which have both implemented and amplified the hope of healing. There is that common thread, weaving through the generations, the partnership of the mind and spirit---always involved in helping a person to overcome, to heal. There is no doubt in my mind that there is "cure by suggestion." Anybody who is skeptical of that---maybe that person just doesn't get it. A perfect example is the cessation of crying and the total change in outlook when a child's "owies" are kissed by the mother. Another example, closer to the adult understanding, is the suggestion, implanted by a pleasant, smiling nurse who passes medications with the hope, "Here, this will make you feel better."

A light turned on! IF nobody really understands the exact nature of healing, or how and why it occurs, why should we then look askance or get our noses out of joint at any alternative approach to healing? Acupuncture, naturopathy, prayer, faith healing, chiropractic---what have you? The list is long, all with devotees who tend to develop a missionary zeal. 40-50 years ago, mainstream medicine fiercely resisted alternative healing concepts. This was tantamount to proclaiming to the world that, "If we can't do it, nobody can." Big problem! The resistance, well financed, seemed to spring more from a desire to protect turf and income than some humanitarian impulse. The rallying cry, of course, was that these resistance efforts were somehow to protect patients. Gradually, in the last two decades, there has been more acceptance of alternative care concepts. The proof of this acceptance is seen in insurance coverage for alternative care. Most striking is the inclusion of alternative care practitioners right within medical clinics.

I hesitate to invoke an overused word but, in my opinion, the word is used properly in describing the mystery of healing, which will come to all of us if we will allow it---AWESOME!

A TIME FOR REFLECTION

Wise, indeed, are the parents who realize that their children's futures are determined not just by parental guidance, but also by the influence of significant others. Surely, if you now re-read the dedication to Henry J. Stengel, M.D, you will recognize a seed implanted. As you've followed my description of a medical odyssey, you perhaps have seen Henry's threads woven into my fabric.

Henry was a graduate of Loyola Medical School in Chicago, returning to his home town to begin his medical practice. Choice of doctor in the Hudson family was given to my mother---and Esther was a bit disapproving of Henry because he was known to play the ponies occasionally at Arlington Park racetrack. My close encounter with Henry at the time of my close encounter with the pneumonia angel in 8th grade, therefore, was obviously dictated by Dr. Dumont's unavailability. Henry was a tall, athletic figure and, later in life, I reminded Henry that, as a boy, I had perceived him to be foreboding. Then I added, "but now, I think you're just Henry---a colleague." Henry liked the "colleague" bit, evoking his guttural German, "Gut!"

I've often worried that the Mt. Morris citizenry didn't fully appreciate Henry's talent---his contribution. To me, he was the exemplary diagnostician, using all his senses, especially common sense, without much lab testing or x-ray imaging. Noteworthy, even when he was a medical student, was his diagnosis of an elusive rheumatic fever in a young girl. Especially mind-boggling was his accurate awareness of an intra-abdominal, extra-uterine pregnancy, an obstetrical rarity. The obstetrical specialists must have been astonished at the astuteness of this small town "doc"---and the diagnosis was made without the aid of ultra-sound.

With the unpredictability of the human body, but with the predictability of human nature, it is well-nigh impossible to please every patient. Just so! Henry told me of his disappointment when an obstetrical patient, caught in a very difficult labor, was upset by the prolonged discomfort. The truth is that Henry, with a short umbilical cord tangled around the baby's neck, performed admirably, accomplishing a high forceps delivery. That little girl turned out to be a straight-A student, but when the mother became pregnant again, those parents engaged a different physician for obstetrical care. A colleague of Henry's offered this tongue-in-cheek explanation, "I don't blame them at all, Henry. If it was me, I'd do the same thing--look for a doctor who can create a longer umbilical cord."

A multi-talented person, Henry liked to play the piano and organ. He also was a perpetual student---of medicine, of world affairs, of Shakespeare. I'm a literary dropout, so I could only marvel at Henry's memorization and quoting of the bard's writings. In Henry, Shakepeare came to life---with meaning for the present day.

Henry and I were among the few physicians slightly to the left of center on the political spectrum. With his humanitarian spirit and an appreciation of public health, Henry found it woefully unfortunate that, with our large military budget, there were still problems in finding the funds to immunize those poor kids in Chicago.

In retirement, Henry became non-officially entrenched as resident philosopher at the Senior Center. There was no designated head table---it just happened to be wherever Henry sat. Understanding and tolerant of others' opinions, he managed to inject a Democratic tone into that bastion of Republicanism.

I chuckle as I recall an incident which increased my stature in Mt. Morris. Unbeknownst to me, Henry had fallen down stairs, injuring his back---this occurring after his retirement. In the best "physician, heal thyself" mode, Henry secluded himself at home, absenting himself from Mt. Morris society. It coincidentally happened that, about two weeks after Henry's fall, Peggy and I were in Mt. Morris for the memorial services of J.H. Florea, my Sunday school teacher. I, of course, called Henry from our room, receiving firsthand the scoop about his injury and his self-imposed confinement. When I suggested that I make a house call, Henry seemed strangely reluctant, and I wished to respect his privacy.

After Mr. Florea's memorial service, a gentleman pleaded with me, "Please go see Doc---he talks about you all the time." This was enough to warrant an unannounced house call. Henry was in bed, but he'd been walking around the house with increased ease, albeit cautiously. I inquired, "Henry, have you thought of an x-ray or going to the hospital?" His reply, "Half the people in this town think I should be in the hospital, but they'd just do CT scans and want me in a nursing home."

Examining carefully, I massaged the lower back, lifted him gently off the bed, and then dropped him abruptly back onto the bed---with no pain! "Henry," I said, "your back muscles are soft, without spasm, and I have no doubt that you'll be back uptown in a day or so." Wouldn't you know it? The next day Henry resumed his customary place at the Senior Center with the proclamation, "Ralph examined me, gave me a chiropractic treatment, and I'm well." Harlan and Marion Baker, my eyes and ears regarding Henry's welfare, informed me that my actions had earned me a place on the community's scroll of honor.

When Henry finally died, after a painfully slow downhill course, there was that very thin line between grief and relief---the grief of separation, but the relief that accompanies release from the torments of this life. How to honor Henry? A thought crossed my mind that somebody should write a book about Henry---to keep him alive in our memories. That simply wasn't to be! What do you think? In this time for reflection, is it possible that this book is also Henry's book?

A THOUGHT I LEAVE WITH YOU

So much has been said. Does more need to be said? How better to wrap up my thoughts than by including the addendum I wrote to my monograph, "How Do I Talk To My Doctor?" These words have had and still have value for me. Hopefully, by reading and musing, your vision will become more focused and acute as you look to the other side---whenever and wherever you might find that other side.

Addendum: It is a great feeling to be free, realizing both your capabilities and your weaknesses, and not confined to any particular mold. As you read these personal philosophies, you should know that, in some way, they have helped me through some troublesome times. Each one of us is a unique person. Therefore, it would be a mistake for you to copy blindly but, knowing your own unique place in life, you might be stimulated to re-think your own philosophies of life.

Life, indeed, is a spiritual adventure and is to be lived by FAITH. Life is unpredictable and is beset with unknowns. Life should be appreciated casually, not fiercely as if trying to cling to it. The butterfly you chase will surely fly away and elude you---but, if you are calm, unhurried, and patient, the butterfly just might light on your shoulder. It has happened to me. Paraphrasing scripture, you may unravel a mystery when you find that only in losing your life will you finally gain your life. It's found in losing that awful preoccupation with existence. At some time, this may be revealed to you in the mellowing which will come to you when you cease your frantic concerns---and reach even a reasonable sense of your own self worth.

Just so, we should approach our health concerns

with a casual attitude, abandoning that frantic, fierce pursuit of perfection. Perfection, after all, is only an idea! Wholeness and healing are far beyond perfection. Perhaps the truth of these thoughts will come to you as you realize that "human being" is more a verb than a noun. With our present appreciation of everything and everybody around us, with a feeling of awe for the environmental creation provided us, there's just no hurry in living in this world or in leaving this world.

There are lifelong questions which never go away, bobbing up again even as we approach the end of life. The concerns I've heard haven't had as much to do with dying, the event, as with the "how, where, why, and when?" Treasuring rational mental function, we fear loss of control and the inability to communicate with others. Is it not a rational extension of all these philosophies to resist and resent living (if it can be called "living") in a physical shell, a physical prison---with no communication or appreciation of who we are or who we have been?

Celebrate life! Enjoy life! After all, death WILL come sometime as physiological aging takes its toll. Only those who have learned how to live casually can understand the mystery of dying---and only those who are comfortable with the thought of dying can be released from the anxieties of living. Guess what? We need not be afraid!